New Directions in Mathematical Finance

New Directions in Mathematical Finance

Edited by

Paul Wilmott and Henrik Rasmussen

JOHN WILEY & SONS, LTD

Other Wiley Editorial Offices

John Wiley & Sons, Inc., 605 Third Avenue,
New York, NY 10158-0012, USA

WILEY-VCH GmbH, Pappelallee 3,
D-69469 Weinheim, Germany

John Wiley & Sons Australia Ltd, 33 Park Road, Milton,
Queensland 4064, Australia

John Wiley & Sons (Asia) Pte Ltd, 2 Clementi Loop #02-01,
Jin Xing Distripark, Singapore 129809

John Wiley & Sons (Canada) Ltd, 22 Worcester Road,
Rexdale, Ontario M9W 1L1, Canada

Library of Congress Cataloging-in-Publication Data

New directions in mathematical finance/edited by Paul Wilmott and Henrik Rasmussen.
        p. cm.
    Includes Index.
    ISBN 0-471-49817-3
    1. Securities–Mathematical models. 2. Investments–Mathematical models. 3. Risk
management–Mathematical models.   I. Wilmott, Paul. II. Rasmussen, Henrik O., 1996

HG4515.2.N49 2002
332.6′01′5118–dc21   2001055797

British Library Cataloguing in Publication Data

A catalogue record for this book is available from the British Library

ISBN 0-471-49817-3

Typeset in 10/12pt Times by Laserwords Private Limited, Chennai, India

This book is printed on acid-free paper responsibly manufactured from sustainable forestry,
in which at least two trees are planted for each one used for paper production.

Contents

Preface

This book is based around material presented at the European Consortium for Mathematics in Industry Conference in Milan, Italy, at the end of 1999. The conference was organized officially by Paul Wilmott and Vincenzo Capasso. It was Henrik Rasmussen, however, who put in the effort to make the conference the great success that it was.

At the time of the conference Dr Wilmott was a financial consultant, researcher, trainer and occasional writer. Professor Capasso was a professor of mathematics. Dr Rasmussen was a post-doctoral researcher commuting between Oxford and Milan. Their interests in mathematical finance came about in various ways. Wilmott had once been a generalist mathematical modeller, but converted to finance in the late 1980s. Capasso was new to the subject, but again, had the applied mathematical background. Rasmussen had been a fluid mechanic specializing in turbulence, but had decided that finance was an easier subject.

Rasmussen was right when he said that finance is easier than fluid mechanics. In this book we are going to see the difference between these two 'scientific' disciplines. But why should you be interested? Many people reading this book have gone from a scientific background to a career in finance. There are more jobs available in the private sector and the rewards are far greater. It is natural to consider the subject of quantitative finance from the perspective of just such a typical career-changing scientist.

Finance, as represented in most textbooks and lecture courses, is really rather basic, built around a simple framework that allows theorists and practitioners to solve important problems in real time. It's a fast-moving business and for obvious reasons, accuracy and pseudo-scientific rigour does not rate as highly as making the deal.

Throughout this book we shall see the conflict between the scientific and the pragmatic. In our notes between sections we will probably be stressing the importance of the scientific side and we will usually have our scientific hats on rather than our practitioner hats. This is partly because of our scientific upbringing—we put the truth at the top of our list of priorities—and partly because we never had to get in 7 o'clock in the morning to hedge our trades.

Paul Wilmott has now added to his duties the job of editing a webzine bearing his name. Vincenzo Capasso is ECMI's big boss. Henrik Rasmussen works for Schroder Salomon Smith Barney (Citigroup).

As an introduction, there follows a lightning tour of the history of quantitative finance. To contact us, you can email <paul@paulwilmott.com>.

1
The quantitative finance timeline

Paul Wilmott

There follows a speedy, roller coaster of a ride through the subject of quantitative finance, passing through both the highs and lows. Where possible we give dates, name names and refer to the original sources.

1827 Brown

The Scottish botanist gave his name to the random motion of small particles in a liquid. This idea of the random walk has permeated many scientific fields and is commonly used as the model mechanism behind a variety of unpredictable continuous-time processes. The lognormal random walk is the basic paradigm for the stock market. See Brown (1827).

1900 Bachelier

Bachelier was the first to quantify the concept of Brownian motion. He developed a mathematical theory for random walks, a theory rediscovered later by Einstein. He proposed a model for equity prices, a simple normal distribution, and built on it a model for pricing the almost unheard-of options. His model contained many of the seeds for later work, but lay 'dormant' for many, many years. It is told that his thesis was not a great success and, naturally, Bachelier's work was not appreciated in his lifetime. See Bachelier (1995).

1905 Einstein

Einstein proposed a scientific foundation for Brownian motion in 1905. He did some other clever stuff as well. See Stachel (1990).

1923 Wiener

Wiener developed a rigorous theory for Brownian motion, the mathematics of which was to become a necessary modelling device for quantitative finance decades later. The starting point for almost all financial models, the first equation written down in most technical papers, includes the Wiener process as the representation for randomness in asset prices. See Wiener (1923).

1950s Samuelson

The 1970 Nobel Laureate in Economics, the first American so honoured, was responsible for setting the tone for subsequent generations of economists. Samuelson 'mathematised' both macro- and microeconomics. He rediscovered Bachelier's thesis and laid the foundations for later option pricing theories. His approach to derivative pricing was via expectations, real as opposed to the much later risk-neutral ones. See Samuleson (1995).

1951 Itô

Where would we be without stochastic or Itô calculus? Some people even think finance is *only* about Itô calculus. Those people should get out more. One of the starting points for classical derivatives theory is the lognormal stochastic differential equation for the evolution of assets. Itô showed the relationship between this equation and the stochastic differential equation for a function, an option price, say, of that asset.

In mathematical terms, if we have a Wiener process X with increments dX that are normally distributed with mean zero and variance dt, then the increment of a function $F(X)$ is given by

$$dF = \frac{dF}{dX} dX + \frac{1}{2} \frac{d^2F}{dX^2} dt$$

This is a very loose definition of Itô's lemma but will suffice. See Itô (1951).

1952 Markowitz

Markowitz was the first to propose a modern quantitative methodology for portfolio selection. This required knowledge of asset volatilities and the correlation between assets. The idea was extremely elegant, resulting in novel ideas such as efficiency and market portfolios. In this Modern Portfolio Theory, Markowitz showed that combinations of assets could have better properties than any individual assets. What did 'better' mean? Markowitz quantified a portfolio's possible future performance in terms of its expected return and its standard deviation. The standard deviation was to be interpreted as its risk. He showed how to optimise a portfolio to give the maximum expected return for a given level of risk (Figure 1.1). Such a portfolio was said to be 'efficient'. The work later won Markowitz a Nobel Prize for Economics but is rarely used in practice because of the difficulty of measuring the parameters' volatility, and especially correlation, and their instability.

If asset i, out of N assets, has a mean growth of μ_i and a standard deviation of σ_i, then a portfolio Π consisting of w_i of each asset will have an expected growth of

$$\mu_\Pi = \sum_{i=1}^{N} w_i \mu_i$$

and a standard deviation of

$$\sigma_\Pi^2 = \sqrt{\sum_{i,j}^{N,N} w_i w_j \rho_{ij} \sigma_i \sigma_j}.$$

Here ρ_{ij} is the correlation between assets i and j. Markowitz showed how to maximise expected growth for a given risk or standard deviation. See Markowitz (1959).

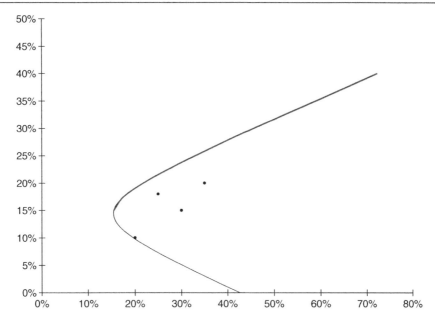

Figure 1.1   Reward versus risk, a selection of risky assets and the efficient frontier (bold)

1963 Sharpe, Lintner and Mossin

Sharpe of Stanford, Lintner of Harvard and Norwegian economist Mossin independently developed a simple model for pricing risky assets. This Capital Asset Pricing Model (CAPM) also reduced the number of parameters needed for portfolio selection from those needed by Markowitz's Modern Portfolio Theory, making asset allocation theory more practical. See Sharpe (1985), Lintner (1965) and Mossin (1966).

1966 Fama

Fama concluded that stock prices were unpredictable and coined the phrase 'market efficiency'. Although there are various forms of market efficiency, in a nutshell the idea is that stock market prices reflect all publicly available information, that no person can gain an edge over another by fair means. A theory beloved of ivory-tower-bound economists, few with experience of the real world have any truck with this notion. See Fama (1965).

1960s Sobol', Faure, Hammersley, Haselgrove, Halton. . .

Many, many people were associated with the definition and development of quasi-random number theory or low-discrepancy sequence theory. The subject concerns the distribution of points in an arbitrary number of dimensions so as to cover the space as efficiently as possible, with as few points as possible (Figure 1.2). The methodology is used in the evaluation of multiple integrals among other things. These ideas would find a use in finance almost three decades later. See Sobol' (1967), Faure (1969), Hammersley and Handscomb (1964), Haselgrove (1961) and Halton (1960).

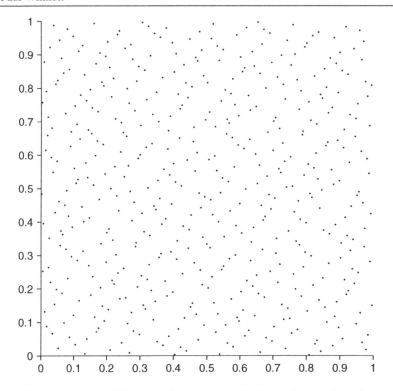

Figure 1.2 They may not look like it, but these dots are distributed deterministically so as to have very useful properties

1968 Thorp

Thorp's first claim to fame was that he figured out how to win at casino blackjack, ideas that were put into practice by Thorp himself and written about in his best-selling *Beat the Dealer*, the 'book that made Las Vegas change its rules'. His second claim to fame is that he invented and built, with Shannon the information theorist, the world's first wearable computer. His third claim to fame is that he was the first to use the 'correct' formulae for pricing options, formulae that were rediscovered and originally published several years later by the next three people on our list. Thorp used these formulae to make a fortune for himself and his clients in the first ever quantitative-finance-based hedge fund. See Thorp (2001) for the true story behind the discovery of the Black–Scholes formulae.

1973 Black, Scholes and Merton

Black, Scholes and Merton derived the Black–Scholes equation for options in the early seventies, publishing it in two separate papers in 1973. The date corresponded almost exactly with the trading of call options on the Chicago Board Options Exchange. Scholes and Merton won the Nobel Prize for Economics in 1997. Black had died in 1995. Scholes and Merton became involved in the hedge fund Long-Term Capital Management, which suffered badly in 1998. See Black and Scholes (1973) and Merton (1973).

The Black–Scholes model is based on geometric Brownian motion for the asset price S:

$$dS = \mu S\, dt + \sigma S\, dX.$$

The Black–Scholes partial differential equation for the value V of an option is then

$$\frac{\partial V}{\partial t} + \frac{1}{2}\sigma^2 S^2 \frac{\partial^2 V}{\partial S^2} + rS\frac{\partial V}{\partial S} - rV = 0.$$

1977 Boyle

Boyle related the pricing of options to the simulation of random asset paths. He showed how to find the fair value of an option by generating lots of possible future paths for an asset and then looking at the average that the option had paid off (Figure 1.3). The future important role of Monte Carlo simulations in finance was assured. See Boyle (1977).

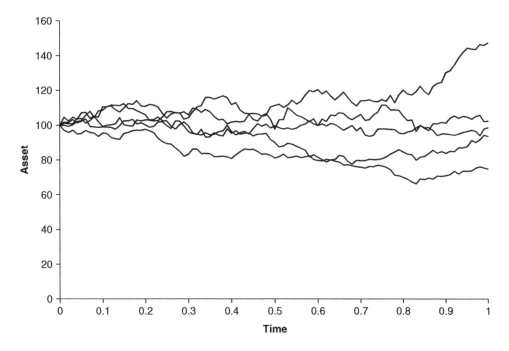

Figure 1.3   Simulations like this can be easily used to value derivatives

1977 Vasicek

So far quantitative finance hadn't had much to say about pricing interest rate products. Some people were using equity option formulae for pricing interest rate options, but a consistent framework for interest rates had not been developed. This was addressed by Vasicek. He started by modelling a short-term interest rate as a random walk and concluded that interest rate derivatives could be valued using equations similar to the

Black–Scholes partial differential equation. This has its plus and its minus points, which we will go into at a more opportune moment.

Vasicek represented the short-term interest rate by a stochastic differential equation of the form

$$dr = \mu(r, t)\, dt + \sigma(r, t)\, dX.$$

The bond pricing equation is a parabolic partial differential equation, similar to the Black–Scholes equation. See Vasicek (1977).

1979 Cox, Ross, Rubinstein

Boyle had shown how to price options via simulations, an important and intuitively reasonable idea, but it was these three who gave option-pricing capability to the masses.

The Black–Scholes equation was derived using stochastic calculus and resulted in a partial differential equation. This was not likely to endear it to the thousands of students interested in a career in finance. At that time these were typically MBA students, not the mathematicians and physicists that are nowadays found on Wall Street. How could MBAs cope? An MBA was a necessary requirement for a prestigious career in finance, but an ability to count beans is not the same as an ability to understand mathematics. Fortunately Cox, Ross and Rubinstein were able to distil the fundamental concepts of option pricing into a simple algorithm requiring only addition, subtraction, multiplication and (twice) division (Figure 1.4). Even MBAs could now join in the fun. See Cox *et al.* (1979).

1979–81 Harrison, Kreps, Pliska

Until these three came onto the scene, quantitative finance was the domain of either economists or applied mathematicians. Harrison and Kreps, in 1979, showed the relationship between option prices and advanced probability theory, originally in discrete time. Harrison and Pliska in 1981 used the same ideas but in continuous time. From that moment until the mid 1990s applied mathematicians hardly got a look in. Theorem, proof everywhere you looked. This is perfectly reasonable as long as you don't lose track of the big picture; reality has a nasty habit of not caring about theorems and proofs.

However, in recent times those of a more practical and applied bent have been responsible for the exciting new theories. See Harrison and Kreps (1979) and Harrison and Pliska (1981).

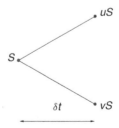

Figure 1.4   The branching structure of the binomial model

1986 Ho and Lee

One of the problems with the Vasicek framework for interest rate derivative products was that it didn't give very good prices for bonds, the simplest of fixed income products. If the model couldn't even get bond prices right, how could it hope to correctly value bond options? Ho and Lee found a way around this, introducing the idea of yield curve fitting or calibration. Again, there are good and bad points about this technique which we will come back to later. See Ho and Lee (1986).

1992 Heath, Jarrow and Morton

Although Ho and Lee showed how to match theoretical and market prices for simple bonds, the methodology was rather cumbersome and not easily generalised. Heath, Jarrow and Morton took a different approach. Instead of modelling just a short rate and deducing the whole yield curve, they modelled the random evolution of the whole yield curve. The initial yield curve, and hence the value of simple interest rate instruments, was an input to the model. The model cannot easily be expressed in differential equation terms and so relies on either Monte Carlo simulation or tree building. The work was well known via a working paper, but was finally published, and therefore made 'respectable', in Heath *et al.* (1992).

1990s Credit risk

If we were to award marks out of 10 for the scientific accuracy of financial models, we would probably give about 7 for the lognormal random walk model for equities. There are one or two problems to do with stability of parameters, serial autocorrelation, the distribution of returns and continuity of asset paths but, what the hell, it's still pretty good. If we were to give a mark for interest rate models, we would have to give them 3, or maybe 4. It doesn't take a statistical genius to show how poor these models actually are. But then again, so what? If they are popular, does it matter? Now, there's a question.... but not one we'll be answering here.

Moving on to credit risk models, we'd be hard pressed to give them even 1 out of 10. Mathematical models for credit risk have taken the same well-worn path trodden successfully by equity product models and, less successfully, by interest rate product models. But credit risk is an entirely different beast. For many different reasons, not least the inability to hedge and the extreme nature of returns, credit risk modelling is a whole new ball game. To spare their blushes, we have not named the guilty parties.

1990s Cheyette, Barrett, Moore, Wilmott

When there are many underlyings, all following lognormal random walks, you can write down the value of any European non-path-dependent option as a multiple integral, one dimension for each asset. Valuing such options then becomes calculating an integral. The usual methods for quadrature are very inefficient in high dimensions, but simulations can prove quite effective. Monte Carlo evaluation of integrals is based on the idea that an integral is just an average multiplied by a 'volume'. And since one way of estimating an average is by picking numbers at random, we can value a multiple integral by picking integrand values at random and summing. With N function evaluations, taking a time of

$O(N)$ you can expect an accuracy of $O(1/N^{1/2})$, independent of the number of dimensions. As mentioned above, breakthroughs in the 1960s on low-discrepancy sequences showed how clever, non-random, distributions could be used for an accuracy of $O(1/N)$, to leading order. (There is a weak dependence on the dimension.) In the early 1990s three groups of people were simultaneously working on valuation of multi-asset options. Their work was less of a breakthrough than a transfer of technology.

They used ideas from the field of number theory and applied them to finance. Nowadays, these low-discrepancy sequences are commonly used for option valuation whenever random numbers are needed. A few years after these researchers made their work public, a completely unrelated group at Columbia University successfully patented the work. See Cheyette (1990) and Barrett *et al.* (1992)

1994 Dupire, Rubinstein, Derman and Kani

Another discovery was made independently and simultaneously by three groups of researchers in the subject of option pricing with deterministic volatility. One of the perceived problems with classical option pricing is that the assumption of constant volatility is inconsistent with market prices of exchange-traded instruments. A model is needed that can correctly price vanilla contracts, and then price exotic contracts consistently. The new methodology, which quickly became standard market practice, was to find the volatility as a function of underlying and time that when put into the Black–Scholes equation and solved, usually numerically, gave resulting option prices which matched market prices. This is what is known as an inverse problem: use the 'answer' to find the coefficients in the governing equation. On the plus side, this is not too difficult to do in theory. On the minus side, the practice is much harder since the sought volatility function depends very sensitively on the initial data. From a scientific viewpoint there is much to be said against the methodology. The resulting volatility structure never matches actual volatility, and even if exotics are priced consistently it is not clear how best to hedge exotics with vanillas so as to minimise any model error. Such concerns seem to carry little weight, since the method is so ubiquitous. As so often happens in finance, once a technique becomes popular it is hard to go against the majority. There is job safety in numbers. See Derman and Kani (1994), Dupire (1994) and Rubinstein (1994).

1996 Avellaneda and Parás

Avellaneda and Parás were, together with Levy and Lyons, the creators of the uncertain volatility model for option pricing. Itself a great breakthrough for the rigorous, scientific side of finance theory, but the best was yet to come. This model, and many that succeeded it, was non-linear. Non-linearity in an option pricing model means that the value of a portfolio of contracts is not necessarily the same as the sum of the values of its constituent parts. An option will have a different value depending on what else is in the portfolio with it, and an exotic will have a different value depending on what it is statically hedged with. Avellaneda and Parás defined an exotic option's value as the highest possible marginal value for that contract when hedged with any or all available exchange-traded contracts. The brilliant result was that the method of option pricing also came with its own technique for static hedging with other options. Prior to their work the only result of an option pricing model was its value and its delta, only dynamic hedging was theoretically necessary. With this new concept, theory became a major step closer to practice. Another result of this technique was that the theoretical price of an exchange-traded option exactly matched its market price. The convoluted calibration of volatility surface models was redundant. See Avellaneda and Parás (1996).

And the Nobel Prize for Economics goes to . . .

We are not going to say who we think will get the Nobel Prizes for Economics in the near future, or even who we think should (almost certainly a completely different list). However, we are sure that some of the above will appear on one or other of these two lists.

BIBLIOGRAPHY

Avellaneda, M. and Buff, R. (1997) Combinatorial implications of nonlinear uncertain volatility models: the case of barrier options. Courant Institute, NYU

Avellaneda, M. and Parás, A. (1994) Dynamic hedging portfolios for derivative securities in the presence of large transaction costs. *Applied Mathematical Finance* **1** 165–94

Avellaneda, M. and Parás, A. (1996) Managing the volatility risk of derivative securities: the Lagrangian volatility model. *Applied Mathematical Finance* **3** 21–53

Avellaneda, M., Levy, A. and Parás, A. (1995) Pricing and hedging derivative securities in markets with uncertain volatilities. *Applied Mathematical Finance* **2** 73–88

Bachelier, L. (1995) *Théorie de la Spéculation*. Jacques Gabay

Barrett, J.W., Moore, G. and Wilmott, P. (1992) Inelegant efficiency. *Risk* **5**(9) 82–84

Black, F. and Scholes, M. (1973) The pricing of options and corporate liabilities. *Journal of Political Economy* **81** 637–59

Boyle, P. (1977) Options: a Monte Carlo approach. *Journal of Financial Economics* **4** 323–38

Brown, R. (1827) *A Brief Account of Microscopical Observations*. London

Cheyette, O. (1990) Pricing options on multiple assets. *Advances in Futures and Options Research* **4** 68–91

Cox, J.C., Ross, S. and Rubinstein, M. (1979) Option pricing: a simplified approach. *Journal of Financial Economics* **7** 229–63

Derman, E. and Kani, I. (1994) Riding on a smile. *Risk* **7**(2) 32–39 (February)

Derman, E., Ergener, D. and Kani, I. (1997) Static options replication. In *Frontiers in Derivatives* (Eds Konishi, A. and Dattatreya, R.E.) Irwin

Dupire, B. (1993) Pricing and hedging with smiles. *Proc. AFFI Conf.*, La Baule, June 1993

Dupire, B. (1994) Pricing with a smile. *Risk* **7**(1) 18–20 (January)

Fama, E. (1965) The behaviour of stock prices. *Journal of Business* **38** 34–105

Faure, H. (1969) Résultat voisin d'un théorème de Landau sur le nombre de points d'un réseau dans une hypersphère. *C. R. Acad. Sci. Paris Sér. A* **269** 383–386

Halton, J.H. (1960) On the efficiency of certain quasi-random sequences of points in evaluating multi-dimensional integrals. *Numerical Mathematics* **2** 84–90

Hammersley, J.M. and Handscomb, D.C. (1964) *Monte Carlo Methods*. Methuen, London

Harrison, J.M. and Kreps, D. (1979) Martingales and arbitrage in multiperiod securities markets. *Journal of Economic Theory* **20** 381–408

Harrison, J.M. and Pliska, S.R. (1981) Martingales and stochastic integrals in the theory of continuous trading. *Stochastic Processes and Their Applications* **11** 215–60

Haselgrove, C.B. (1961) A method for numerical integration. *Mathematics of Computation* **15** 323–37

Heath, D., Jarrow, R. and Morton, A. (1992) Bond pricing and the term structure of interest rates: a new methodology. *Econometrica* **60** 77–105

Ho, T. and Lee, S. (1986) Term structure movements and pricing interest rate contingent claims. *Journal of Finance* **42** 1129–42

Itô, K. (1951) On stochastic differential equations. *Memoirs of the American Mathematical Society* **4** 1–51

Lintner, J. (1965) Security, prices, risk, and maximal gains from diversification. *Journal of Finance* **20**(4) 587–615

Markowitz, H. (1959) *Portfolio Selection: Efficient Diversification of Investment*. John Wiley www.wiley.com

Merton, R.C. (1973) Theory of rational option pricing. *Bell Journal of Economics and Management Science* **4** 141–83

Merton, R.C. (1992) *Continuous-time Finance*. Blackwell

Mossin, J. (1966) Equilibrium in a capital asset market. *Econometrica* **34**(4) 768–83

Niederreiter, H. (1992) *Random Number Generation and Quasi-Monte Carlo Methods*. SIAM

Ninomiya, S. and Tezuka, S. (1996) Toward real-time pricing of complex financial derivatives. *Applied Mathematical Finance* **3** 1–20

Paskov, S. (1996) New methodologies for valuing derivatives. In *Mathematics of Derivative Securities* (Eds Pliska, S.R. and Dempster, M.)

Paskov, S.H. and Traub, J.F. (1995) Faster valuation of financial derivatives. *Journal of Portfolio Management*. Fall 113–20

Rubinstein, M. (1994) Implied binomial trees. *Journal of Finance* **69** 771–818

Samuelson, P. (1955) Brownian motion in the stock market. Unpublished

Sharpe, W.F. (1985) *Investments*. Prentice Hall

Sloan, I.H. and Walsh, L. (1990) A computer search of rank two lattice rules for multidimensional quadrature. *Mathematics of Computation* **54** 281–302

Sobol', I.M. (1967) On the distribution of points in cube and the approximate evaluation of integrals. *USSR Computational Mathematics and Mathematical Physics* **7** 86–112

Stachel, J. (ed.) (1990) *The Collected Papers of Albert Einstein*. Princeton University Press

Thorp, E.O. (1962) *Beat the Dealer*. Vintage

Thorp, E.O. (2001) Private communication

Thorp, E.O. and Kassouf, S. (1967) *Beat the Market*. Random House

Traub, J.F. and Wozniakowski, H. (1994) Breaking intractability. *Scientific American* Jan 102–7

Vasicek, O.A. (1977) An equilibrium characterization of the term structure. *Journal of Financial Economics* **5** 177–88

Wiener, N. (1923) Differential space. *Journal of Mathematics and Physics* **58** 131–74

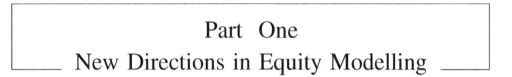

Part One
New Directions in Equity Modelling

2

Introduction

If you can't do a decent job of modelling equities and equity derivatives then you don't stand a chance of being able to model fixed income products or credit derivatives. That's a fairly safe statement. The math tools needed for equity derivative pricing are needed for both fixed income and credit risk, but not necessarily vice versa.

The first part of this book focuses on the modelling of equities and their derivatives. We will be seeing work on fundamentals of modelling, including some completely new concepts. We will also see some techniques of applied mathematics used in novel financial contexts. But first, let's remind ourselves about the basic building blocks of equity derivatives theory.

In the beginning was Bachelier. Circa 1900 he introduced the first stochastic model for equities and developed theories of Brownian motion before other clever people like Einstein. His model was what we'd now call a 'normal', as opposed to 'lognormal', random walk. The distinction is more important in practice than in theory, the key issue being that he pointed people on the right track.

Okay, so despite being pointed on the right track, no one went there. Paul Samuelson and others got close to a decent theory, by examining the expected profit from an option position. Calculating expected payoffs and then present valuing them was suggested as a plausible way to value an option. Such a model has two parameters input from the asset price random walk, the drift rate μ and the volatility σ. The asset price random walk was written down as

$$dS = \mu S\, dt + \sigma S\, dX,$$

with the randomness being contained in the dX term. The option price $V(S, t)$ then becomes the present value of the expected payoff, and so satisfies

$$\frac{\partial V}{\partial t} + \tfrac{1}{2}\sigma^2 S^2 \frac{\partial^2 V}{\partial S^2} + \mu S \frac{\partial V}{\partial S} - dV = 0. \qquad (2.1)$$

Here d is the discount factor. At least this was the proposed option value. But what d to use? You can't justify discounting at the risk-free rate because the option is not risk-free. Discount at the real risk-free rate r? Discount at the rate μ?

In unpublished work—but commercially exploited to great profit—Ed Thorp came up with a pricing formula that essentially solved equation (2.1). What parameters did he choose that resulted in the great profits? He replaced μ with r and discounted at the rate r. Nowadays, we know that this result is exactly the classical Black–Scholes concept, but how did he come up with this? His reasoning, which amounted to the modern idea of risk neutrality, was one of parsimony. He had a way of eliminating risk, delta hedging, so why should the price depend on anything other than the risk-free rate? This is the perfect example of genius at work, going from A to Z without passing through B to Y.

A few years later Fischer Black, Myron Scholes and Robert Merton recast the problem of option pricing and systematically filled in the steps B to Y. Their pricing equation published in 1973 was

$$\frac{\partial V}{\partial t} + \frac{1}{2}\sigma^2 S^2 \frac{\partial^2 V}{\partial S^2} + rS \frac{\partial V}{\partial S} - rV = 0.$$

They formalised risk elimination by delta hedging and using the idea of no arbitrage came up with the equation for which Thorp already had the solution. Scholes and Merton later won the Nobel Prize for their work. (Thorp just made heaps of cash.)

There are many assumptions in this model. These include the lognormal random walk, known volatility (a measure of the randomness), zero transaction costs, etc., etc. The theory, which is a very good theory, is also not bad in practice. Some of the assumptions matter more than others and many people have worked on relaxing these assumptions to make better models. We'll see some of these here.

CHAPTERS 3 TO 6

Asymptotic analysis of stochastic volatility models

Henrik Rasmussen and Paul Wilmott

The basic Black–Scholes equation or Thorp formulae require several inputs, most of which are easily and accurately known. There are three that are not so easy, however. These three are interest rate, volatility and dividend. We will not be worrying about interest rates in this part of the book; the effect they have on equity derivatives is not that great. But volatility and dividends are another matter.

The volatility that is used in the pricing equations and formulae is supposed to be the 'actual' volatility, the annualised standard deviation of returns. Unfortunately this is extremely difficult to measure statistically, and shows every sign of being random itself, or at least highly unstable. Naturally this has provoked the interest of researchers.

Volatility has been modelled to death in the last decade and a half. Deterministic, stochastic actual, stochastic implied, uncertain, jump ... Some of these models make sense, some don't. Some lead to simple models, some don't. Some have to be crunched numerically, some don't. This is not the place for a discussion of all the different volatility models; look through the bibliography for relevant references. But it is the place to mention Henrik and Paul's neat trick for the analysis of stochastic volatility models.

In their model they build upon the common observation that volatility of volatility is much greater than the volatility of the underlying asset. The equity world is therefore one of two timescales, one associated with the dynamics of the asset and one with the dynamics of the volatility of that asset. The latter dynamics are much faster than the former.

A common mathematical methodology in the world outside of finance is 'asymptotic analysis'. This is an approximation technique that systematically exploits the smallness or largeness of a parameter. In the problem under consideration the small parameter is the ratio of the volatility and asset timescales, here called ϵ.

Henrik and Paul find a series solution for a vanilla option price, a power series solution in the square root of the small parameter ϵ. The form of this series solution means that they are able to fit market prices of vanilla options.

How useful is the model? It is still only an approximation, based upon the asymptotic analysis. But that does not matter. There are plenty of popular approximations around, for the prices of American options, say, or Asian options. It is certainly quicker to calibrate than traditional volatility smile models, whether deterministic or stochastic, and almost certainly more stable.

Passport options: a review

Antony Penaud

The original Black–Scholes equation is fine for pricing simple contracts. In particular, contracts that don't depend on the history of the underlying. When the path is important, in exotic option contracts, we need some new mathematics. The simple exotics only need a simple extension to the pricing equation, but the latest generation of exotics need input from another branch of mathematics, stochastic control theory.

Passport options, perfect trader options or simply trader options are just about the most exciting new product in the derivatives supermarket. Imagine a contract that allows you to trade in some asset, buying or selling at will, with the guarantee that whatever happens, however bad you are, you will not lose money. That product is a trader option. Why is this an exciting product? There are at least a couple of reasons.

First, it gives new traders the opportunity to try their hand at trading without running the risk of crippling their bank. It is the perfect starter vehicle, the bicycle with stabilisers.

Second, and more important to us here, it introduces into derivatives theory a whole new branch of stochastic mathematics. That new subject is stochastic control theory. Previously this subject was only seen in derivatives models in the presence of transaction costs. To some extent these cost models were contrived, of some academic interest but little practical interest. But you cannot price and hedge trader options unless you know some stochastic control theory. The gentlemen responsible for originally pricing these contracts are Hyer, Lipton-Lifschitz and Pugachevsky. Good work!

Because the pricing of this contract involves making assumptions about the behaviour of the trader, we find ourselves in this exciting branch of mathematics. The assumptions that we must make are that the trader acts optimally, in some sense. It is the optimality of his trading that makes this a control problem.

Antony shows you the theory in a simple form, using basic partial differential equation modelling. He then goes on to introduce some even more exotic trader options, again showing you how these can be valued in a consistent framework.

It is extremely likely that new products will be designed in the not too distant future that are even more complex than trader options and that require the specialist knowledge which Antony shows us here.

Equity dividend models

David Bakstein and Paul Wilmott

Less modelled, but often more important than volatility, are dividends. In the literature the few models that have been proposed have followed the same well-worn, unimaginative route beloved of the plodders that inhabit the field of quantitative finance research. Bakstein and Wilmott have taken a different route.

Until David and Paul came up with their equity dividend models, the world of equity derivatives had to resort to some pretty naive assumptions about the behaviour of dividends. And as any trader will tell you, dividends can have a major impact on the price of an option contract. These naive assumptions fell into the following categories: (1) dividends are known and constant, and paid at a specified date; (2) the dividend yield is known and constant and paid at a specified date (or spread infinitesimally in time); (3) dividends are stochastic.

The first two assumptions are not too bad but, as is shown in this chapter, a contract's sensitivity to the precise value of the dividend or its yield can be much greater even than the sensitivity to volatility. The third assumption will be recognised as the typical approach taken when all else fails. Any simple observation of dividend data will immediately show you that dividends do not act quite like the typical stochastic variable.

So, in this chapter we are treated to some very interesting new ideas for modelling dividends. What if we don't know what the dividend will be? What if we don't know the precise date of the dividend? What if the dividend date could lie before or after the expiry of a contract we want to price? (We also get shown the classical models as well as these new-fangled ones.)

Isoperimetry, log-concavity and elasticity of option prices

Christer Borell

Christer's chapter concerns technical issues in the elasticity of option prices. The elasticity of an option price tells you about the relative movement in a stock and an option on that stock. This is clearly important from a risk management viewpoint and also to a speculator wanting to know how much leverage he will get from a contract. He extends this idea into arbitrary dimensions, that is for options on many underlying stocks, the basket options.

MODELS NEEDED

And what next? Have the finishing touches been applied to the shopping mall of equity derivatives theory or are we still constructing the basement? There's still a belief in quantitative finance circles that finance is a branch of physics, that there are 'laws of nature' out there just waiting for another Newton to find them. That's not how it is, though, is it? When an apple falls from a tree its path is predictable; the same result will be found again and again. When the stock market falls, each time is different: the degree of the fall, its longevity, its impact on the world economy.

And there are others who believe that finance is a branch of probability theory. Such people are even more deranged. Let us not confuse a theory, which can exist on Mars where, as far as we know, there is no currency let alone a stock market, with reality. An axiomatic approach to finance is a luxury that can be afforded only by those in the public sector.

Chances are that future models, of which there will be many, will move away from the simplicity of traditional stochastic models, with their assumptions about probabilistic behaviour. Future models will draw from a wider range of mathematical tools.

Here are a couple of issues we'd like to see addressed. First, the evolution of an idea. Second, the weakest link in our beloved business.

An idea is born, in the bathtub perhaps. A paper is written. The methodology is implemented. Profits are made. Or are they? Please, can someone check these models in practice, using real data? We don't believe that people really know (or care) whether models work. Please let's try to find some models that don't need patch after patch after patch to get them to work.

Where is the weakest link in the profit-making chain? Is it the data collection? The mathematical model? The numerical result? The computational time? The hedging procedure? The patches? Sales? The trader? The quant? Risk management? The back office? IT? The management? The compensation package? Where is most money made and where is most lost? There is nothing that can't be quantified, and with so much money in this business it's got to be worth the effort.

BIBLIOGRAPHY

Ahn, H. and Wilmott, P. (1998) On trading American options. Working Paper, Oxford University

Ahn, H., Penaud, A. and Wilmott, P. (1998) Various passport options and their valuation. MFG Working Paper, Oxford University

Ahn, H., Arkell, R., Choe, K., Holstad, E. and Wilmott, P. (1999) Optimal static vega hedge. MFG Working Paper, Oxford University

Ahn, H., Hua, P., Penaud, A. and Wilmott (1999) Compensating traders and bonus maximization. Wilmott Associates Working Paper

Avellaneda, M. and Buff, R. (1997) Combinatorial implications of nonlinear uncertain volatility models: the case of barrier options. Courant Institute, NYU

Avellaneda, M. and Parás, A. (1994) Dynamic hedging portfolios for derivative securities in the presence of large transaction costs. *Applied Mathematical Finance* **1** 165–94

Avellaneda, M. and Parás, A. (1996) Managing the volatility risk of derivative securities: the Lagrangian volatility model. *Applied Mathematical Finance* **3** 21–53

Avellaneda, M., Levy, A. and Parás, A. (1995) Pricing and hedging derivative securities in markets with uncertain volatilities. *Applied Mathematical Finance* **2** 73–88

Avellaneda, M., Friedman, C., Holmes, R. and Samperi, D. (1997) Calibrating volatility surfaces via relative-entropy minimization. *Applied Mathematical Finance* **4** 37–64

Bakstein, D. and Wilmott, P. (1999) Equity dividend models. Wilmott Associates Working Paper

Bergman, Y.Z. (1995) Option pricing with differential interest rates. *Review of Financial Studies* **8** 475–500

Black, F. and Scholes, M. (1973) The pricing of options and corporate liabilities. *Journal of Political Economy* **81** 637–59

Bowie, J. and Carr, P. (1994) Static simplicity. *Risk* **7** 45–49

Boyle, P., Evnine, J. and Gibbs, S. (1989) Numerical evaluation of multivariate contingent claims. *Review of Financial Studies* **2** 241–50

Carr, P., Ellis, K. and Gupta, V. (1998) Static hedging of exotic options. *Journal of Finance*, forthcoming

Derman, E., Ergener, D. and Kani, I. (1997) Static options replication. In *Frontiers in Derivatives* (Eds Konishi, A. and Dattatreya, R.E.). Irwin

Derman, E. and Kani, I. (1994) Riding on a smile. *Risk* **7**(2) 32–39 (February)

Derman, E. and Kani, I. (1997) Stochastic implied trees: arbitrage pricing with stochastic term and strike structure of volatility. Goldman Sachs Quantitative Strategies Technical Notes April 1997

Derman, E. and Zou, J. (1997) Predicting the response of implied volatility to large index moves. Goldman Sachs Quantitative Strategies Technical Notes November 1997

Dumas, B., Fleming, J. and Whaley, R.E. (1998) Implied volatility functions: empirical tests. *Journal of Finance*, forthcoming

Dupire, B. (1993) Pricing and hedging with smiles. *Proc. AFFI Conf.*, La Baule, June 1993

Dupire, B. (1994) Pricing with a smile. *Risk* **7**(1) 18–20 (January)

Eberlein, E. and Keller, U. (1995) Hyperbolic distributions in finance. *Bernoulli* **1** 281–99

Geske, R. (1978) Pricing of options with stochastic dividend yield. *Journal of Finance* **33** 617–25

Hoggard, T., Whalley, A.E. and Wilmott, P. (1994) Hedging option portfolios in the presence of transaction costs. *Advances in Futures and Options Research* **7** 21–35

Hyer, T., Lipton-Lifschitz, A. and Pugachevsky, D. (1997) Passport to success. *Risk* **10**(9) 127–32

Miller, M. and Modigliani, F. (1961) Dividend policy, growth and the valuation of shares. *Journal of Business* **34** 411–33

O'Hara, M. (1995) *Market Microstructure Theory*. Blackwell

Penaud, A., Wilmott, P. and Ahn, H. (1998) Exotic passport options. MFG Working Paper, Oxford University

Rubinstein, M. (1994) Implied binomial trees. *Journal of Finance* **69** 771–818

Wilmott, P. (1995) Volatility smiles revisited. *Derivatives Week* **4**(38) 8

3

Asymptotic analysis of stochastic volatility models

Henrik Rasmussen and Paul Wilmott

INTRODUCTION

In this chapter we consider the pricing of options when the underlying asset value S and its volatility σ are described by the stochastic differential equations

$$dS/S = r\,dt + \sigma\,dX \qquad (3.1)$$

$$d\sigma = A\,dt + B\,dY \qquad (3.2)$$

$$dX \cdot dY = \rho\,dt \qquad (3.3)$$

where X and Y are Brownian motions, r is the short rate, and where the coefficients A and B are functions of only σ. When calibrating such a stochastic volatility model to market prices, one usually finds that the volatility of volatility B/σ is greater than the volatility σ of the underlying. For instance (Wiggins, 1987)

$$\sigma \propto 0.2$$

$$B \propto 0.2,$$

in which case the ratio between volatility and the volatility of volatility becomes

$$\frac{B}{\sigma^2} \propto 5.$$

Accordingly, we introduce a small parameter ϵ,

$$B = \frac{\beta}{\sqrt{\epsilon}},$$

such that (for characteristic values of σ)

$$\frac{\beta}{\sigma^2} \propto 1.0$$

which implies

$$\epsilon \propto 0.04.$$

The parameter ϵ can be interpreted as a ratio of timescales for fluctuations in volatility σ and in the asset price S. If T is a characteristic timescale for S, then ϵT is a characteristic timescale for the volatility process σ. Since we would like to think of ϵ as a ratio of characteristic timescales, we let the drift term A scale like

$$A = \alpha/\epsilon,$$

and thereby arrive at the equations

$$dS/S = r\, dt + \sigma\, dX \tag{3.4}$$

$$d\sigma = \frac{\alpha}{\epsilon}\, dt + \frac{\beta}{\sqrt{\epsilon}}\, dY \tag{3.5}$$

$$dX \cdot dY = \rho\, dt. \tag{3.6}$$

Let now V denote the value of a European option on S. It satisfies Garman's equation (Garman, 1976; Wilmott, 1998):

$$\frac{\partial V}{\partial t} + \frac{\sigma^2 S^2}{2}\frac{\partial^2 V}{\partial S^2} + rS\frac{\partial V}{\partial S} - rV + \rho\frac{S\sigma\beta}{\sqrt{\epsilon}}\frac{\partial^2 V}{\partial S\,\partial\sigma} + \frac{\beta^2}{2\epsilon}\frac{\partial^2 V}{\partial\sigma^2} + \frac{\alpha}{\epsilon}\frac{\partial V}{\partial\sigma} = 0. \tag{3.7}$$

In the following, we first seek a regular pertubation series solution of Garman's equation up to and including order ϵ^2,

$$V(S,\sigma,t) \sim \sum_{n=0}^{N} \epsilon^{n/2} V_n(S,\sigma,t), \qquad N = 4. \tag{3.8}$$

We next estimate the implied volatility for a vanilla option (these are used for calibration). Our approximation to the implied volatility is a fifth-order polynomial in moneyness with coefficients depending on the time to expiry and on the current volatility.

Our results extend those of Fouque *et al.* (1998a, 1998b, 1999) and Sircar and Papanicolaou (1998) in being valid for many more models and in going to higher orders in ϵ (where model differences become important). The motivation for going to higher orders in ϵ is to fit better the 'smiles' observed in the market. Specifically, Fouque *et al.* (2000) solve Garman's equation to order $\epsilon^{1/2}$ for the case of a volatility being a deterministic function of an Ornstein–Uhlenbeck process. But the corresponding approximation to the implied volatility only grows linearly with log-moneyness (log of forward over strike), whereas the implied volatility observed in the market often has significant curvature with respect to log-moneyness (the smile). To capture curvature in the implied volatility, we need an approximation that is at least quadratic in log-moneyness.

CONDITIONS ON THE MODELS

The volatility process should be autonomous in the sense that α and β are functions of only σ,

$$\alpha = \alpha(\sigma) \tag{3.9}$$

$$\beta = \beta(\sigma) \tag{3.10}$$

In addition, the risk-neutral probability density of volatility should have a stationary limit and this limit should be well behaved. Let p denote the stationary limit of the risk-neutral probability density of volatility. It is a function of σ only and it satisfies (if it exists) the stationary version of the Kolmogorov forward equation for the volatility process,

$$\frac{1}{2} \frac{\partial^2}{\partial \sigma^2} \left[\beta^2 p \right] - \frac{\partial}{\partial \sigma} \left[\alpha p \right] = 0. \tag{3.11}$$

A stationary density exists if the solution of this equation is normalisable,

$$p(\sigma) = \frac{C}{\beta^2(\sigma)} \exp\left\{ \int_{\sigma_0}^{\sigma} \frac{2\alpha(x)}{\beta^2(x)} \, dx \right\} \in L^1. \tag{3.12}$$

Here C is a constant needed for normalisation,

$$\|p\|_1 = 1.$$

This density p should be well behaved in the sense that certain integrals must be finite. In particular,

$$\hat{\sigma}^2 = \int_0^\infty \sigma^2 p(\sigma) \, d\sigma < \infty, \tag{3.13}$$

i.e. the risk-neutral volatility process has a finite root mean square value with respect to the stationary density. When this condition is satisfied, $\hat{\sigma}$ becomes an effective long-term volatility, around which the real volatility σ fluctuates with a characteristic timescale of order ϵ.

EXAMPLES OF MODELS

Many of the common models satisfy the above conditions. An important exception is the lognormal model (without mean reversion), for which no stationary probability density exists. Table 3.1 gives some examples of stochastic volatility models (the C_i are constants).

Table 3.1 Examples of stochastic volatility models

Authors	Model
Hull and White; Zhu and Avellaneda	$d\sigma^2 = C_1 \sigma^2 \, dt + C_2 \sigma^2 \, dY$
Scott *et al.*	$d\ln\sigma = C_1(C_2 - \ln\sigma) \, dt + C_3 \, dY$
Stein and Stein	$\sigma = |Z|$ where $dZ = C_1(C_2 - Z) \, dt + C_3 \, dY$
Ball and Roma; Heston	$d\sigma^2 = C_1(C_2 - \sigma^2) \, dt + C_3 \sigma \, dY$
Ravanelli	$d\sigma^2 = C_1(C_2 - \sigma^2) \, dt + C_3 \sigma^2 \, dY$

Scott's model

In this model, $\ln(\sigma_t)$ is a mean-reverting Ornstein–Uhlenbeck process,

$$d\ln(\sigma) = C_1(C_2 - \ln(\sigma)) \, dt + C_3 \, dY \tag{3.14}$$

(assuming volatility non-dimensionalised). A stationary density exists for $C_1 > 0$ and is given by

$$p(\sigma) = CC_3^2 \, \sigma^{-1+2C_1C_2/C_3^2} \exp\left[-C_1 \ln^2(\sigma)/C_3^2\right].$$
(3.15)

$C_1 > 0$ ensures that the log of volatility is mean-reverting, at rate C_1 and towards the level C_2/C_1.

The Heston/Ball–Roma model

This model is given by

$$d\sigma^2 = C_1(C_2 - \sigma^2)\,dt + C_3\,\sigma\,dY.$$
(3.16)

The stationary density is given by

$$p(\sigma) = \frac{4C}{C_3^2} \, \sigma^{4C_1(C_2-C_3^2/4)/C_3^2} \exp(-2C_1\sigma^2/C_3^2),$$
(3.17)

and it exists for $C_1 > 0$ and $C_2 - C_3^2/4 > 0$. The Heston model is perhaps the most popular model in applications, since it allows semi-closed-form solutions for option prices.

NOTATION

To simplify the notation, we introduce the differential operators

$$D_0^\sigma = \frac{\partial}{\partial t} + \frac{1}{2}\sigma^2 S^2 \frac{\partial^2}{\partial S^2} + rS \frac{\partial}{\partial S} - r$$

$$D_1 = S\frac{\partial}{\partial S}$$

$$D_2 = \sigma\frac{\partial}{\partial \sigma}$$

$$D_3 = \frac{1}{2}\beta^2\frac{\partial^2}{\partial \sigma^2} + \alpha\frac{\partial}{\partial \sigma}$$

$$D_4 = S^2\frac{\partial^2}{\partial S^2}$$

It is easily shown that

$$D_4 D_0^\sigma = D_0^\sigma D_4$$
(3.18)

$$D_4 D_1 = D_1 D_4$$
(3.19)

$$D_0^\sigma = D_0^{\hat\sigma} + \frac{1}{2}\left(\sigma^2 - \hat\sigma^2\right)D_4$$
(3.20)

$$D_3^{-1}(f) = -\int_\sigma^\infty \frac{1}{\beta^2(y)p(y)} \int_0^y f(x)p(x)\,dx\,dy.$$
(3.21)

To prove (3.18) and (3.19), we simply note that

$$x = \ln(S/S_0),$$

where S_0 is a constant with the same dimension as S, transforms D_0^σ and D_4 into operators with constant coefficients. Equation (3.20) follows immediately from the definitions, while (3.21) can be proved by first applying D_3 on both sides, and then simplifying using the definition of the stationary density p.

Finally, we define

$$F_1(\sigma) = \frac{1}{2} \int_\sigma^\infty \frac{1}{\beta^2(y)p(y)} \int_0^y p(x)(\hat{\sigma}^2 - x^2)\,dx\,dy$$

$$\gamma = \int_0^\infty p(x)\beta(x)D_2(F_1)[x]\,dx$$

$$F_2(\sigma) = \int_\sigma^\infty \frac{1}{\beta^2(y)p(y)} \int_0^y p(x)\big(\gamma - \beta(x)\big)D_2(F_1)[x]\big)\,dx\,dy$$

$$F_3(\sigma) = \frac{1}{2} \int_\sigma^\infty \frac{1}{\beta^2(y)p(y)} \int_0^y p(x)(\hat{\sigma}^2 - x^2)F_1(x)\,dx\,dy$$

$$F_4(\sigma) = \int_\sigma^\infty \frac{1}{\beta^2(y)p(y)} \int_0^y p(x)\beta(x)D_2[F_1](x)\,dx\,dy$$

$$F_5(\sigma) = \int_\sigma^\infty \frac{1}{\beta^2(y)p(y)} \int_0^y p(x)\beta(x)F_2(x)\,dx\,dy.$$

These functions are all straightforward to evaluate in closed form, or by analytical or numerical approximation.

ASYMPTOTIC ANALYSIS

Using the above notation, Garman's equation becomes

$$\epsilon D_0^\sigma(V) + \sqrt{\epsilon}\rho\beta D_1 D_2(V) + D_3(V) = 0. \tag{3.22}$$

Inserting the perturbation series (3.8) into (3.22), we find that

$$D_3(V_0) = 0 \tag{3.23}$$

$$\rho\beta D_1 D_2(V_0) + D_3(V_1) = 0 \tag{3.24}$$

$$\forall n \geqslant 2: \quad D_0^\sigma(V_{n-2}) + \rho\beta D_1 D_2(V_{n-1}) + D_3(V_n) = 0. \tag{3.25}$$

To satisfy the expiry condition at time $t = T$, we need the expiry conditions

$$V_0(S, \sigma, T) = V(S, T)$$

$$V_n(S, \sigma, T) = 0 \quad \text{for} \quad n \geqslant 1.$$

The solution has a thin expiry layer for t near T. However, we are only interested in the solution outside this expiry layer, so we need only impose the expiry condition for $n = 0$.

Equations (3.23) and (3.24) together imply that V_0 and V_1 are independent of σ. It then follows from the definition of D_2 above that the second term in (3.25) vanishes for $n = 2$, so that

$$D_0^\sigma(V_0) + D_3(V_2) = 0. \tag{3.26}$$

After multiplying by the stationary density $p(\sigma)$ and then integrating with respect to σ over $[0, \infty]$, the contribution from the second term is going to be zero. To see this, integrate by parts and note that p satisfies the Kolmogorov forward equation. Since V_0 is independent of σ, we obtain

$$D_0^{\hat{\sigma}}(V_0) = 0. \tag{3.27}$$

This is just the Black–Scholes equation with volatility equal to the root mean square volatility $\hat{\sigma}$,

$$\frac{\partial V_0}{\partial t} + \frac{1}{2}\hat{\sigma}^2 S^2 \frac{\partial^2 V_0}{\partial S^2} + rS\frac{\partial V_0}{\partial S} - r V_0 = 0, \tag{3.28}$$

so that

$$V_0(S, t) = V_{BS}(S, \hat{\sigma}, t), \tag{3.29}$$

where $V_{BS}(S, \sigma, t)$ denotes a Black–Scholes price at volatility σ. The expiry condition for V_0 is the original expiry condition $V(S, T)$.

Since V_0 is known, we may solve for V_2 in (3.26). We first subtract (3.27) from (3.26), and then invert D_3,

$$V_2 = \frac{1}{2}\left[D_3^{-1}(\hat{\sigma}^2 - \sigma^2) \right] D_4(V_B S). \tag{3.30}$$

By definition of F_1,

$$V_2(S, \sigma, t) = F_1(\sigma) D_4(V_{BS}). \tag{3.31}$$

Note that V_2 does not satisfy the expiry condition $V_2 = 0$ at $t = T$. The reason is that V has a thin expiry layer, and our series in (3.8) converges only outside this layer.

Consider now (3.25) for $n = 3$,

$$D_0^\sigma(V_1) + \rho \beta D_1 D_2(V_2) + D_3(V_3) = 0. \tag{3.32}$$

As before, we multiply by p and integrate with respect to σ. Since V_1 too is independent of σ,

$$D_0^{\hat{\sigma}}(V_1) + \rho \int_0^\infty p(\sigma)\beta(\sigma)D_1 D_2(V_2)[\sigma]\, d\sigma = 0. \tag{3.33}$$

It then follows from (3.31) that

$$D_0^{\hat{\sigma}}(V_1) + \rho \left\{ \int_0^\infty p(\sigma)\beta(\sigma) D_2(F_1)[\sigma]\, d\sigma \right\} D_1 D_4(V_{BS}) = 0. \tag{3.34}$$

By the definition of γ,

$$D_0^{\hat{\sigma}}(V_1) + \rho\gamma D_1 D_4(V_{BS}) = 0. \tag{3.35}$$

To solve this equation, we first note that $D_1(f)$ and $D_4(f)$ are both solutions of the Black–Scholes equation if f is a solution. Therefore, since V_{BS} satisfies the Black–Scholes equation with volatility $\hat{\sigma}$,

$$D_0^{\hat{\sigma}} D_1 D_4(V_{BS}) = 0. \tag{3.36}$$

Using this fact, it is easily checked that

$$V_1(S, t) = \rho\gamma(T - t) D_1 D_4(V_{BS}) \tag{3.37}$$

is the solution of (3.35). In the next section we determine $D_1 D_4(V_{BS})$ explicitly for the case of a European vanilla option, and we shall see that the expiry condition $V_1 = 0$ is satisfied. In contrast to V_2, V_0 and V_1 do not depend on the current volatility σ, but only on current stock price S and date t. Note also that, to the leading order, the deviation from a Black–Scholes price increases linearly with the correlation coefficient ρ.

To get an even better approximation, we calculate two more terms in (3.8). The method is the same as before. To determine V_3, subtract (3.35) from (3.32),

$$D_0^{\sigma}(V_1) - D_0^{\hat{\sigma}}(V_1) + \rho\beta D_1 D_2(V_2) - \rho\gamma D_1 D_4(V_{BS}) + D_3(V_3) = 0. \tag{3.38}$$

Using (3.20) for the first and second term, and (3.31) to simplify the third term, we obtain

$$\frac{1}{2}(\sigma^2 - \hat{\sigma}^2) D_4(V_1) + \rho\left(\beta D_2(F_1) - \gamma\right) D_1 D_4(V_{BS}) + D_3(V_3) = 0. \tag{3.39}$$

Insert now V_1 from (3.37) and invert D_3,

$$V_3(S, \sigma, t) = \rho\gamma(T - t) F_1(\sigma) D_1 D_4^2(V_{BS}) + \rho F_2(\sigma) D_1 D_4(V_{BS}). \tag{3.40}$$

Here we used (3.19) to change the order of D_1 and D_4 and simplified the inverse of D_3 by means of the above definitions of F_1 and F_2. We see that V_3, like V_1, vanishes when $\rho = 0$. In fact, it is true in general that odd-order terms vanish for $\rho = 0$. Finally, by a similar argument as used for V_3, we find that

$$V_4(S, \sigma, t) = F_3(\sigma) D_4^2(V_{BS}) + \rho^2 \gamma(T - t) F_4(\sigma) D_1^2 D_4^2(V_{BS})$$
$$- \rho^2 F_5(\sigma) D_1^2 D_4(V_{BS}). \tag{3.41}$$

In this section we have shown that

$$V(S, \sigma, t) = V_{BS}(S, \bar{\sigma}, t)$$
$$+ \epsilon^{1/2} \rho\gamma(T - t) D_1 D_4(V_{BS})$$
$$+ \epsilon F_1(\sigma) D_4(V_{BS})$$
$$+ \epsilon^{3/2} \rho\left\{ \gamma(T - t) F_1(\sigma) D_1 D_4^2(V_{BS}) + F_2(\sigma) D_1 D_4(V_{BS}) \right\}$$

$$+ \epsilon^2 \left\{ F_3(\sigma) D_4^2(V_{BS}) + \rho^2 \gamma (T - t) F_4(\sigma) D_1^2 D_4^2(V_{BS}) \right.$$

$$\left. - \rho^2 F_5(\sigma) D_1^2 D_4(V_{BS}) \right\}$$

$$+ O(\epsilon^{5/2}).$$

Note that the first term is a Black–Scholes value with volatility equal to the risk-neutral root mean square $\bar{\sigma}$ of volatility. This RMS value is also the effective volatility for the asset price S in the limit of an infinitesimal characteristic timescale for the volatility process. See Skorokhod (1987) and Khasminskii and Yin (1996) for discussions of 'homogenisation' of a slow process in the presence of a fast process.

VANILLA OPTIONS: ASYMPTOTICS FOR VALUES

Stochastic volatility models are often calibrated to vanilla options, so let us consider these in detail, i.e. a European call or put. Since gamma of such options is given by

$$\Gamma(S, \hat{\sigma}, t) = \frac{1}{S \hat{\sigma} \sqrt{T - t}} n(d_1)$$

$$d_1 = \frac{\ln(S/K) + (r + \hat{\sigma}^2/2)(T - t)}{\hat{\sigma} \sqrt{T - t}}$$

$$n(x) = \frac{1}{\sqrt{2\pi}} e^{-x^2/2},$$

we get

$$D_4(V_{BS}) = \frac{S}{\hat{\sigma} \sqrt{T - t}} n(d_1) \tag{3.42}$$

where V_{BS} is the Black–Scholes price with volatility $\hat{\sigma}$. To simplify the notation, let

$$x = d_2/\sqrt{2} \tag{3.43}$$

$$d(t) = \frac{K}{\sqrt{2\pi}} \exp\left[-r(T - t) + \hat{\sigma}^2(T - t)/2\right] \tag{3.44}$$

$$\tau = 2\hat{\sigma}^2 (T - t), \tag{3.45}$$

where

$$d_2 = \frac{\ln(S/K) + (r - \hat{\sigma}^2/2)(T - t)}{\hat{\sigma} \sqrt{T - t}}. \tag{3.46}$$

Then

$$D_4(V_{BS}) = d(t) e^{-x^2} \tag{3.47}$$

and

$$D_1(f) = \tau^{-1/2} \frac{\partial f}{\partial x}$$

$$D_1^2(f) = \tau^{-1} \frac{\partial^2 f}{\partial x^2}$$

$$D_4(f) = \tau^{-1} \frac{\partial^2 f}{\partial x^2} - \tau^{-1/2} \frac{\partial f}{\partial x}$$

$$D_1 D_4(f) = \tau^{-3/2} \frac{\partial^3 f}{\partial x^3} - \tau^{-1} \frac{\partial^2 f}{\partial x^2}$$

$$D_1^2 D_4(f) = \tau^{-2} \frac{\partial^4 f}{\partial x^4} - \tau^{-3/2} \frac{\partial^3 f}{\partial x^3}.$$

Using

$$\frac{d^n}{dx^n} e^{-x^2} = (-1)^n H_n(x) e^{-x^2}, \tag{3.48}$$

where H_n is the nth Hermite polynomial, and the fact that

$$H_0 = 1$$
$$H_1 = 2x$$
$$H_2 = 4x^2 - 2$$
$$H_3 = 8x^3 - 12x$$
$$H_4 = 16x^4 - 48x^2 + 12,$$

we get

$$D_1 D_4(V_{BS}) = -\tau^{-1/2} H_1(x) D_4(V_{BS})$$

$$D_1^2 D_4(V_{BS}) = -\tau^{-1} H_2(x) D_4(V_{BS})$$

$$D_4^2(V_{BS}) = \tau^{-1} \left[H_2(x) + \tau^{1/2} H_1(x) \right] D_4(V_{BS})$$

$$D_1 D_4^2(V_{BS}) = -\tau^{-3/2} \left[H_3(x) + \tau^{1/2} H_2(x) \right] D_4(V_{BS})$$

$$D_1^2 D_4^2(V_{BS}) = \tau^{-2} \left[H_4(x) + \tau^{1/2} H_3(x) \right] D_4(V_{BS}).$$

Then, inserting in the formulae from the previous section, we obtain the correction terms to the Black–Scholes prices V_0:

$$V_1(S, \sigma, t) = -\frac{1}{2} \rho \gamma \hat{\sigma}^{-2} \tau^{1/2} H_1(x) S^2 \Gamma$$

$$V_2(S, \sigma, t) = F_1(\sigma) S^2 \Gamma$$

$$V_3(S, \sigma, t) = -\frac{1}{2} \rho \gamma \hat{\sigma}^{-2} \tau^{-1/2} F_1(\sigma) \left[H_3(x) + \tau^{1/2} H_2(x) \right] S^2 \Gamma$$

$$+ \tau^{-1/2} F_2(\sigma) H_1(x) S^2 \Gamma$$

$$V_4(S, \sigma, t) = \tau^{-1} F_3(\sigma) \left[H_2(x) + \tau^{1/2} H_1(x) \right] S^2 \Gamma$$

$$+ \frac{1}{2} \rho^2 \gamma \hat{\sigma}^{-2} \tau^{-1} F_4(\sigma) \left[H_4(x) + \tau^{1/2} H_3(x) \right] S^2 \Gamma$$

$$- \rho^2 \tau^{-1} F_5(\sigma) H_2(x) S^2 \Gamma,$$

where the volatility used in Γ is $\hat{\sigma}$. From the definitions of the first Hermite polynomial H_1, of x and of Γ, it follows that V_1 vanishes at expiry, i.e. both V_0 and V_1 satisfy their corresponding expiry conditions. But this is not the case for terms V_n with $n \geqslant 2$.

VANILLA OPTIONS: IMPLIED VOLATILITIES

In this section we look for an asymptotic expansion of the implied volatility

$$I = \hat{\sigma} + \epsilon^{1/2} I_1 + \epsilon I_2 + \epsilon^{3/2} I_3 + \epsilon^2 I_4 + O(\epsilon^{5/2}). \tag{3.49}$$

Since the implied volatility I satisfies

$$V_{BS}(S, I, t) = V(S, \sigma, t), \tag{3.50}$$

we determine $\{I_1, I_2, I_3, I_4\}$ by Taylor expanding on the LHS, inserting previous results on the RHS, and then equating terms of equal powers in ϵ. On the LHS we use

$$V_{BS}(S, I, t) = \sum_{n=0}^{4} \left(\epsilon^{1/2} I_1 + \epsilon I_2 + \epsilon^{3/2} I_3 + \epsilon^2 I_4 \right)^n \frac{\partial^n V_{BS}}{\partial \hat{\sigma}^n} + O(\epsilon^{5/2}). \tag{3.51}$$

Since vega for a European vanilla option is given by

$$\frac{\partial V_{BS}}{\partial \hat{\sigma}} = S \sqrt{T - t}\, n(d_1), \tag{3.52}$$

and since

$$\frac{\partial d_1}{\partial \hat{\sigma}} = -\hat{\sigma}^{-1} d_2$$

$$\frac{\partial d_2}{\partial \hat{\sigma}} = -\hat{\sigma}^{-1} d_1,$$

we get

$$\frac{\partial^2 V_{BS}}{\partial \hat{\sigma}^2} = \eta_2 \frac{\partial V_{BS}}{\partial \hat{\sigma}}$$

$$\frac{\partial^3 V_{BS}}{\partial \hat{\sigma}^3} = \eta_3 \frac{\partial V_{BS}}{\partial \hat{\sigma}}$$

$$\frac{\partial^4 V_{BS}}{\partial \hat{\sigma}^4} = \eta_4 \frac{\partial V_{BS}}{\partial \hat{\sigma}},$$

where we have used the 'vega coefficients'

$$\eta_1 = 1$$

$$\eta_2 = \hat{\sigma}^{-1} d_1 d_2$$

$$\eta_3 = -\hat{\sigma}^{-2}\left(1 + d_1 + d_2 - d_1 d_2\right)$$

$$\eta_4 = \hat{\sigma}^{-3} d_1 d_2 \left([d_1 d_2 - 1]^2 - d_1^2 d_2 - d_1 d_2^2 - d_2^2 - d_1^2 + 2d_2 + 2d_1\right).$$

Equation (3.51) now becomes

$$V_{BS}(S, I, t) = V_{BS}(S, \hat{\sigma}, t)$$

$$+ \left[\sum_{n=1}^{4}\left(\epsilon^{1/2}I_1 + \epsilon I_2 + \epsilon^{3/2}I_3 + \epsilon^2 I_4\right)^n \eta_n\right] \frac{\partial V_{BS}}{\partial \hat{\sigma}} + O(\epsilon^{5/2}). \quad (3.53)$$

Since

$$\frac{\partial V_{BS}}{\partial \hat{\sigma}} = \hat{\sigma}\,(T - t)\,S^2\,\Gamma, \quad (3.54)$$

and after collecting terms of equal order in ϵ, we get

$$V_{BS}(S, I, t) = V_{BS}(S, \hat{\sigma}, t)$$

$$+ \epsilon^{1/2}\hat{\sigma}(T - t)I_1 S^2 \Gamma$$

$$+ \epsilon\hat{\sigma}(T - t)(I_2 + I_1^2\eta_2)S^2 \Gamma$$

$$+ \epsilon^{3/2}\hat{\sigma}(T - t)(I_3 \eta_1 + 2I_1 I_2\eta_2 + I_1^3\eta_3)S^2\Gamma$$

$$+ \epsilon^2\hat{\sigma}(T - t)(I_1^4\eta_4 + 3I_1^2 I_2\eta_3 + 2I_1 I_3\eta_2 + I_2^2\eta_2 + I_4\eta_4)S^2\Gamma$$

$$+ O(\epsilon^{5/2}).$$

Setting this equal to

$$V_{BS}(S, I, t) = V(S, \hat{\sigma}, t)$$

$$= V_0 + \epsilon^{1/2}V_1 + \epsilon V_2 + \epsilon^{3/2}V_3 + \epsilon^2 V_4 + O(\epsilon^{5/2}),$$

it is straightforward to determine $\{I_1, I_2, I_3, I_4\}$ in terms of $\{V_1, V_2, V_3, V_4\}$. In particular, using the results for V_1 and V_2, we obtain for I_1 and I_2,

$$I_1 = -\rho\gamma\hat{\sigma}^{-2}(T - t)^{-1/2} d_2$$

$$I_2 = \frac{1}{2\hat{\sigma}(T - t)} \int_{\sigma}^{\infty} \frac{1}{\beta^2(y)p(y)} \int_{0}^{y} p(x)(\hat{\sigma}^2 - x^2)\,dx\,dy$$

$$- \rho^2\gamma^2\hat{\sigma}^{-5}(T - t)^{-1}d_1 d_2^2,$$

where we now use standard notation. Since

$$d_1 = \frac{M + \hat{\sigma}^2(T-t)/2}{\hat{\sigma}\sqrt{T-t}}$$

$$d_2 = \frac{M - \hat{\sigma}^2(T-t)/2}{\hat{\sigma}\sqrt{T-t}}$$

$$d_1 d_2 = \frac{M^2 - \hat{\sigma}^4(T-t)^2/4}{\hat{\sigma}^2(T-t)},$$

we get

$$I = \hat{\sigma} - \epsilon^{1/2}\rho\gamma\hat{\sigma}^{-3}(T-t)^{-1}\big(M - \hat{\sigma}^2(T-t)/2\big)$$

$$+ \frac{\epsilon}{2\hat{\sigma}(T-t)} \int_\sigma^\infty \frac{1}{\beta^2(y)p(y)} \int_0^y p(x)(\hat{\sigma}^2 - x^2)\,dx\,dy$$

$$- \epsilon\rho^2\gamma^2\hat{\sigma}^{-8}(T-t)^{-4}\big(M - \hat{\sigma}^2(T-t)/2\big)\big(M^2 - \hat{\sigma}^4(T-t)^2/4\big) + O(\epsilon^{3/2})$$

$$(3.55)$$

where

$$M = \ln(Se^{r(T-t)}/K) \qquad (3.56)$$

is the 'forward moneyness'. In terms of M,

$$I = \hat{\sigma} + \frac{1}{2}\epsilon^{1/2}\rho\gamma\hat{\sigma}^{-1} - \frac{1}{8}\epsilon\rho^2\gamma^2\hat{\sigma}^{-2}(T-t)^{-1}$$

$$+ \frac{\epsilon}{2\hat{\sigma}(T-t)} \int_\sigma^\infty \frac{1}{\beta^2(y)p(y)} \int_0^y p(x)(\hat{\sigma}^2 - x^2)\,dx\,dy$$

$$+ \left\{ \frac{1}{4}\epsilon\rho^2\gamma^2\hat{\sigma}^{-4}(T-t)^{-2} - \epsilon^{1/2}\rho\gamma\hat{\sigma}^{-3}(T-t)^{-1} \right\} M$$

$$+ \left\{ \frac{1}{2}\epsilon\rho^2\gamma^2\hat{\sigma}^{-6}(T-t)^{-3} \right\} M^2$$

$$- \epsilon\rho^2\gamma^2\hat{\sigma}^{-8}(T-t)^{-4}M^3 + O(\epsilon^{3/2}),$$

which is the main result in this chapter. Using (3.57), we can easily calibrate a stochastic volatility model to the implied volatilities of traded options. We considered only vanilla options, but a similar analysis can be carried out for any option with a closed-form solution in the Black–Scholes world (like digitals, barriers, ladders and certain compound options). Finally, we note that (3.57) fails for small $T - t$. The reason is that (3.57) only holds if the time to expiry, $T - t$, is much larger than the characteristic timescale for volatility fluctuations. See Hull and White (1987), Taylor and Xu (1994), Zhu and Avellaneda (1998), Hagan and Woodward (1998) and Lewis (2000) for approximations that can be used when $T - t$ is small.

ACKNOWLEDGEMENT

HOR would like to thank the European Union for a TMR fellowship. The work was carried out at OCIAM (Mathematical Institute) in Oxford and at the department of mathematics at Universita degli Studi di Milano.

REFERENCES

J.P. Fouque, G. Papanicolaou, and K.R. Sircar (1998a) Asymptotics of a two-scale stochastic volatility model

J.P. Fouque, G. Papanicolaou, and K.R. Sircar (1998b) Financial modeling in a fast mean-reverting stochastic volatility environment

J.P. Fouque, G. Papanicolaou, and K.R. Sircar (1999) Mean-reverting stochastic volatility. *International Journal of Theoretical and Applied Finance*

M. Garman (1976) A general theory of asset valuation under diffusion state processes, Technical Report 50, Center for Research in Management Science, Berkeley

P.S. Hagan and D.E. Woodward (1998) Equivalent Black Volatilities

S.L. Heston (1993) A closed-form solution for options with stochastic volatility with application to bond and currency options. *Review of Financial Studies*, **6**, 327–43

J. Hull and A. White (1987) The pricing of options on assets with stochastic volatilities. *Journal of Finance*, **42**, 281–300

J. Hull and A. White (1988) An analysis of the bias in option pricing caused by a stochastic volatility. *Advances in Futures and Options Research*, **3**, 29–61

R.Z. Khasminskii and G. Yin (1996) Asymptotic series for singularly perturbed Kolmogorov–Fokker–Planck equations. *SIAM Journal of Applied Mathematics*, **56**, 1766–93

A.L. Lewis (2000) *Option Valuation under Stochastic Volatility*. Finance Press

C. Ravanelli (1999) MSc dissertation, Universita degli Studi di Milano

K.R. Sircar and G.C. Papanicolaou (1998) Stochastic volatility, smile and asymptotics. *Applied Mathematical Finance*

A.V. Skorokhod (1987) *Asymptotic Methods in the Theory of Stochastic Differential Equations* Nauka. Translated by the American Mathematical Society, Monograph 78 (1989)

E. Stein and J. Stein (1991) Stock price distributions with stochastic volatility: an analytic approach. *Review of Financial Studies*, **4**, 727–52

S.J. Taylor and X. Xu (1994) The magnitude of implied volatility smiles: theory and empirical evidence for exchange rates. *Review of Futures Markets*, **13**

J. Wiggins (1987) Option values and stochastic volatility, *Journal of Financial Economics*, **19**, 351–72

P. Wilmott (1998) *Derivatives*. Wiley

Y. Zhu and M. Avellaneda (1998) A risk-neutral stochastic volatility model. *International Journal of Theoretical and Applied Finance*, **1**(2) 289–310

4

Passport options: a review

Antony Penaud

INTRODUCTION

Market participants trade risky assets for better returns, at least on average. As long as the risk remains significant, however, investment in these assets does not guarantee a positive payoff and traders are prone to become a victim of their own strategies. Nowadays, a variety of financial instruments allow traders to generate non-linear returns and hence enable them to avoid extreme financial loss to some extent. An example of such an instrument is the passport or perfect trader option.

The noteholder is allowed to trade a particular asset (of price S) during the life of the option, T. The number of assets he holds at a particular time t is denoted q and can be positive or negative. There is, however, a constraint (specified in the contract) on q; this is the position limit $L : |q| \leqslant L$. So q can be any value in $[-L, L]$ and it is the noteholder who decides its value; he can change it whenever he wants and as many times as he wants. However, at each time t, the issuer must have knowledge of q, the trading strategy of the noteholder. According to this strategy, the issuer has to hedge; the noteholder does not actually buy or sell anything: he just tells his q to the issuer, and the issuer has to deal with it. Depending on q and dS, the trading account (denoted by π) of the noteholder changes:

$$d\pi = r\pi \, dt + q(dS - rS \, dt) \qquad (4.1)$$

where we have assumed that the cost of borrowing is equal to the risk-free interest rate r. Hyer *et al.* (1997) and Nagayama (1999) study the more general case. We assume that the asset price S follows the lognormal random walk

$$dS = \mu S \, dt + \sigma S \, dX \qquad (4.2)$$

where μ is the drift of the asset, σ its volatility, and dX is a Gaussian random variable with mean 0 and variance dt. At expiry (time T) the issuer has to pay to the noteholder $\max(\pi, 0)$. This implies that the noteholder cannot lose more than the premium he spent at $t = 0$ for buying the passport option. The passport option can be seen as a call on the trading account of the noteholder, the value of the trading account representing how well the noteholder is doing.

In the case where the trading strategy is known in advance, one can price the option using standard techniques. But in the contract of the option, the issuer does not know in advance what strategy the noteholder will follow. To overcome this obstacle, the issuer prices the option by assuming that the noteholder will follow the trading strategy which maximizes the option price. This trading strategy is called the optimal strategy.

In the first part of the chapter, we study in depth the (vanilla) passport option. We look at the two approaches: the stochastic control approach and the martingale approach.

For the stochastic control approach, we follow the work of Hyer *et al.* (1997). For the martingale approach we follow the work of Henderson and Hobson (2000) and Delbaen and Yor (1999). Finally, we see how the noteholder utilizes his option and how much the issuer gains by selling the option. In this last section we follow Ahn *et al.* (1999).

In the second part we look at different exotic features we can add to the original passport option. We start by generalizing the passport option to the multi-asset passport option: the noteholder can trade different assets (Ahn *et al.* 1999). Then we look at different trading constraints. In particular, we study the case where the noteholder is only allowed to trade N times during the life of the option (Ahn *et al.* 1999; Andersen *et al.* 1998). We then follow Shreve and Vecer (2000) to study the case where the constraint on q is more general, i.e. $q \in [\alpha, \beta]$. In the last section we look at more exotic passport options (Penaud *et al.* 1999; Penaud 2001).

THE VANILLA PASSPORT OPTION

The stochastic control approach

The passport option is a call option on the trading account. Let's call $V(t, S, \pi)$ the price of this option. Note that V does not depend on the paths $S(t)$ and $q(\cdot)$ because equations (4.1) and (4.2) show that the trading account π is Markovian in the state variables S, π and q; since the option payoff does not depend on the paths of S and π, neither may V and the optimal strategy q^* (Fleming and Soner 1992).

Let $V^q(t, S, \pi)$ denote the value corresponding to the trading strategy $q(\cdot)$, where q does not need to be optimal. We can write a stochastic differential equation for V^q:

$$dV^q = V_t^q \, dt + V_S^q \, dS + V_\pi^q \, d\pi + \frac{\sigma^2 S^2}{2} (V_{SS}^q + 2q V_{\pi S}^q + q^2 V_{\pi\pi}^q) dt \qquad (4.3)$$

Now, consider the following portfolio:

$$\Pi = -V^q + \Delta S \qquad (4.4)$$

Over a small time step, the change in this portfolio is

$$d\Pi = -V_t^q \, dt - V_S^q \, dS - V_\pi^q \, d\pi - \frac{\sigma^2 S^2}{2} (V_{SS}^q + 2q V_{S\pi}^q + q^2 V_{\pi\pi}^q) + \Delta \, dS \qquad (4.5)$$

Rearranging, we get

$$d\Pi = -V_t^q \, dt + (\Delta - V_S^q - q V_\pi^q) \, dS - V_\pi^q (r\pi - qrS) \, dt$$

$$- \frac{\sigma^2 S^2}{2} (V_{SS}^q + 2q V_{\pi S}^q + 2q^2 V_{\pi\pi}^q) \, dt \qquad (4.6)$$

The following choice of Δ makes the change in the portfolio deterministic:

$$\Delta = V_S^q + q V_\pi^q \qquad (4.7)$$

With this choice of Δ, the portfolio is risk-free. The hypothesis of no arbitrage (Wilmott 1998) states that all risk-free portfolios should grow at the risk-free rate. This enables us to write the pricing equation for the passport option:

$$d\Pi = r \Pi \, dt \qquad (4.8)$$

which leads to the PDE

$$-V_t^q = -rV^q + rSV_S^q + r\pi V_\pi^q + \frac{\sigma^2 S^2}{2} V_{SS}^q + \frac{\sigma^2 S^2}{2} [q^2 V_{\pi\pi}^q + 2q V_{S\pi}^q] \qquad (4.9)$$

after division by dt.

Note that V^q can be expressed as the present value of the expected payoff under the risk-neutral measure as well (Harrison and Pliska 1981):

$$V^q(t, S, \pi) = E[e^{-r(T-t)} \max(\pi_T, 0)] \qquad (4.10)$$

In order to price the option for when we don't know $q(\cdot)$, we assume that the noteholder will follow the strategy which maximizes the option price:

$$V(t, S, \pi) = \max_{|q| \leqslant L} V^q(t, S, \pi) \qquad (4.11)$$

where V is the price of the passport option. So

$$V(t, S, \pi) = \max_{|q| \leqslant L} E[e^{-r(T-t)} \max(\pi_T, 0)] \qquad (4.12)$$

where E is the expectation under the risk-neutral measure.

For the above stochastic control problem, Bellman's principle of dynamic programming (Fleming and Rishel 1975) is formulated as

$$V(t, S, \pi) = \max_{|q| \leqslant L} E[e^{-r\delta t} V(t + \delta t, S(t + \delta t), \pi(t + \delta t))] \qquad (4.13)$$

where the expectation is maximized by proceeding optimally over the short time interval $[t, t + \delta t]$. This principle states that we find the optimal strategy at a given time by assuming that we already know the optimal strategy at all future times: in other words, that backward induction works. Bellman's principle can be used to derive a PDE for V, the Hamilton–Jacobi–Bellman (HJB) equation (Fleming and Rishel 1975):

$$-V_t = -rV + rSV_S + r\pi V_\pi + \frac{\sigma^2 S^2}{2} V_{SS} + \frac{\sigma^2 S^2}{2} \max_{|q| \leqslant C} [q^2 V_{\pi\pi} + 2V_{S\pi}] \qquad (4.14)$$

with final condition

$$V(T, S, \pi) = \max(\pi, 0) \qquad (4.15)$$

This equation defines the option price and the optimal strategy q^* which is the maximizer of the term in brackets. Once this strategy is found, the PDE for V is defined. The verification result for the HJB equation, which demonstrates that the value $V(\cdot)$ is attainable with some strategy and cannot be exceeded, follows a standard derivation (Karatzas and Shreve 1998).

Throughout the chapter we assume $L = 1$. We do not lose generality because $V_{L=L^*}(t, S, \pi) = V_{L=1}(t, L^* S, \pi)$.

Now, the HJB equation can be simplified thanks to the symmetry of the problem; indeed, if we introduce the variable $z = \pi/S$, then $V(t, S, \pi) = S\phi(t, z)$, where ϕ satisfies

$$-\phi_t = \frac{\sigma^2}{2} \max_{|q| \leqslant 1} [(z - q)^2 \phi_{zz}] \qquad (4.16)$$

with the final condition $\phi(T, z) = \max(z, 0)$.

The payoff being convex, the maximum of the term in brackets is attained on $|q| = 1$ (Hyer *et al.* 1997) and the pricing equation is therefore simplified to the linear PDE

$$-\phi_t = \frac{\sigma^2}{2}(1 + |z|)^2 \phi_{zz} \qquad (4.17)$$

Note the following properties:

- On $\pi = 0$, V is linear in S and therefore $V_{C=C^*}(t, S, 0) = C^* V_{C=1}(t, S, 0)$
- The passport option price does not depend on the interest rate
- $SV_S + \pi V_\pi = V$

Using Green's functions, Hyer *et al.* derive a complicated explicit formula for the option price. The case where the asset pays dividends is studied by Hyer *et al.* and Andersen *et al.*

The martingale approach

The pricing of the passport option was first tackled by Hyer *et al.* using stochastic control techniques. But it has not taken long for martingale people to tackle the problem with their beloved tools. This approach was used by Henderson and Hobson and by Delbaen and Yor independently.

We assume that the market is complete with a unique martingale measure $\mathbb{P}$ under which the discounted asset price is a martingale. So the price of any option can be expressed as the present value of the expected payoff under $\mathbb{P}$.

Under the risk-neutral measure, the price follows

$$\frac{dS_t}{S_t} = r \, dt + \sigma \, dW_t \qquad (4.18)$$

We consider the discounted price process $P_t = e^{-rt} S_t$ which solves

$$dP_t = P_t \sigma \, dW_t \qquad (4.19)$$

so P_t is a martingale.

Define the discounted value of the trading account $G_t(q) = e^{-rt} \pi_t(q)$. Note that $G(q)$ is a local martingale under $\mathbb{P}$ (in fact a martingale for each q) and

$$dG_t(q) = q_t \sigma P_t \, dW_t = q_t \, dP_t \qquad (4.20)$$

Now we price the option by assuming that the noteholder will follow the optimal strategy. So

$$V(t, S, \pi) = \max_{q_t \leqslant L} e^{-r(T-t)} E[\pi_T^+(q)] \qquad (4.21)$$

where $\pi_T^+(q) = \max(\pi_T(q), 0)$ and E is the expectation under $\mathbb{P}$.

We use Tanaka's formula for continuous semimartingales (Revuz and Yor 1991, Theorem VI.1.2):

$$G_T^+(q) = G_0^+(q) + \int_0^T I_{(G(q)>0)} \, dG(q) + \frac{1}{2} L_T^{G(q)}(0) \qquad (4.22)$$

where $L_T^{G(q)}(0)$ is the local time of process $G(q)$ at level zero between time 0 and time T. This representation enables us to write

$$E[\exp(-rT)\pi_T^+(q)] = EG_T^+(q) = \frac{1}{2}E[L_T^{G(q)}(0) + G_0^+(q)] \qquad (4.23)$$

where we have used the fact that $\int_0^T I_{(G(q)>0)}q_u \, dP_u$ is a martingale for all strategies q (Revuz and Yor 1991, Exercise IV.4.22).

Let $M_u(q) = \int_0^u -q_r \, \mathrm{sgn}(G_r(q)) \, dS_r$ and $M_r^*(q) = \sup_{0\leqslant u\leqslant r} M_u(q)$. Applying Skorokhod's lemma (Karatzas and Shreve 1988) leads to

$$L_T^{G(q)}(0) = (M_T^*(q) - |G_0(q)|)^+ \qquad (4.24)$$

so

$$E[G_T^+(q)] = \frac{1}{2}E[M_T^*(q) - |G_0(q)|]^+ + G_0^+(q) \qquad (4.25)$$

Now setting $v = -q \, \mathrm{sgn}\,(G(q))$ allows us to rewrite the pricing problem as follows:

- Find the strategy v, with $|v| \leqslant 1$, such that $E[M_T^*(q) - g]^+$ is maximized, where $M_r^*(v) = \sup_{0\leqslant s\leqslant r} M_s(v)$ and $M_s(v) = \int_0^s v_u \, dP_u$.
- Find the associated value for the passport option as given by the formula $\frac{1}{2}E[M_T^*(\tilde{v}) - |G_0(q)|)^+] + G_0^+(q)$, where $\tilde{v}$ is the optimal strategy.

Using coupling arguments Henderson and Hobson show that the optimal strategy is $v = 1$. The option price is then $\frac{1}{2}E[\sup_{0\leqslant r\leqslant T} S_r - S_0 - |G_0(q)|)^+] + G_0(q)^+$. Note that this price is related to the price of a lookback call option with strike $S_0 + |G_0(q)|$.

An explicit formula is available for the option price:

$$\pi_t^+(q) + \frac{1}{2}[S_t N(d) - N(d - \sigma\sqrt{\tau}) + \sigma\sqrt{\tau}(N'(d) + dN(d)) - |\pi_t(q)|N(d - \sigma\sqrt{\tau})] \qquad (4.26)$$

where $\tau = T - t$ and

$$d = \frac{-\log(1 + |\pi_t(q)|/S_t) + \frac{1}{2}\sigma^2\tau}{\sigma\sqrt{\tau}} \qquad (4.27)$$

and N is the cumulative normal distribution function.

Henderson and Hobson study the case where the underlying follows a more general diffusion process and find that the optimal strategy is still the same (long when behind, short when ahead).

Utility of trading passport

In this section we examine how the option holder utilizes his option and how much the issuer gains by selling the option. The investor who owns a passport option may construct his trading strategy to maximize his utility, predicting the market movement. When the physical trend of the market differs from the risk-neutral drift significantly, the option holder will benefit as long as he has a correct view on the market. At the same time, the issuer will gain from the difference between the price-maximizing trading strategy and the trading strategy performed by his customer.

Perfectly specified drift model

Modeling the gain by investors may be fictitious when one assumes a perfectly specified drift μ. However, the presumption allows us to evaluate the gain by selling passport options to a transcendental investor who trades ideally. Therefore, if the gain turns out to be significant in this case, then the result remains persuasive.

First we assume that the option holder finds his strategy by solving the value of the maximum expected utility of the payoff:

$$u(t, S, \pi) = \sup_{|q| \leqslant 1} E\left[e^{-r(T-t)}U\left(\max(\pi_T(q), 0)\right)\right] \qquad (4.28)$$

where E is the expectation under the physical measure and U is the option holder's utility function which is increasing in its argument. In fact, we will only concentrate on the case $U(x) = x$, i.e. the option holder maximizes his expected payoff. The reason for this choice of utility function is that the investor's portfolio is insured by the passport option. So it makes sense to take risks. One can check that u satisfies the following HJB equation. The same equation arises in Ahn *et al.* (2000). The function u represents the expected end-of-the-year bonus of a trader and q is the strategy he should follow in order to maximize his expected bonus.

$$-u_t = r\pi u_\pi + \mu S u_S - ru$$

$$+ \sup_{|q| \leqslant 1}\left(qS(\mu - r)u_\pi + \frac{1}{2}\sigma^2 S^2\{q^2 u_{\pi\pi} + 2q u_{\pi S} + u_{SS}\}\right) \qquad (4.29)$$

$$u(T, S, \pi) = \max(\pi, 0)$$

where μ is the physical drift of the underlying asset. Note that u is homogeneous of degree 1 in space variables, hence it has a similarity solution of the form $u(t, S, \pi) = Sh(t, \pi/s)$. Furthermore $h(t, z)$ satisfies the following HJB equation:

$$-h_t = (\mu - r)(h - zh_z) + \sup_{|q| \leqslant 1}\left(\frac{1}{2}\sigma^2(z - q)^2 h_{zz} + q(\mu - r)h_z\right) \qquad (4.30)$$

with the terminal data $\max(z, 0)$. From this we obtain the option holder's trading strategy:

$$q = \text{sign}\left(\frac{\mu - r}{\sigma^2} \cdot \frac{h_z}{h_{zz}} - z\right) \qquad (4.31)$$

When μ coincides with the risk-free rate r, then (4.30) agrees with the price-maximizing value function for the option (4.17), and q in (4.31) coincides with the price-maximizing strategy q_*. If μ differs from r, then the option holder's choice will be different from the price-maximizing strategy.

Next we discuss the issuer's hedging strategy, Δ. Earlier we explained that the hedging strategy must be in tune with the actual trading strategy performed by the option holder, and that it is given by $\Delta = V_S + q V_\pi$ where V solves the HJB equation (4.14). Then the profit of the issuer becomes

$$P = V(0, S_0, 0) + \int_0^T e^{-rt} \Delta (dS - rS\,dt) - e^{-rT} V(T, S_T, \pi_T) \qquad (4.32)$$

The first term is the price of the option he collects in cash, the second is the result of the delta hedging, and the third is the present value of the potential liability. Applying Itô's formula to V yields

$$P = -\int_0^T dt\, e^{-rt} \cdot \left(V_t + \frac{1}{2}\sigma^2 S^2 \{V_{SS} + 2q V_{\pi S} + q^2 V_{\pi\pi}\} \right)$$

$$= \frac{1}{2}\sigma^2 \int_0^T dt\, e^{-rt} S_t^2 \cdot \left((q^{*2} - q^2) V_{\pi\pi} + 2(q^* - q) V_{\pi S} \right) \qquad (4.33)$$

where q^* is the price-maximizing strategy and q is the strategy performed by the option holder. Here we have exploited (4.14) as well as $\pi V_\pi + S V_S - V = 0$. Recall that $V(t, S, \pi)$ has a similarity solution $S\pi(t, \pi/s)$ where ϕ is defined in (4.17). In particular, we have

$$V_{\pi S} = -\frac{\pi}{S^2}\phi_{zz} \quad \text{and} \quad V_{\pi\pi} = \frac{1}{S}\phi_{zz}$$

Also recall that $q^* = -\text{sign}(z)$. Thus we have a further reduction in the integrand of (4.33):

$$S^2 \cdot \left((q^{*2} - q^2) V_{\pi\pi} + 2(q^* - q) V_{\pi S} \right) = \phi_{zz}(t, \frac{\pi}{S}) \cdot \left(2|\pi| + 2q\pi + (1-q)^2 S \right)$$

$$\qquad (4.34)$$

Now suppose that the option holder finds his strategy by maximizing the expected return. Then, as we computed earlier in (4.31), the option holder's strategy q depends on π and S only through the ratio π/s and has a value of ± 1. Hence the last term in (4.34) drops out, and the profit of the issuer becomes

$$P = \sigma^2 \int_0^T dt\, e^{-rt} S_t \cdot (|z_t| + q(t, z_t) z_t)\, \phi_{zz} \qquad (4.35)$$

where z is the ratio π/S. To obtain the expected profit $E[P]$ of the issuer, we define

$$g(t, S, \pi) = \sigma^2 E\left[\int_t^T d\tau\, e^{-r\tau} S_\tau \cdot (|z_\tau| + q(\tau, z_\tau) z_\tau)\, \phi_{zz} \right]$$

Again we observe that g has a similarity solution of the form $g(t, S, \pi) = S\psi(t, \pi/S)$ and that $\psi(t, z)$ satisfies the following PDE:

$$-\psi_t = (\mu - r)(q - z)\psi_z + \mu\psi + \frac{1}{2}\sigma^2(q - z)^2 \psi_{zz} + \sigma^2 e^{-rt}(|z| + zq(t, z))\phi_{zz}$$

subject to $\psi(T, z) = 0$. To solve this equation, we need to obtain ϕ from (4.17) and q from (4.31).

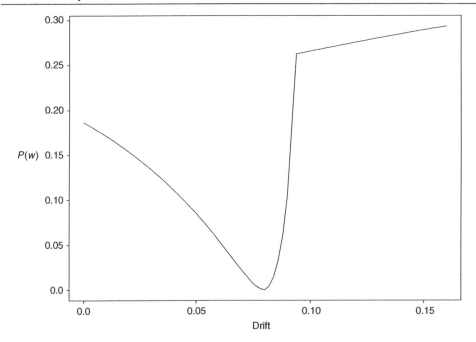

Figure 4.1 Issuer's expected gain versus the drift of the underlying asset

Figure 4.1 shows the expected gain by the issuer as a function of μ, the physical drift, that is $\psi(0,0)$ against μ. The asset volatility is 20% per annum and the maturity of the option is 6 months. We calculate the profit $100 \cdot \psi$ at 81 different values of the physical drift from zero to 16%. When the drift coincides with the risk-free rate $r = 0.08$ (i.e. 8% annum), the gain vanishes. As we explained earlier, the issuer gains more as the gap between the drift and the risk-free rate becomes larger.

Imperfect information model

When the physical drift is positive, the price of the asset increases in the long run. In a short period, however, the volatility dictates the price behavior and the effect of the drift is reduced. Thus, even if the drift is positive, the price may fall in a short period. We use the term *market direction* for the direction of the price in a short period to distinguish it from the drift.

We investigate how an investor benefits from buying passport options in the environment where he must guess the market direction from imperfect information. Thus the strategy performed by the option holder will be different from the one that maximizes the price and the issuer gains as long as he hedges well. In the following, we describe our simulation model. Suppose that the price of the asset is a lognormal diffusion with physical drift μ and volatility σ. Then the probability that the price at time τ is greater than the price at time 0 is given by

$$N\left(\sqrt{\tau}\left(\frac{\mu}{\sigma} - \frac{1}{2}\sigma\right)\right) \tag{4.36}$$

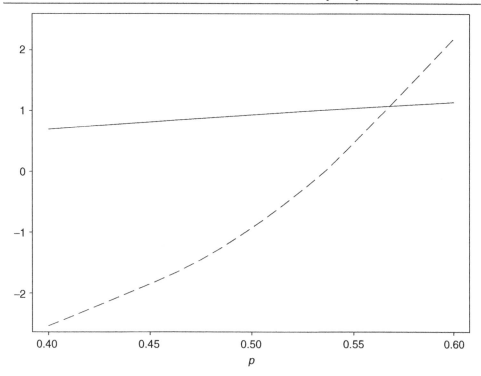

Figure 4.2   Profits and correct guessing probabilities

where N is the distribution function for the standard normal random variable. For example, if $\sigma = 0.2$ (i.e. 20% annum) and $\tau = 0.05$ (18 days, roughly), then $\mu_+ = 0.2466$ yields 60% chance of rise and $\mu_- = -0.2066$ yields 60% chance of fall. Thus, if the investor guesses a rising market when $\mu_+ = 0.2466$ (or a falling market when $\mu_- = -0.2066$), then he will be correct only 60% of the time. In general, we may choose $\mu_+(p)$ and $\mu_-(p)$ so that the probability of a correct guess becomes p. As we alternate μ_+ and μ_-, the investor guesses the market direction correctly only $100 \cdot p\%$ of the time.

Figure 4.2 shows the mean profit made by the issuer (the thin line) and the mean profit made by the option holder (the broken line), as a function of the guessing probability. We alternate μ_+ and μ_- 10 times during the life of the option which we set at 6 months. As before, the volatility is 20% per annum and the initial asset price is $100. The curves in the picture are in fact the present values of the mean profits (i.e. it is already discounted). Thus the issuer beats the risk-free rate regardless of the correct guessing probability. If the option holder guesses correctly 53.8% of the time, then he beats the risk-free rate as well.

Figure 4.3 shows a scatterplot of 5000 simulations when the option holder guesses correctly 60% of the time. The horizontal axis is for the issuer (writer) and the vertical axis is for the option holder. The price of the option is 2.94. The mean profit is 1.14 for the issuer and 2.16 for the option holder. Thus the mean return for the option holder is 72%. The few points at which the issuer loses money are the result of discrete hedging in simulation (100 rebalancings) and of errors in numerical computations.

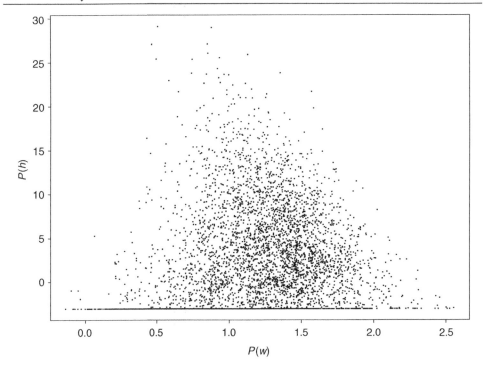

Figure 4.3 Profits of writer (w) and holder (h)

EXOTIC PASSPORT OPTIONS

Multi-asset passport option

In this section we generalize the vanilla passport option to the multi-asset passport option
In what follows we will use rather abstract notation: ∇ and ∇^2 are the gradient (the first
derivative) and the Hessian (the second derivative), respectively.

We designate X to be the vector of size $n + 1$ consisting of π and S. We define the
value function of the problem as follows:

$$V(t, X) = \max_{|q| \leqslant 1} E \left[e^{-r(T-t)} \max(\pi_T(q), 0) \right] \tag{4.37}$$

where E is the expectation under the risk-neutral measure. We have the following result.

Let $X = (\pi, S_1, \dots, S_n)'$. The value function $V(t, X)$ defined in (4.37) satisfies the
following HJB equation:

$$-V_t = r \left(\langle \nabla V, X \rangle - V \right) + \frac{1}{2} \cdot \max_{|q| \leqslant 1} \left\{ \langle q, C_q \rangle V_{\pi\pi} + 2 \langle \nabla_0^2 v, C_q \rangle + \langle S, DS \rangle \right\} \tag{4.38}$$

$$V(T, X) = \max(\pi, 0)$$

where $C = [\rho_{ij}\sigma_i\sigma_j S_i S_j]_{n \times n}$, $D = [\rho_{ij}\sigma_i\sigma_j \nabla_{ij}^2 V]_{n \times n}$, and $\nabla_0^2 V = (\nabla_{01}^2 V, \dots, \nabla_{0n}^2 V)'$.
The dimensionality of the above equation can be reduced (Ahn *et al.* 1999). As for the
single-asset passport option, the multi-asset passport option does not depend on r and

we have

$$\langle \nabla V, X \rangle = V \tag{4.39}$$

Next we discuss the behavior of q^*, the price-maximizing trading strategy. Since the terminal data $\max(\pi, 0)$ is convex in π, $V_{\pi\pi}$ stays positive as long as the solution of (4.36) does not explode. Also note that C is a positive definite matrix. Therefore the supremum in the HJB equation (4.38) is always attained in the boundary of the feasible set: the price-maximizing trading strategy q^* satisfies $|q_t^*| = 1$ for all t almost surely. Of course this will fail when the terminal data is not convex.

Example 4.1: Dual passport ($n = 2$)
In the following numerical example, $\sigma_1 = 0.2$, $\sigma_2 = 0.4$ and $\rho = 0.5$.

Figure 4.4 is a graph of the price of the 6 month dual passport option with constraint $q^{(1)}q^{(2)} = 0$, i.e. the option holder may use his passport to enter into different territories, but given any time the physical presence has to be in either one of them. Intuitively this constraint reduces the effect of correlation by not allowing the two assets to coalesce with each other in the trading account. Thus pricing and hedging are somewhat less sensitive to the possible misspecification of the correlation. In this example the volatility of $S^{(2)}$ dominates that of $S^{(1)}$. Thus, when the price of $S^{(2)}$ is greater than that of $S^{(1)}$, the price of the option is robust to the change of prices in $S^{(1)}$.

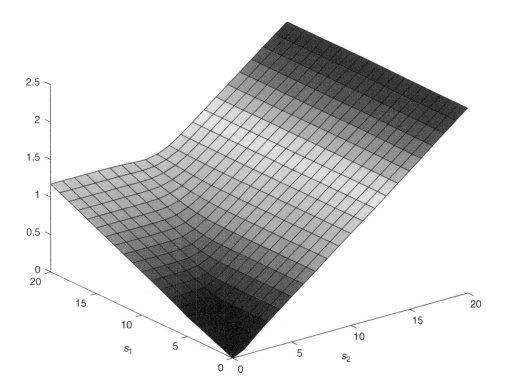

Figure 4.4 Price of dual passport option with constraints $q^{(1)}q^{(2)} = 0$

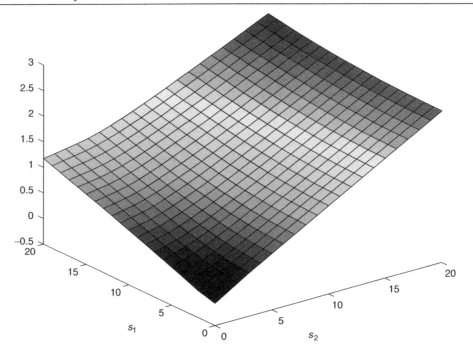

Figure 4.5   Price of dual passport option without constraints

Figure 4.5 is the case when there is no constraint. Obviously the contract without the constraint $q^{(1)}q^{(2)} = 0$ is more expensive than the contract with the constraint.

Discrete trading constraints

In this section we discuss trading constraints which force the option holder to trade only a maximum number of times. Two constraints to be considered here are a specification of the total number of trades and a restriction on the time between trades. In both cases it is clear that the price-maximizing strategy has its value (i.e. the amount of holding) equal to one of the limits ± 1. Then the price-maximizing strategy can be identified by a sequence of optimal stopping times. We will describe the option price with multiple layers of free boundary PDEs. We refer to Van Moerbeke (1976) for the justification of the equivalence of the optimal stopping problems and free boundary PDEs.

Limited number of trades

Our goal is to describe the price-maximizing value function when only a finite number of trades are permitted. The model that we present is different from those of Andersen *et al.* and Delbaen and Yor. Indeed their model allows the strategy q to be modified at N discrete times $(t_0, t_1, \ldots, t_{N-1})$ where $t_0 = 0$ and $t_N = T$. The one we are going to describe here allows the noteholder to change his trading position at any time. When only one trade is permitted, the worst case for the issuer is when his customer demands a trade at the very moment he signs the contract (see Ahn *et al.* 1999). So for the time being, we will assume that one trade is made at time 0.

We consider $V^{(n+)}$ and $V^{(n-)}$, where n is the number of trades to be made and $+/-$ indicates the current position, long or short. Then the price of the option is the maximum of $V^{(n+)}(0, S, 0)$ and $V^{(n-)}(0, S, 0)$, if $n + 1$ trades are allowed, because we assumed one trade is made at time 0. These functions are homogeneous of degree 1 in space variables, hence $\pi V_\pi^{(n\pm)} + S V_S^{(n\pm)} = V^{(n\pm)}$ regardless of n. If the option holder is not allowed to trade any more ($n = 0$), the value functions evolve without an obstacle:

$$\mathcal{L}^+ V^{(0+)} = V_t^{(0+)} + \frac{1}{2}\sigma^2 S^2 \left(V_{SS}^{(0+)} + 2V_{\pi S}^{(0+)} + V_{\pi\pi}^{(0+)} \right) = 0$$

$$\mathcal{L}^- V^{(0-)} = V_t^{(0-)} + \frac{1}{2}\sigma^2 S^2 \left(V_{SS}^{(0-)} - 2V_{\pi S}^{(0-)} + V_{\pi\pi}^{(0-)} \right) = 0$$

with terminal data $V^{(0\pm)}(T, S, \pi) = \max(\pi, 0)$. Now we investigate $V^{(n+)}$ for $n > 0$. Suppose that $\Pi = \Delta S - V^{(n+)}$ is the riskless portfolio for the issuer. As we described earlier, the issuer must choose $\Delta = V_S^{(n+)} + q V_\pi^{(n+)}$ where q is the actual trading strategy performed by his customer. Since the riskless portfolio must grow at least at the risk-free rate r,

$$\mathcal{L}^+ V^{(n+)} = V_t^{(n+)} + \frac{1}{2}\sigma^2 S^2 \left(V_{\pi\pi}^{(n+)} + 2V_{\pi S}^{(n+)} + V_{SS}^{(n+)} \right) \leqslant 0 \qquad (4.40)$$

The equality must hold at least in one case to avoid arbitrage, and when it does, it is the worst case for the issuer. Suppose that $\mathcal{L}^+ V^{(n+)}$ is strictly less than 0 in a situation. This means that the option holder staying with long position is no longer the worst case for the issuer. Thus the value $V^{(n+)}$ must coincide with the residual value $v^{((n-1)-)}$. On the other hand, if $V^{(n+)}$ exceeds $V^{(n-1)-}$, the trade demanded by the option holder does not provoke the worst case for the issuer. Thus $\mathcal{L}^+ V^{(n+)}$ vanishes. Combining these, we obtain

$$\mathcal{L}^+ V^{(n+)} \cdot \left(V^{(n+)} - V^{((n-1)-)} \right) = 0, \quad \mathcal{L}^+ V^{(n+)} \leqslant 0, \quad V^{(n+)} \geqslant V^{((n-1)-)} \qquad (4.41)$$

with the terminal condition $V^{(n+)}(T, S, \pi) = \max(\pi, 0)$. This is known as a variational formulation of a free boundary PDE (i.e. linear complementary problem). For the theoretical aspects of the problem such as regularity conditions, we refer to Friedman (1988). Similarly, $V^{(n-)}$ satisfies the following:

$$\mathcal{L}^- V^{(n-)} \cdot \left(V^{(n-)} - V^{(n-1)+} \right) = 0, \quad \mathcal{L}^- V^{(n-)} \leqslant 0, \quad V^{(n-)} \geqslant V^{(n-1)+} \qquad (4.42)$$

with terminal data $V^{(n-)}(T, S, \pi) = \max(\pi, 0)$. If the contract specifies a fixed amount of penalty, say p, on each trade the option holder engages, then we replace the free boundary conditions in (4.41) and (4.42) by

$$V^{(n+)} \geqslant V^{((n-1)-)} + p \quad \text{and} \quad V^{(n-)} \geqslant V^{((n-1)+)} + p$$

Now we discuss how the issuer hedges the option. Suppose that n trades are allowed so that the maximum of $V^{((n-1)+)}$ and $V^{((n-1)-)}$ is the price. When we construct $V^{(k\pm)}$, $k \geqslant 0$, we assume that the option holder trades at time 0 while he may not have to. If the option holder indeed trades at time 0, the issuer follows $V^{(k\pm)}$, $k = n - 1, \ldots, 0$, tracking his customer's position ($+/-$ as long/short) and the number of trades to be made. For example, if the customer holds 0.7 shares of the underlying and if he is allowed to engage 3 more trades, the issuer holds $\Delta = V_S^{(3+)} + 0.7 V_\pi^{(3+)}$. If the noteholder does not trade at time 0, the issuer makes a profit (Ahn *et al.* 1999).

Restrictions on time between trades

Now the contract states that the option holder is allowed to trade only after a specified time, say ω, has elapsed since the last trade. We introduce the idea of a clock which keeps track of time since the last trade. The clock is reset to zero immediately after each time the option holder trades, and it keeps ticking until its hand reaches ω, where it remains until the next trade. To model this, we introduce an additional time variable θ:

$$\theta(t) = \begin{cases} t - \tau_i & \text{if } \tau_i \leqslant t < \tau_i + \omega \\ \omega & \text{if } \tau_i + \omega \leqslant t < \tau_{i+1} \end{cases}$$

where τ_i and τ_{i+1} are adjacent trading times. The option holder is allowed to trade only when the clock is dormant, i.e. $\theta = \omega$.

We will describe the value of the option using price-maximizing value functions, $V^{(+)}$ and $V^{(-)}$. The status described by $V^{(+)}(t, S, \pi, \theta)$, for $\theta \in (0, \omega)$, is that the option holder is currently long in asset, but not allowed to trade. $V^{(+)}(t, S, \pi, \omega)$ is for the case when the option holder is currently long in asset and he is allowed to trade, which puts him in a short position in asset. $V^{(+)}(t, S, \pi, 0)$ describes the very moment the option holder puts himself in a long position in asset. $V^{(-)}$ describes the opposite case. As before, these functions are homogeneous of degree 1 in space variables, hence $\pi V_\pi^{(\pm)} + S V_S^{\pm} = V^{\pm}$.

The evolution of the price-maximizing value functions $V^{(\pm)}$ will depend on the status of the clock, active or dormant. First we consider the case when the clock is active ($\theta < \omega$). The option holder is not allowed to trade and all he can do is to watch the clock ticking anxiously. The price-maximizing value functions evolve naturally (i.e. without any obstacles) as the clock ticks:

$$V_t^{(+)} + V_\theta^{(+)} + \frac{1}{2}\sigma^2 S^2 \left(V_{SS}^{(+)} + 2 V_{\pi S}^{(+)} + V_{\pi\pi}^{(+)} \right) = 0$$

$$V_t^{(-)} + V_\theta^{(-)} + \frac{1}{2}\sigma^2 s^2 \left(V_{SS}^{(-)} - 2 V_{\pi S}^{(-)} + V_{\pi\pi}^{(-)} \right) = 0$$

Next we suppose that the clock is dormant ($\theta = \omega$), hence the option holder is allowed to trade. Then the value functions evolve with several rules. First, the price-maximizing value functions must stay above the residual values:

$$V^{(+)}(t, S, \pi, \omega) \geqslant V^{(-)}(t, S, \pi, 0) \quad \text{and} \quad V^{(-)}(t, S, \pi, \omega) \geqslant V^{(+)}(t, S, \pi, 0) \quad (4.43)$$

Second, the riskless portfolio for the issuer grows at least at the risk-free rate:

$$\mathcal{L}^+ V^{(+)} = V_t^{(+)} + \frac{1}{2}\sigma^2 S^2 \left(V_{SS}^{(+)} + 2 V_{\pi S}^{(+)} + V_{\pi\pi}^{(+)} \right) \leqslant 0 \quad (4.44)$$

$$\mathcal{L}^- V^{(-)} = V_t^{(-)} + \frac{1}{2}\sigma^2 S^2 \left(V_{SS}^{(-)} - 2 V_{\pi S}^{(-)} + V_{\pi\pi}^{(-)} \right) \leqslant 0 \quad (4.45)$$

where each function is evaluated at (t, S, π, ω). Here we dropped $V_\theta^{(\pm)}$ as the clock is no longer ticking. The third rule combines the first two in the following sense. $\mathcal{L}^+ V^{(+)} < 0$ indicates that trading demand does not provoke the worst case. This happens only when $V^{(+)}(t, S, \pi, \omega) = V^{(-)}(t, S, \pi, 0)$. On the other hand, if $V^{(+)}(t, S, \pi, \omega)$ exceeds $V^{(-)}(t, S, \pi, 0)$, waiting does provoke the worst case. In summary,

$$\mathcal{L}^+ V^{(+)}(t, S, \pi, \omega) \cdot \left(V^{(+)}(t, S, \pi, \omega) - V^{(-)}(t, S, \pi, 0) \right) = 0 \qquad (4.46)$$

In the opposite case, we have

$$\mathcal{L}^- V^{(-)}(t, S, \pi, \omega) \cdot \left(V^{(-)}(t, S, \pi, \omega) - V^{(+)}(t, S, \pi, 0) \right) = 0 \qquad (4.47)$$

Conditions (4.43) to (4.47) define a linear complementary problem. As in the case without clock, the price is the maximum of $V^{(+)}(0, S, 0, 0)$ and $V^{(-)}(0, S, 0, 0)$, and hedging is a matter of tracking the position of the option holder. If there is a fixed penalty p on each trade, we replace the free boundary conditions in (4.43) by

$$V^{(+)}(t, S, \pi, \omega) \geqslant V^{(-)}(t, S, \pi, , 0) + p \quad \text{and} \quad V^{(-)}(t, S, \pi, \omega) \geqslant V^{(+)}(t, S, \pi, 0) + p$$

Numerical results

The price of the single-asset passport option is proportional to the price of the underlying asset, even with discrete trading constraints. Let $\phi(n)$ be the proportional constant when n trades are permitted (i.e. the maximum of $v^{(n-1)+}$ and $v^{(n-1)-}$) and $\phi_c(\omega)$ for the clock. Figure 4.6(a) shows the value of $100 \cdot \phi$, thus the price of the option when the underlying asset price is 100, for $n = 1, \ldots, 10$. The dotted line is the price of the passport option without trading constraints, i.e. $n = \infty$. The volatility is 20% per annum and the maturity is six months. Figure 4.6(b) is the price of the passport option with clock, $100 \cdot \phi_c$. Parameters are the same as in (a). We have chosen the variable T/ω for the horizontal axis. Thus the number of permitted trades is the greatest integer not more than the variable T/ω. Again the dotted line is the case when there is no clock, i.e. $\omega = 0$. Note that the option with clock is less expensive. This is because it has more restriction even when the same number of trades are allowed.

Also it is noteworthy that the price of the option with 10 trades is already close to the price of the unconstrained passport option. In practice, however, it is customary that the contract compels the option holder to refrain from frequent trades. In order to maintain a delta-neutral position, the issuer of the passport option needs to trade the underlying asset at least as often as his customer. When the customer trades very often, the issuer is burdened with an excessive transaction cost.

Vacation calls and vacation puts

So far we have assumed that $q \in [-L, L]$ and have actually looked at the case $q \in [-1, 1]$ because there was no loss of generality. In this section we look at the more general case $q \in [\alpha, \beta]$. This problem was studied by Shreve and Vecer (2000).

The option price is still the maximum over all possible strategies:

$$V(t, S, \pi) = \max_{q \in [\alpha, \beta]} E[e^{-r(T-t)} \max(\pi_T, 0)] \qquad (4.48)$$

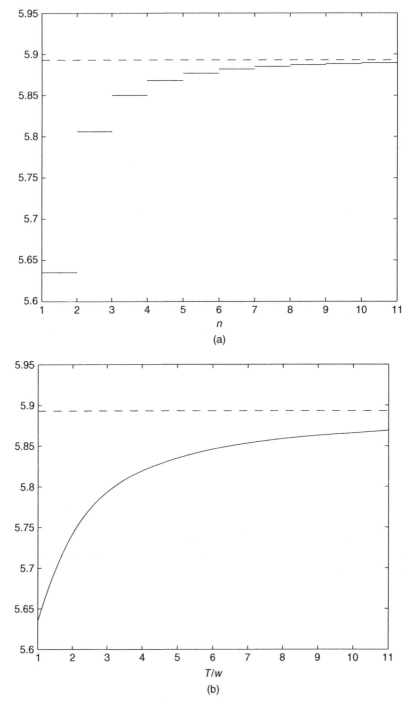

Figure 4.6 Discrete trading constraints: (a) limited number of trades, (b) clock

where E is the expectation under the risk-neutral measure. The corresponding HJB equation is

$$-V_t = -rV + rSV_S + r\pi V_\pi + \frac{\sigma^2 S^2}{2} V_{SS} + \frac{\sigma^2 S^2}{2} \max_{q \in [\alpha, \beta]} [q^2 V_{\pi\pi} + 2V_{S\pi}] \quad (4.49)$$

with final condition

$$V(T, S, \pi) = \max(\pi, 0) \quad (4.50)$$

The dimensionality of the problem can be reduced using the change of variable $z = \pi/S - \frac{1}{2}(\alpha + \beta)$. We get $V(t, S, \pi) = S\phi(t, z)$, where ϕ satisfies

$$\phi_t + \frac{\sigma^2}{2} \max_{q \in [\alpha, \beta]} \left(\left(z + \frac{\alpha + \beta}{2} - q \right)^2 \phi_{zz} \right) = 0 \quad (4.51)$$

with the final condition

$$\phi(T, z) = \max\left(z + \frac{\alpha + \beta}{2}, 0 \right) \quad (4.52)$$

Using a mean comparison theorem of Hajek (1985), Shreve and Vecer find the optimal strategy:

$$q^* = \alpha I_{\pi \geqslant \frac{\alpha+\beta}{2}} + \beta I_{\pi \leqslant \frac{\alpha+\beta}{2}} \quad (4.53)$$

So ϕ satisfies the PDE

$$\phi_t + \frac{\sigma^2}{2} \left(|z| + \frac{\beta - \alpha}{2} \right)^2 \phi_{zz} = 0 \quad (4.54)$$

One of the main properties of these exotic passport options is the generalized put/call parity:

$$V^{(\alpha,\beta)}(t, S, \pi) - V^{(-\beta,-\alpha)}(t, S, -\pi) = \pi \quad (4.55)$$

Shreve and Vecer derive a complicated explicit formula for V as well. They study in depth the case $q \in [0, 1]$ (vacation call) and the case $q \in [-1, 0]$ (vacation put).

Miscellaneous exotic

In this section we explore more exotic features we could add to the passport option.

The smooth trader passport options

Hedging a passport option can be difficult for the issuer. Indeed, if the noteholder decides to change his strategy, then the issuer has to change his Δ accordingly. The Δ does not evolve continuously if q is not continuous. So Δ-hedging would be very expensive in the presence of transaction costs. In this section we introduce the smooth trading passport option as a remedy to this problem. This option does not have a constraint on q, but on q_t

instead: $|q_t| \leqslant L'$. This means that the noteholder cannot change his position from $q = 1$ to $q = -1$ (for example) instantaneously. Indeed, there is a maximum speed (namely L') at which q can be changed by the noteholder. If L' and T are not too large, this option will be cheaper than the vanilla one and may be more attractive to the noteholder who does intend to trade smoothly.

The option price depends on q and the HJB equation for V becomes

$$-V_t = \frac{\sigma^2 S^2}{2}(V_{SS} + q^2 V_{\pi\pi} + 2q V_{\pi S}) + \max_{|q_t| \leqslant L'} [V_q q_t]$$

with the usual final condition $V(T) = \max(\pi, 0)$. Indeed, it is now q_t that the noteholder can choose and it is therefore among all possible (Markovian) q_t that the maximization takes place.

Using $V(t, S, \pi, q) = S\phi(t, z, q)$, where $z = \pi/S$, the HJB equation satisfied by the similarity solution ϕ is

$$-\phi_t = \frac{\sigma^2}{2}(z - q)^2 \phi_{zz} + L'|\phi_q|$$

with $\phi(T) = \max(z, 0)$ as usual.

The piecewise smooth trader passport option

In the smooth trader passport option, the constraint on the slope of q might be too restrictive in certain circumstances: imagine he suddenly changes his mind about the direction of the asset. He would be stuck in a position he does not like at all. As a remedy to this rather annoying feature, we introduce an extra clause in the contract which allows the noteholder a certain number of jumps (say N) in $q(t)$. In order to avoid large jumps, we reintroduce the position limit $L : |q| \leqslant L$.

We call V^n the option price when n jumps are allowed; V^0 is just the pure smooth trading passport option described in the previous section.

For each t^*, S^*, π^*, q^*, the option price $V^n(t^*, S^*, \pi^*, q^*)$ should be larger than $V^{n-1}(t^*, S^*, \pi^*, q)$ for all q in $[-L, L]$. Indeed, if the noteholder decides to exercise his right to have a jump in q^* at t^*, then $q^*(t^* + dt)$ could be any q allowed in the contract.

In terms of the similarity solution ϕ, the linear complementary problem is

$$\mathcal{L}\phi^n \leqslant 0$$
$$\phi^n \geqslant \max_{|q| \leqslant L}\{\phi^{n-1}\}$$
$$\mathcal{L}\phi^n \cdot (\phi^n - \max_{|q| \leqslant L}\{\phi^{n-1}\}) = 0$$

with $\phi(T) = \max(z, 0)$ and where $\mathcal{L}$ is such that

$$\mathcal{L}\phi = \begin{cases} \phi_t + \frac{1}{2}\sigma^2(z - q)^2 \phi_{zz} + \max_{|q_t| \leqslant L'}[\phi_q q_t] & \text{if } |q| < L \\ \phi_t + \frac{1}{2}\sigma^2(z - q)^2 \phi_{zz} + \max_{0 \leqslant q_t \leqslant L'}[\phi_q q_t] & \text{if } q = -L \\ \phi_t + \frac{1}{2}\sigma^2(z - q)^2 \phi_{zz} + \max_{-L' \leqslant q_t \leqslant 0}[\phi_q q_t] & \text{if } q = L \end{cases}$$

Let's briefly explain financially the linear complementary problem: either it is optimal for the noteholder to exercise his right to have a jump, in which case $\phi^n = \max_{|q| \leqslant L}\{\phi^{n-1}\}$

and as a consequence $\mathcal{L}\phi^n < 0$, or it is not optimal for the noteholder to exercise his right to have a jump and the 'smooth trader passport option equation' is valid together with the constraint $\phi^n > \max_{|q|\leqslant L}\{\phi^{n-1}\}$.

More connections between financial products, free boundary problems and linear complementary problems can be found in Wilmott (1998). Rigorous justification between equivalence of the optimal stopping problems and free boundary PDEs can be found in Van Moerbeke (1976); theoretical aspects of free boundary PDEs can be found in Friedman (1988).

The double-stake passport option

This exotic passport option allows the noteholder to change his position limit from 1 to 2 during a period of time specified in the contract (say D).

Imagine that at a time during the life of the option the noteholder, for some reason, is pretty sure which direction the asset is going to go. Then he can decide to enter the double-stake period and can therefore make more profit if he is right (but more loss if he is wrong).

If $S\phi(t, z)$ is the price of the double-stake passport option, it must be larger than $S\Phi(t, z, 0)$, the price of the option which specifies that the position limit is 2 from time t to time $t + D$. The linear complementary problem for ϕ is therefore

$$\mathcal{L}\phi \leqslant 0$$

$$\phi(t, z) \geqslant \Phi(t, z, 0)$$

$$\mathcal{L}\phi \cdot (\phi(t, z) - \Phi(t, z, 0)) = 0$$

where $\mathcal{L}$ is as in the previous section and $\phi(T) = \max(z, 0)$. But we need to find Φ as well; between t and $t + D$, a clock τ is ticking and $L = 2$:

$$-\Phi_t - \Phi_\tau = \tfrac{1}{2}\sigma^2(2 + |z|^2)\Phi_{zz} \quad \text{if } 0 \leqslant \tau < D$$

$$-\Phi_t = \tfrac{1}{2}\sigma^2(1 + |z|^2)\Phi_{zz} \quad \text{if } \tau = D$$

$$\Phi(T) = \max(z, 0)$$

Figure 4.7 gives an example of a double-stake passport option. In this example, $T = 0.5$ $\sigma = 0.2, S = 100$. When $D = T$ the price is, as expected, twice as expensive as when $D = 0$.

CONCLUSION

Leland (1980) explained that investors whose risk tolerance grows with wealth more rapidly than that of the average investor would benefit from portfolio insurance. Nowadays, a variety of options serve market participants as portfolio insurance as well as investment tools. Unlike people who buy and hold vanilla options to protect their static portfolio, investors equipped with passport options can actively rectify their market position more aggressively as well, with a limited downside. Thus passport options could attract the investors with below average risk aversion as well.

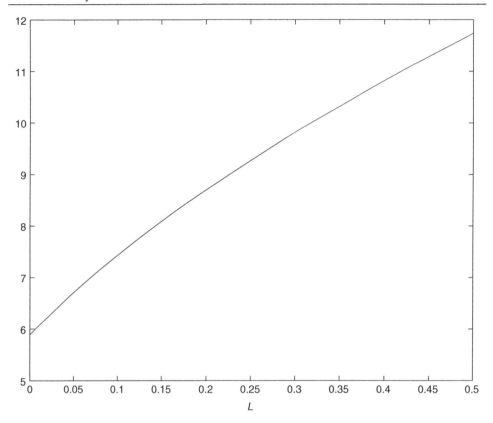

Figure 4.7   Price of double-stake passport option in function of D

REFERENCES

Ahn, H., A. Penaud, and P. Wilmott (1999) Various passport options and their valuation. *Applied Mathematical Finance*, **6**(4), 275–92

Ahn, H., J. Dewynne, P. Hua, A. Penaud, and P. Wilmott (2000). The end-of-the-year bonus: how to optimally reward a trader? Preprint, http://www.maths.ox.ac.uk/penaud/

Andersen, L., J. Andreasen, and R. Brotherton-Ratcliffe (1998). The passport option *Journal of Computational Finance*, **1**(3), 15–36

Delbaen, F. and M. Yor (1999) Passport options, preliminary manuscript, Dept. Math., ETH-Zurich, http://ww.math.ethz.ch/delbaen/.

Fleming, W.H. and R.W. Rishel (1975) *Deterministic and Stochastic Optimal Control*. Springer-Verlag, New York

Fleming, W.H. and H.M. Soner (1992) *Controlled Markov Processes and Viscosity Solutions*. Springer-Verlag, New York

Friedman, A. (1988) *Variational Principles and Free Boundary Problems*. Robert E. Kreiger, New York

Hajek, B. (1985) Mean stochastic comparison of diffusions. *Z. Wahrscheinlichkeitstheorie verw. Gebiete*, **68**, 315–29

Harrison, J.M. and S.R. Pliska (1981) Martingales and stochastic integrals in the theory of continuous trading. *Stochastic Processes and Their Applications* **11**, 215–60

Henderson, V. and D. Hobson (2000) Local time, coupling and the passport option. *Finance and Stochastics*, **4**(1), 63–80

Hyer, T., A. Lipton-Lifschitz, and D. Pugachevsky (1997) Passport to success. *Risk*, **10**(9), 127–31

Karatzas, I. and S.E. Shreve (1988) *Brownian Motion and Stochastic Calculus*. Springer-Verlag, New York

Leland, H.E. (1980) Who should buy portfolio insurance? *Journal of Finance*, **35**(2), 581–94

Nagayama, I. (1999) Pricing of passport options. *J. Math. Sci. Univ. Tokyo*, **5**, 747–85

Penaud, A. (2001) Optimal decisions in finance: passport options and the bonus problem. Dphil thesis, Oxford University

Penaud, A., P. Wilmott and H. Ahn (1999) Exotic passport options. *Asia-Pacific Financial Markets*, **6**, 171–82

Revuz, D. and M. Yor (1991) *Continuous Martingales and Brownian Motion*. Springer-Verlag, New York

Shreve, S. and J. Vecer (2000) Options on a traded account: vacation calls, vacation puts and passport options. *Finance and Stochastics*, May, pp. 255–74

Van Moerbeke, P. (1976) On optimal stopping and free boundary problems. *Archives of Rational Mechanical Analysis*, **60**, 101–48

Wilmott, P. (1998) *Derivatives*. Wiley, New York

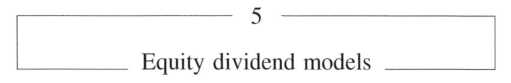

5

Equity dividend models

David Bakstein and Paul Wilmott

INTRODUCTION

One reason why dividends take an important place in the financial literature is the perfect market hypothesis (PMH), stating that stocks are valued as their future dividend stream discounted by an appropriate cost of capital rate. Many equity analysts use modifications of this discounted cash flow model to estimate the current fair value of a firm and forecast its future performance. Numerous empirical studies have been conducted to test if the PMH holds in reality, but with inconclusive results. See Fama (1970) for the PMH and Copeland and Weston (1988) for an extensive survey of valuation models. In fact, if the value of a stock is dependent on its future dividend stream, then the stock itself can be regarded as a derivative on the dividends. But, on the other hand, equity derivative traders and quantitative analysts normally regard the stock price as the exogenous underlying process and separately require, among other parameters, and assuming it is available, the exact schedule of dividends over the life of the option in order to value and hedge equity-linked positions. As an additional business activity, many banks and hedge funds specialise in dividend stripping and arbitrage, by either swapping dividends between traders with different marginal tax rates or taking bets on the market reaction to dividends.

Most academic literature on derivatives usually treats dividends as a minor modification to the Black–Scholes (BS) formula. In fact, comparing the amount of research available on models for spot, interest rate or volatility processes, the literature on dividend models is scarce. Nonetheless, as Figure 5.1 indicates, the correct evaluation of dividends may be crucial. Other major fields of research in the derivatives literature are the modelling of jumps and risk management frameworks like Value at Risk (VaR). The first modifies the BS world of continuous Brownian motion, the second measures and aggregates market risk on a macro level. Since dividends are in fact regular and by far the most common, albeit partly predictable, jumps in a financial variable, their modelling approaches may also be applicable in the other fields. One could measure the risk of jumps due to earnings announcements, currency revaluations, interest rate changes, etc., or any other event that leads to a jump in a variable analogously and reflect it in appropriate hedging strategies. Bakstein and Wilmott (2000) point out the similarities between dividends and crashes.

In this chapter we attempt to give a concise summary of the relation between dividends and the valuation of equity derivatives. We present various approaches to modelling the dividend process of a security or an index, elaborating on existing models and presenting new approaches. Choices normally have to be made about whether to use deterministic or stochastic models and discrete dates or a continuous yield. We describe the appropriateness of each of the models under various market circumstances and list their respective advantages and limitations.

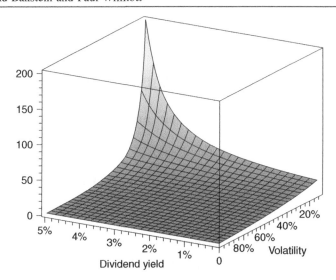

Figure 5.1 Dividend sensitivity/vega for an at-the-money binary call with a risk-free rate of 5% and an expiry of 6 months

EFFECTS OF DIVIDENDS ON ASSET PRICES

Frictionless markets

If we assume the spot price S of the stock to follow a geometric Brownian motion

$$\frac{dS}{S} = \mu \, dt + \sigma \, dX,$$

with constant drift μ, volatility σ and dX a Wiener process, then the contingent claim $V(S, t)$ on the underlying follows a process with separate, possibly non-constant, drift $\tilde{\mu}$ and volatility $\tilde{\sigma}$,

$$dV = \tilde{\mu}(V, t) \, dt + \tilde{\sigma}(V, t) \, dX,$$

but is driven by the same Wiener process. Because both processes are continuous, in this basic form the model would not be suitable for equity that pays dividends at discrete points in time. In that case there will be at least one and possibly two points in time for each dividend, when either S or V jump discontinuously.

Firstly, on the ex-dividend date t_D, if markets are frictionless, the spot should drop by exactly the amount of the dividend D,

$$S_{t_D^-} = S_{t_D^+} + D,$$

where t_D^- and t_D^+, respectively, denote the left and right limits, i.e. the instants just before and after an ex-dividend time, usually termed cum and ex. Because D and t_D are normally announced some time in advance and, unlike for the holder of the equity, the holder of an option does not receive any cash flow, we have that

$$V(S, t_D^-) = V(S - D, t_D^+).$$

Secondly, on the announcement date t_A of the dividend, the new information will directly have an impact on V, if the actual D and t_D deviate from the implied values. On the other hand, the effect on the spot price itself is not directly determined by non-arbitrage arguments. Depending on subjective expectations the spot can move in any direction. In a slightly different context, the famous theorem of Miller and Modigliani (1961) states that equity returns should not change with dividend policy. Therefore, hedging a derivative with the spot is not perfect across the announcement date. It can, however, be hedged with another option or a forward contract, if available. Some option exchanges also offer contracts that are dividend protected. The standard protection clause is that the strike of the option will be reduced by exactly the amount of the dividend. However, it can be shown that this underprotects a call option unless it is well in the money and overprotects the put (Harpaz, 1988). A perfect protection would require increasing the number of underlying stock by a factor $1 + D/S_{t_D^+}$ instead.

Market frictions

In practice the drop in the spot price across the ex-dividend date is

$$S_{t_D^-} = S_{t_D^+} + D + O(S),$$

due to various non-arbitrage relationships in the market. In the literature the last term is mainly attributed to differences in marginal tax rates for dividends (τ_D) and capital gains (τ_C), the so-called tax-clientele hypothesis (Elton and Gruber, 1970). The tax-modified jump condition is derived through

$$S_{t_D^-}(1 - \tau_C) = S_{t_D^+}(1 - \tau_C) + D(1 - \tau_D)$$

thus

$$S_{t_D^-} = S_{t_D^+} + \alpha D,$$

where $\alpha \equiv (1 - \tau_D)/(1 - \tau_C)$ is the tax ratio. Empirical tests of α (e.g. Lakonishok and Vermaelen, 1983), however, are inconclusive. The alternative hypothesis is that around ex-dividend dates, arbitrageurs allocate equity with high dividend yield to investors with low marginal tax rates, possibly even with tax credits. This would damp the effect of α. In general, trading across ex-dividend dates tends to be high, as in Figure 5.2, where a special dividend was paid on top of the ordinary one. For example, Barone-Adesi and Whaley (1986) fail to reject the hypothesis that $\alpha = 1$ for US stocks. But Kaplanis (1986) finds significant differences for implied dividends in option prices on UK stocks with $1 > \alpha > 0.5$ and argues that setting $\alpha = 1$ would lead to option mispricing. Moreover, in the German legislation, domestic investors receive a tax credit on top of the dividend, so for this market α tends to be larger than 1. Overall, there is thus an additional parameter that needs to be estimated whose true value is only revealed after the ex-dividend date. Therefore the price of the derivative across the ex-dividend date may be discontinuous as well unless α was anticipated correctly.

A second market friction occurs if the dividend payout date t_P is not the same as the ex-dividend date. Typically, German companies pay their dividend on the ex-date or within a few days, UK companies 5 weeks after and other European companies up to 6

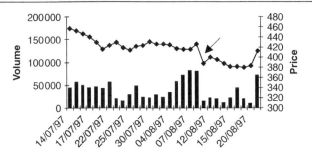

Figure 5.2   Ex-dividend day behaviour of BT plc stock price and trading volume

months in arrears. Hence the stock price should in fact jump by the discounted amount of the dividend, $De^{-r(t_P - t_D)}$. If the payment date is uncertain, it is an additional factor that needs to be estimated.

NON-STOCHASTIC DIVIDEND MODELS

Known dividends

The dividend-modified process for the spot can be written as

$$dS = (\mu S - D(S, t)) \, dt + \sigma S \, dX, \tag{5.1}$$

i.e. with the asset's drift reduced by the dividend. If the dividend process $D(S, t)$ is predictable, i.e. $t > t_A$ so the dividend amount and the exact timing are known, then the price and hedging strategy of options can be found exactly. One can follow the risk-neutral valuation approach by Black and Scholes (1973) of delta-hedging to arrive at the dividend-modified BS partial differential equation (PDE):

$$V_t + \frac{1}{2}\sigma^2 S^2 V_{SS} + (rS - D(S, t))V_S - rV = 0$$

here V_t and V_S represent partial derivatives. Apart from choosing the exact functional form of $D(S, t)$, we also need to decide which S we are referring to.

If, for example, n discrete dividends D_i are paid at times t_i, in the absence of frictions, the backward jump condition at each dividend date is $V(S_x + D_i, t_i^-) = V(S_x, t_i^+)$, where S_x denotes the ex-dividend stock price. Conversely, we define by S_c the cum-dividend stock price or total gains process, that is a sum of S_x and dividends. Under the assumption that S_x is lognormally distributed with volatility σ_x, i.e. that it satisfies

$$\frac{dS_x}{S_x} = \mu \, dt + \sigma_x \, dX,$$

then solving backwards from the terminal condition $V(S_x, T) = V(S_c, T)$:

$$V(S_x, t_n^+) = e^{-r(T - t_n)} \int_0^{\infty} \frac{V(S', t) \, dS'}{2\sigma S' \sqrt{\pi(T - t_n)}} \exp\left\{ \frac{\left(\ln(S'/S_x) + \left(r - \frac{1}{2}\sigma_x^2\right)(T - t_n) \right)^2}{4\sigma_x^2(T - t_n)} \right\}$$

$$= V(S_x + D_n, t_n^-).$$

Because D_n is not random, solving backwards until t_{n-1} yields

$$e^{-r(t_n-t_{n-1})} \int_0^\infty \frac{V(S'+D_n,t_n)\,dS'}{2\sigma S'\sqrt{\pi(t_n-t_{n-1})}} \exp\left[\frac{\left(\ln(S'/S_x)+\left(r-\frac{1}{2}\sigma_x^2\right)(t_n-t_{n-1})\right)^2}{4\sigma_x^2(t_n-t_{n-1})}\right]$$

$$= V\left(S_x + D_n e^{-r(t_n-t_{n-1})}\chi_{[t_{n-1},t_n]}(t), t_{n-1}^+\right)$$

$$= V\left(S_x + D_n e^{-r(t_n-t_{n-1})}\chi_{[t_{n-1},t_n]}(t) + D_{n-1}, t_n^-\right).$$

Continuing the backward solution procedure to $t_0 = t$, we obtain

$$V\left(S_x + \sum_{i=1}^n D_i e^{-r(t_i-t)}\chi_{[t,t_i]}(t), t\right) = V(S_c,t),$$

where $\chi_{[A]}(x) = 1$ if $x \in A$, else 0, is the characteristic function. Hence we arrive at the modified (BS) option value, by subtracting the discounted future dividends from the current (cum-dividend) spot,

$$V(S_x,t) = V\left(S_c - \sum_{i=1}^n D_i e^{-r(t_i-t)}\chi_{[t,t_i]}(t), t\right), \tag{5.2}$$

and treat the stock as non-dividend-paying. It can be shown (e.g. Musiela and Rutkowski, 1998) that this is equivalent to increasing all the strike prices in a portfolio by the future value of the dividends:

$$\hat{K} = K + \sum_{i=1}^n D_i e^{r(T-t_i)}\chi_{[t_i,T]}(t). \tag{5.3}$$

In (5.2) care has to be taken that the present value of the dividends does not exceed the current spot, since this would imply arbitrage opportunities. In fact, $D_i \geqslant 0$, $\forall i$ and in the limit $S = \sum_{i=1}^\infty D_i e^{-r(t_i-t)}$; a central result of the PMH.

But if instead we assume that S_c is lognormally distributed, then by Itô's lemma

$$dS_x = d\left(S_c - \sum_{i=1}^n D_i e^{-r(t_i-t)}\chi_{[t,t_i]}(t)\right)$$

$$= dS_c + \left(r\sum_{i=1}^n D_i e^{-r(t_i-t)}\chi_{[t,t_i]}(t) + \sum_{i=1}^n D_i e^{-r(t_i-t)}\delta(t_i-t)\right)dt,$$

S_x is not and the dividend modification is slightly more difficult. Then the corrections (5.2) or (5.3) do not hold and numerical methods like finite differences, trees or Monte Carlo simulations have to be applied, as demonstrated in depth by Shaw (1998) and Hull (1999), for example. Most notably, care has to be taken because in general $\sigma_x \neq \sigma_c$. Depending on the estimation method of the volatility, the dividend jump contributions have to be added to σ_x, in order to obtain σ_c.

It is common practice to model the dividend amount as a fraction of the spot: $D = y(S,t)S$. This leads to the non-arbitrage jump condition $V(S,t_D^-) = V(S(1-y),t_D^+)$.

If we assume that the fraction is constant and dividends are paid in regular intervals $\delta t = [t_{i-1}, t_i]$, then similarly to the derivation of (5.2) the corresponding solution is

$$V(S_x, t) = V(S_c(1 - y)^n, t). \tag{5.4}$$

Now, writing the yield in annualised terms $\hat{y} = my$, where m is the number of dividends per annum, we have $n = m(T - t)$. Substituting both into (5.4) and taking limits gives

$$V\left(\lim_{m \to \infty} S_c\left(1 - \frac{\hat{y}}{m}\right)^{m(T-t)}, t\right) = V\left(S_c e^{-\hat{y}(T-t)}, t\right). \tag{5.5}$$

The latter is the most common dividend correction proposed in standard textbooks. Its main advantage is simplicity and the fact that if we assume S_x to be lognormally distributed, this implies that so is S_c, and vice versa, because by Itô's lemma

$$dS_c = d\left(S_x e^{\hat{y}(T-t)}\right) = e^{\hat{y}(T-t)}dS_x - \hat{y}S_x e^{\hat{y}(T-t)}dt$$

$$= (\mu - \hat{y})S_c\,dt + \sigma_c S_c\,dX.$$

Here also $\sigma_x = \sigma_c$. The correction terms in (5.2) and (5.5) are related by

$$\hat{y} = -\frac{\ln(S_c) - \ln\left(S_c - \sum_{i=1}^{n} D_i e^{-r(t_i - t)} \chi_{[t, t_i]}(t)\right)}{T - t}.$$

The disadvantage of the single yield correction is that, even for large equity indices, dividends are not uniformly distributed throughout the year, but instead exhibit a seasonal pattern, as Table 5.1 shows. This becomes particularly important if there are multiple cash flow dates in a portfolio of derivatives. Therefore, by writing the dividend term as a time-

Table 5.1 Ex-dividend dates for a sample of 46 large European stocks

	Jan	Feb	Mar	Apr	May	Jun	Jul	Aug	Sep	Oct	Nov	Dec
1999	5	2	5	5	12	8	3	3	0	4	4	2
1998	3	4	5	4	12	10	7	5	3	2	6	1
1997	5	5	3	4	10	10	8	7	3	2	3	1
1996	2	3	6	9	9	10	3	6	4	2	2	2

dependent fraction of the (index) stock price $D(S, t) = y(t)S$, we incorporate a term structure of dividends. For a European call option, the dividend modified BS formula can easily be derived as

$$V = Se^{-\int_t^T y(s)ds}N(d_1) - Ke^{-r(T-t)}N(d_2),$$

where

$$d_{1/2} = \frac{\ln(S/K) + (r \pm \frac{1}{2}\sigma^2)(T - t) - \int_t^T y(s)\,ds}{\sigma\sqrt{T - t}} \quad \text{and} \quad N(x) = \int_{-\infty}^{x} e^{-s^2/2}ds.$$

Closed-form solutions exist if the dividend yield integral can be solved.

But instead of estimating every single dividend and all its parameters in an index, which for a large equity index like the S&P 500 may potentially imply up to 2000 dividends and their weightings, the term structure of dividends can be inferred from traded index futures or OTC forwards, through the following relation:

$$y(t, T) = r(t, T) - \frac{\ln(F/S)}{T - t}.$$

But at any point in time there will only be a limited number of implied yields available. Hence, as is also the practice for the interest rate term structure, interim points will have to be interpolated through various techniques like linear interpolation, polynomial splines, exponential splines, etc., which are also standardly used for interest rate yield curve fitting. However, through this technique the dividend yield may be difficult to obtain, partly because of the frictions accompanying dividends and also due to the illiquidity of the forward markets themselves.

Non-Markovian models

In addition to representing the fair value of a company or a signal of future stock returns, dividends may reflect the performance of the firm in the past accounting period. Intuitively, firms may be inclined to increase their dividends if earnings were good, and vice versa. Wilmott (1998) suggests two models that in one way or the other depend on the path that the stock price has taken in a period prior to the announcement date. Thereby the stock price performance is treated as a proxy for the profitability of the company.

In the first model, since dividends are announced at t_A, several weeks before the ex-dividend date t_D, one could assume that the company's dividend policy may be dependent on the level of S on the day that the dividend is announced. The value of an option would follow its specific PDE with the additional dividend jump condition

$$V(S, t_D^-) = V(S(1 - y(S_{t_A})), t_D^+).$$

To see if this relation holds and the exact functional form of the dividend term would be a statistical exercise of testing and calibration.

A second possible model, described in Wilmott *et al.* (1993), is to let the dividend be functionally dependent on the performance of the stock over the past accounting period. If we assume there is positive correlation between spot and dividend level, then this may damp the price of a long-dated call option, because spot and dividends have opposite effects on it. Moreover, depending on the exact functional form, it could ensure that any one discrete dividend will not exceed the spot on the ex-dividend day.

Under this assumption the model would need to keep track of certain properties of the path that the stock price has taken. This gives the contract the characteristic of an Asian option, i.e. an option functionally dependent on the average of a particular parameter over a time period. The required information about the parameter is captured in the integral

$$D = \int_{t_{A_{i-1}}}^{t_{A_i}} f(S, s, y) \, ds,$$

in $(t_{A_{i-1}}, t_{A_i})$, $\forall i$. Performing a Taylor expansion to leading order gives

$$dD = f(S, t, y) \, dt.$$

Hence the BS PDE can be appended by the additional term to give

$$V_t + \frac{1}{2}\sigma^2 S^2 V_{SS} + rSV_S + fV_D - rV = 0,$$

along with the jump condition $V(S, t_D^-) = V(S - D, t_D^+)$. An obvious choice for the dividend would be the arithmetic average $f = yS$.

If a continuous dividend yield is modelled in the non-Markovian way, then the entire path of S needs to be recorded, because expanding the integral

$$y_t = \int_{t-\tau}^{t} f(S, s) \, ds$$

leads to

$$dy = (f(S, t) - f(S, t - \tau)) \, dt,$$

resulting in the delay PDE

$$V_t + \frac{1}{2}\sigma^2 S^2 V_{SS} + (r - y)SV_S + (f(t) - f(t - \tau))V_y - rV = 0.$$

For non-Markovian dividend models the option value is dependent on an additional variable and hence strongly path-dependent. Therefore, in general, solutions have to be found numerically. For the first model, a finite-difference grid with an updating rule would be sufficient; for the second, implementing a Monte Carlo simulation is straightforward.

Non-linear models

Bid/ask spreads exist in all financial markets. On the one hand they represent transaction costs, but on the other hand they also constitute a buffer for the market-maker against the counterparty's asymmetric information about the exact value of, possibly non-observable, future parameters that an asset depends on. Employing an uncertain parameter model replicates the price spread effect due to the latter reason and it also provides a measure of the risk of a portfolio of assets. Then, by employing hedging strategies that go beyond the standard delta-hedge, these spreads can be minimised, so that they may become suitable pricing tools.

The uncertain parameter modelling approach is based on a system of non-linear PDEs that span an incomplete market. Instead of estimating a vector of constant parameters $\theta = \{\theta_1, \ldots, \theta_n\}$, or alternatively, the processes that they follow, it may be easier and more robust to come up with estimates of, possibly time-dependent, intervals whose bounds they cannot breach:

$$\theta(\omega, t) : \Omega \times [t, T] \to \{[\theta_i^-, \theta_i^+]\}, \qquad \forall i, \tag{5.6}$$

where ω are paths adapted to a filtration $\mathcal{F}_t$ generated by the parameters in their space Ω. In its most general form, we assume that a contract $V(\theta, t)$ is dependent on the parameter vector (5.6), which follows the, possibly random, system of processes

$$d\theta = \mu(\theta, t)\, dt + \sigma(\theta, t)\, dX.$$

Within the specified parameter ranges (5.6) it is possible to fix two (vectors of) paths ω^+ and ω^- that will result in a maximum and a minimum of $V(\theta, t)$, respectively:

$$V^+ = \max_{\theta^- \leqslant \theta \leqslant \theta^+} \{E_Q[V]\} = E_Q[V(\theta(\omega^+), t],$$

$$V^- = \min_{\theta^- \leqslant \theta \leqslant \theta^+} \{E_Q[V]\} = E_Q[V(\theta(\omega^-), t].$$

Here the expectations are taken with respect to a risk-neutral Q-measure. The spread can be shown to be non-arbitrageable, as long as the parameters do not breach their ranges.

Avellaneda *et al.* (1995) and Lyons (1995) first developed this modelling approach for volatility ranges. Epstein and Wilmott (1997) employ it in the modelling of the short rate and Hua (1997) uses it to find worst times for crashes. Finally, Bakstein and Wilmott (2000) applied the approach to model dividend magnitude, timing and yield.

Discrete uncertain dividends

Usually, prior to a dividend announcement, the dividend amount and often the ex-dividend date are uncertain, but estimates lie within some reasonable ranges $D^- \leqslant D \leqslant D^+$ and $t_D^E \leqslant t_D \leqslant t_D^L$. Many companies try to hold the growth of their dividend amount and ex-date constant, but nonetheless changes happen from year to year due to poor earnings, merger activity, management changes, etc.

To derive the minimum value of a portfolio V^-, under the assumptions of uncertainty, we define two functions V_B^- and V_A^- on the interval $[t_D^E, t_D^L]$, denoting the value of the portfolio before and after a dividend, respectively. Both are governed by the BS PDE almost everywhere. On the dividend interval's right limit, these functions are initialised through the conditions

$$V_A^- \left(S, t_D^L\right) = V^- \left(S, t_D^L\right)$$

and

$$V_B^- \left(S, t_D^L\right) = \min_D \left\{ V^- \left(S - D, t_D^L\right) \right\}, \qquad \forall S.$$

Throughout the interval (t_D^E, t_D^L) the minimising condition that has to hold is

$$V_B^-(S, t) \leqslant \min_D \left\{ V_A^-(S - D, t) \right\}, \qquad \forall S.$$

Finally, at the left limit

$$V^- \left(S, t_D^E\right) = \min \left\{ V_B^- \left(S, t_D^E\right), \min_D \left\{ V_A^- \left(S - D, t_D^E\right) \right\} \right\} \qquad \forall S,$$

to ensure that the dividend has been paid during the interval. The system is analogous for V^+. Finding the extreme points is a free-boundary problem, similar to determining the early exercise time of an American option. The free-boundary $t_D^*(S)$ itself is given by

$$t_D^*(S) = \min\left\{t : V_B^-(S,t) = \min_D\left\{V_A^-(S-D,t)\right\}\right\}, \qquad \forall S$$

and therefore V^- is determined both through its governing (BS) PDE and the jump condition

$$V^-\left(S,t_D^{*-}\right) = V\left(S-D,t_D^{*+}\right), \qquad \forall S.$$

Uncertain dividend yield

If dividends are modelled in the form of a continuous, time-dependent yield, the uncertain parameter model becomes slightly more tractable than in the discrete case. If the yield $y(t)$ lies within the time-homogeneous range $[y^-, y^+]$, finding the minimum value for a contract is equivalent to minimising the change to the hedged portfolio $\Pi = V - \Delta S$:

$$\min_{y(t)}\{d\Pi\} = \min_{y(t)}\left\{\left(V_t + (\mu - y)(V_S - \Delta)S + \frac{1}{2}\sigma^2 S^2 V_{SS} - \Delta y(t)S\right)dt\right.$$
$$\left. + (V_S - \Delta)\sigma S\, dX\right\}$$
$$= r(V - \Delta)\, dt. \tag{5.7}$$

Thereby (5.7) can be justified by choosing $\Delta = V_S$, which makes the random terms cancel one another. After rearrangement this leads to

$$\min_{y(t)}\left\{V_t + \frac{1}{2}\sigma^2 S^2 V_{SS} + (r - y(t))SV_S - rV\right\} = 0, \tag{5.8}$$

similarly for the maximisation case with max replacing min. Equation (5.8) is a standard equation of stochastic control (e.g. Øksendal, 1998) and for it to reach its extreme value V^- the optimal process of the controls $y(t, \omega^-)$ can be inferred from optimising the function

$$f(y) = V_t + (r - y(t, \omega))SV_S + \frac{1}{2}\sigma^2 S^2 V_{SS} - rV, \qquad \forall S, t$$

subject to the constraints on the controls. The function is linear in y and therefore it takes its extremes at the limits of the control ranges, depending on the sign of V_S. Hence the solution satisfies the non-linear PDE

$$V_t^- + rSV_S^- + \frac{1}{2}\sigma^2 S^2 V_{SS}^- - rV^- = y(\Delta)SV_S^-,$$

where $y(\Delta) = y^+$ if $V_S > 0$ and vice versa. The result is the converse for V^+. Closed-form solutions are only available in the trivial case, when the delta of the portfolio is single-signed. Figure 5.3 shows the spread between the maximum and the minimum for a butterfly spread.

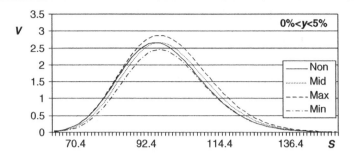

Figure 5.3   Best/worst scenario value spreads

Hedging dividend uncertainty

Unlike in the BS world, due to the non-linearity of the governing PDEs, the value of a portfolio of derivatives is not equal to the sum of the values of its components. This fact can be exploited by adding contracts to the portfolio that reduce the best/worst case spreads of the original portfolio and serve as static hedges. For an extensive account of static hedging and a guide to its implementation, see the relevant chapters in Wilmott (1998). The objective of this type of hedge is to minimise or maximise the marginal value $M^{+/-}$ of the portfolio $V^{+/-}$ by choosing optimal quantities λ_i of liquidly traded additional contracts V_i to be included in the extended portfolio $\tilde{V}^{+/-}$. The Lagrangian is therefore formulated as

$$M^{-} = \min_{\lambda_i, \forall i} \left\{ \tilde{V}^{-} - \sum_i \lambda_i V_i \right\},$$

conversely for M^{+}. Finding the optimal quantities λ_i normally requires an optimisation algorithm. Figure 5.4 shows the marginal value of a butterfly spread hedged with an at-the-money (ATM) call option. The possibility of tightening the initial spread allows a trader to sell the initial portfolio to a client and hedge it with other contracts as well as the stock. This reduces the cost of hedging and may help in attracting counterparties through tighter spreads. Also, these minimum spreads are useful for detecting arbitrage opportunities in the market, should another market-maker's bid/ask spreads be too wide.

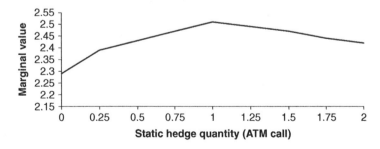

Figure 5.4   Hedged portfolio values: Lagrangian

STOCHASTIC DIVIDEND MODELS

Diffusive dividend processes

Usually dividends are not predictable. In the PMH they are formulated in terms of Markovian expectations, implying that they are of stochastic nature. In its most general form, we can write the dividend yield process as

$$dy = \mu_y(S, y, t)\, dt + \sigma_y(S, y, t)\, dX_y.$$

To derive a PDE we set up a hedged portfolio

$$\Pi(S, y, t) = V(S, y, t) - \Delta S - \hat{\Delta}\hat{V}(S, y, t)$$

with an additional asset that depends on the dividend yield as for instance another option or a future. Then over a time period dt, invoking Itô's formula, the portfolio changes like

$$d\Pi = dV - \Delta\, dS - \hat{\Delta}\, d\hat{V} - \Delta y S\, dt$$

$$= \left(V_t + \frac{1}{2}\sigma^2 S^2 V_{SS} + \frac{1}{2}\sigma_y^2 V_{yy} + \rho\sigma_y\sigma S V_{Sy}\right) dt + V_S\, dS + V_y\, dy - \Delta\, dS$$

$$- \hat{\Delta}\left(\left(\hat{V}_t + \frac{1}{2}\sigma^2 S^2 \hat{V}_{SS} + \frac{1}{2}\sigma_y^2 \hat{V}_{yy} + \rho\sigma_y\sigma S \hat{V}_{Sy}\right) dt + \hat{V}_S\, dS + \hat{V}_y\, dy\right) - \Delta y S\, dt,$$

where $dX\, dX_y = \rho\, dt$, to leading order, is the correlation between the random terms. Choosing the hedge quantities as

$$\Delta = V_S - V_y \hat{V}_S / \hat{V}_y$$

$$\hat{\Delta} = V_y / \hat{V}_y,$$

setting the then deterministic change equal to risk-free growth and rearranging gives

$$\left(V_t + \frac{1}{2}\sigma^2 S^2 V_{SS} + \frac{1}{2}\sigma_y^2 V_{yy} + \rho\sigma_y\sigma S V_{Sy} + (r - y)S V_S - rV\right)\Big/ V_y$$

$$= \left(\hat{V}_t + \frac{1}{2}\sigma^2 S^2 \hat{V}_{SS} + \frac{1}{2}\sigma_y^2 \hat{V}_{yy} + \rho\sigma_y\sigma S \hat{V}_{Sy} + (r - y)S \hat{V}_S - r\hat{V}\right)\Big/ \hat{V}_y.$$

Because one side depends only on V and the other only on $\hat{V}$, it is possible to drop the distinction and set one of the sides equal to $\mu_y - \lambda\sigma_y$, where $\lambda(S, y, t)$ is the market price of dividend risk, i.e. the market's required excess return for every unit of dividend risk, as measured by its volatility. Rearranging the PDE eventually leads to

$$V_t + \frac{1}{2}\sigma^2 S^2 V_{SS} + \frac{1}{2}\sigma_y^2 V_{yy} + \rho\sigma_y\sigma S V_{Sy} + (r - y)S V_S + (\mu_y - \lambda\sigma_y)V_y - rV = 0.$$

In order to solve the PDE, firstly, the payoff at expiry as well as its boundary conditions need to be specified. Secondly, it is required to parameterise the risk-neutralised dividend process. The latter is at the heart of the discussion about market efficiency. Still if we only specify the first requirement, we can formulate the solution in a general form. For instance, the value of a call option struck at K, with deterministic short rate r is given by the Feynman–Kac type formula

$$V(S, y, t) = e^{-r(T-t)} E_Q[\max(S - K, 0)]$$

$$= E_Q\left[S_T e^{-\int_t^T y_s\, ds}\right] N(d_3) - K e^{-r(T-t)} N(d_4),$$

with

$$d_{3/4} = \frac{\ln\left(E_Q\left[S_T e^{-\int_t^T y_s\, ds}\right]\Big/K\right) \pm \frac{1}{2}\,\mathrm{Var}_Q\left[S_T e^{-\int_t^T y_s\, ds}\right]}{\sqrt{\mathrm{Var}_Q\left[S_T e^{-\int_t^T y_s\, ds}\right]}}$$

To arrive at a fully closed-form solution, tractable expressions for the integrals need to be found; this is shown for one of the processes below. But it becomes apparent that even for simple processes, analytic solutions become very complex, assuming they are available. In most cases the solutions have to be found numerically.

It is counterintuitive that dividend yields go either negative or above one. In both cases the stock price would not reflect the true value of the firm and theoretically there would be arbitrage opportunities. Taking these factors into account, Geske (1978) suggested a lognormal process for the dividend yield:

$$dy = \mu_y y\, dt + \sigma_y y\, dX_y.$$

Even though this process does not guarantee that the yield won't exceed one, he states actual cases where it did. Moreover, this process would be consistent with the PMH, which states that dividends and stock prices are lognormal and therefore also their ratio. But many empirical studies (e.g. Shiller, 1981; DeJong and Whiteman, 1991) find this is not consistent with actual observations. They suggest that a trend-stationary, namely a mean-reverting, process for dividends may be more appropriate. Intuitively, this also follows from an assumed positive correlation between stock prices and dividends. Often mean reversion is also employed in the modelling of (stochastic) convenience yields (Hilliard and Reis, 1998; Miltersen and Schwartz, 1998), into which dividends belong. The standard mean-reverting Ornstein–Uhlenbeck process is

$$dy = a(\overline{y} - y)\, dt + \sigma_y\, dX_y, \tag{5.9}$$

where $\overline{y}$ is the mean of the yield and a governs the speed of reversion. The risk-neutralised version of the mean-reverting process (5.9) is

$$dy = (a(\overline{y} - y) - \lambda\sigma_y)\, ds + \sigma_y\, dX_y,$$

with the solution

$$y_T = \overline{y} - \frac{\lambda\sigma_y}{a} + \left(y_t - \overline{y} + \frac{\lambda\sigma_y}{a}\right) e^{-a(T-t)} + \sigma_y e^{-a(T-t)} \int_t^T e^{as}\, dX_s.$$

Now

$$E_Q\left[S_T e^{-\int_t^T y_s\, ds}\right] = E_Q\left[e^{\ln S_T - \int_t^T y_s\, ds}\right]$$

$$= \exp\left\{E_Q\left[\ln S_T - \int_t^T y_s\, ds\right] - \frac{1}{2}\,\mathrm{Var}_Q\left[\ln S_T - \int_t^T y_s\, ds\right]\right\}$$

because the exponent is normally distributed. It can be shown (e.g. Hilliard and Reis, 1998) that

$$E_Q\left[\ln S_T - \int_t^T y_s\,ds\right] = \ln S_t + \left(r - \frac{1}{2}\sigma^2 - \overline{y} - \frac{\lambda\sigma_y}{a}\right)(T-t)$$

$$\times \left(y_t - \overline{y} + \frac{\lambda\sigma_y}{a}\right)\left(\frac{1 - e^{-a(T-t)}}{a}\right)$$

and

$$\mathrm{Var}_Q\left[\ln S_T - \int_t^T y_s\,ds\right] = \sigma^2(T-t) - \frac{\sigma_y^2}{2a}\left(\frac{1 - e^{-a(T-t)}}{a}\right)^2$$

$$+ \left(T - t - \frac{1 - e^{-a(T-t)}}{a}\right)\left(\frac{\sigma_y^2}{a^2} - \frac{2\rho\sigma_y\sigma}{a}\right).$$

This also turns out to be the total variance v. This process is also employed in the interest rate model of Vasicek (1977) and it is well known that, in this case, y may become negative. Whereas this is impossible in theory, it is sometimes observed in practice due to a so-called negative basis between the underlying and the derivative written on it. The basis may occur due to tax accounting differences between the assets, difficulties with hedging or other frictions. Since it is difficult to estimate what part of the implied basis error is due to dividends, a mean-reverting one-factor model for the combined basis that may become negative may be more appropriate than a two-factor model for dividends and other effects.

Random jump processes

One phenomenon that may occur during the life of an equity option is the announcement of a special, i.e. non-recurring, dividend. Those tend to be paid out when the firm is changing its financial structure, after a year with good earnings, after mergers, to wind up its operations, etc. These types of dividend announcements should lead to jumps in option prices since they are rarely anticipated. A standard way of incorporating the possibility of random jumps into option prices is through a Poisson process, or its doubly stochastic extension, a Cox process. Initially the jump-diffusion model was introduced by Merton (1976) for modelling stock market crashes. Stochastic jump processes are also used in the modelling of short rate resets, the default of bonds or jumps in volatility. In fact, dividends are the most common jumps in the stock market and a terminal dividend has mathematically the same effect as a default on a bond.

Incorporating a Poisson element, the new risk-neutralised random walk for the stock price is

$$dS = (r - y + \eta\tilde{y})S\,dt + \sigma S\,dX - \tilde{y}S\,dq, \tag{5.10}$$

where $\tilde{y} \in [0,1]$ is the (possibly random) special dividend as a fraction of the asset and dq is a Poisson process with intensity η and probability measure $P : dq \in \{0,1\} \to \{\eta\,dt, 1-\eta\,dt\}$, as well as $E[dX\,dq] = 0$. Hence (5.10) is diffusive and almost everywhere continuous away from jumps at random times caused by special dividends.

Following the standard delta-hedging strategy, it will not be possible to hedge the jumps. The change to a delta-hedged portfolio Π has a residual risk term

$$d\Pi = \left(V_t + \frac{1}{2}\sigma^2 S^2 V_{SS}\right) dt + (V((1 - \tilde{y})S, t) - V(S, t) - \tilde{y}SV_S) \, dq. \qquad (5.11)$$

Assuming, not unreasonably, that the risk of the special dividend is non-systematic, hence diversifiable, it is possible to take expectations and set (5.11) equal to risk-free growth. The ensuing PDE is

$$V_t + \frac{1}{2}\sigma^2 S^2 V_{SS} + (r - y - \eta E[\tilde{y}])SV_S + \eta E[V((1 - \tilde{y})S, t) - V(S, t)] = 0.$$

Its solution depends on the distribution of $\tilde{y}$ and it is tractable if, for example, $\ln \tilde{y}$ is normal with mean $\tilde{\mu}$ and variance $\tilde{\sigma}^2$. The value of, say, a European call option can then be written as a probability-weighted sum of jump effects:

$$V(S, t) = \sum_{n=1}^{\infty} \frac{e^{-\eta(1 - \tilde{\mu})(T - t)}(\eta(1 - \tilde{\mu})(T - t))^n}{n!} \left(Se^{-(y + \eta\tilde{\mu})(T - t) + n\ln(1 - \tilde{\mu})} N(d_5) \right.$$

$$\left. -Ke^{-r(T - t)}N(d_6) \right), \qquad (5.12)$$

where

$$d_{5/6} = \frac{\ln(S/K) + (r - y - \eta\tilde{\mu} \pm \frac{1}{2}\sigma^2)(T - t) + n(\ln(1 - \tilde{\mu})\tilde{\sigma}^2)}{\sqrt{\sigma^2(T - t) + n\tilde{\sigma}^2}};$$

see Wilmott (1998) for a derivation. In the extreme case of the firm paying a terminal dividend with the stock subsequently being delisted, $\tilde{y} = 1$ and $n = 1$. Then (5.12) collapses to

$$\tilde{V}(S, t) = e^{-\eta(T - t)} V(Se^{\eta(T - t)}, t)$$

$$= V(S, t, r + \eta),$$

i.e. the BS value with an increased risk-free rate.

In reality, as DeAngelo *et al.* (2000) find, special dividends are rare and therefore the numerous parameters are hard to estimate. For instance, in 1999 only one of the 50 biggest quoted European firms paid a special dividend. But if a particular OTC derivative will be exposed to a substantial future dividend stream, like for example a long-dated basket option, then instead of estimating the future dividends exactly, they could be treated as a random future sequence of jumps and combined with the modelling of actual crashes.

CRITERIA FOR MODEL CHOICE AND SUMMARY

In this chapter we presented a variety of approaches to modelling the dividend on equity applied to pricing, hedging and risk management of (portfolios of) derivatives, along with references of their origin. The models ranged from constant over non-Markovian and uncertain to stochastic. What particular model to choose in what situation is subject to certain criteria. Below we identify those that may be most significant.

Sensitivity ratios

The sensitivity of the option price with respect to the dividend may be significantly higher than the sensitivity of any of the other parameters for certain instruments and parameter ranges. This remains true even when weighting the sensitivities by the volatilities of the respective parameters. This should be taken into consideration when establishing priorities about the accurate determination and neutralisation of the risk attributed to each parameter. Dividends are particularly significant in barriers and American options.

Time to expiry

Most traded (vanilla) stock options only have a time to expiry of a few months that will encapsulate an overseeable number of dividends. In this case it might be best to value the product assuming discrete non-stochastic dividend estimates taken from fundamental research. Uncertain dividend modelling may be vital if there is a non-negligible uncertainty that a dividend will be paid before expiry or not. In this case the difference between best and worst possible values of an option may be big, and appropriate hedging strategies will be required.

The majority of products like convertible bonds, warrants or OTC baskets have a time to maturity of several years, some exceeding 20 years, some even perpetual. Thus dividends become difficult to predict and they will rarely stay constant. In this case a stochastic dividend model may be appropriate, introducing some volatility to the dividend process and therefore increasing the value of the option. If statistical analysis would show a significant trend in the dividend policy, then a Markovian model may be a suitable alternative.

Computational cost

There always exists a trade-off between sophisticated modelling and accuracy on the one side as well as implementation and computation speed on the other. Often, when quoting prices or hedging in real time, it is not suitable to make a model more complex, e.g. by adding an extra stochastic factor for the sake of accuracy. Conversely, when structuring and pricing an OTC contract it may be worthwhile to pay attention to every single risk factor. The basic deterministic discrete and continuous modifications are of little complexity, thus implemented and computed instantly, whereby the parameter maintenance, depending on the number of dividends, may be the most significant time factor. For the uncertain model, especially when hedging statically, the computation time may be significant, especially when performing a non-linear optimisation over a large set of possible hedging instruments. Finally, for stochastic models the calibration may be the most time-consuming factor.

Type of instrument

Whereas for options on individual stocks or small baskets it may be relatively quick to implement exact dividend corrections, for index options the same method may be very time-consuming, dependent on the size of the index and availability of fundamental research. Alternatively, implied dividend yields taken from prices of traded futures or OTC forwards may be a quicker method. Most data providers also give dividend yield forecasts and consensus estimates for single stocks and indices. But none of these are official and may vary from provider to provider. In general, all types of options with knockout features like barriers or American options may be very sensitive to dividends. For a call option it is only optimal to exercise early prior to a dividend. The papers by Adams *et al.* (1994) and Broadie *et al.* (2000) look at the effects of both deterministic and stochastic dividends on the valuation of American options.

Finally, for convertible bonds the dividends can be a significant factor because of the perceived positive correlation between dividends on stock price level. If the stock underlying a convertible bond is above the exercise price, then it is likely it will eventually be exercised, hence the credit risk of the bond is lower, but dividends may be higher. On the other hand, if the stock trades below the conversion price, then the credit risk is higher, but the firm, should it not be able to pay a coupon, or the principal of the bond, will most likely scrap the dividend first. These two effects, i.e. dividend size and credit risk, have opposite sign on the value of the convertible. Any model should reflect this.

To conclude, we would like to argue that dividends are of non-negligible significance when assessing the risk of portfolios of derivatives. Besides monitoring the risk of a portfolio by the delta, gamma and vega, the sensitivity with respect to changes in the underlying cost of carry, namely dividends, may be significant and should therefore be included in any type of VaR calculation.

REFERENCES

Adams, P.D., Wyatt, S.B. and Walker, M.C. (1994) Dividends, dividend policy and option valuation: a new perspective. *Journal of Business, Finance and Accounting*, **21**, 945–62

Avellaneda, M., Levy A. and Parás, A. (1995) Pricing and hedging derivative securities in markets with uncertain volatilities. *Applied Mathematical Finance*, **2**, 73–88

Bakstein, D. and Wilmott, P. (2000) Non-probabilistic jump modelling for financial derivatives. *Proceedings of ECMI 2000*. Springer

Barone-Adesi, G. and Whaley, R.E. (1986) The valuation of American call options and the expected ex-dividend stock price decline. *Journal of Financial Economics*, **17**, 91–111

Black, F. and Scholes, M. (1973) The pricing of options and corporate liabilities. *Journal of Political Economy*, **81**, 637–54

Broadie, M., Detemple, J., Ghysels, E. and Torres, O. (2000) American options with stochastic dividends and volatility: a nonparametric investigation. *Journal of Econometrics*, **94**, 53–92

Copeland, T.E. and Weston, J.F. (1988) *Financial Theory and Corporate Policy*. Addison-Wesley

DeAngelo, H., DeAngelo, L. and Skinner, D.J. (2000) Special dividends and the evolution of dividend signalling. *Journal of Financial Economics*, **57**, 309–54

DeJong, D.N. and Whiteman, C.H. (1991) The temporal stability of dividends and stock prices: evidence from the likelihood function. *American Economic Review*, **81**, 600–617

Elton, E.J. and Gruber, M.J. (1970) Marginal stockholder tax rates and the clientele effect. *Review of Economics and Statistics*, **52**, 68–74

Epstein, D. and Wilmott, P. (1997) Yield envelopes. *Net Exposure*, no. 2

Fama, E.F. (1970) Efficient capital markets: a review of theory and empirical work. *Journal of Finance*, **25**, 383–417

Geske, R. (1978) The pricing of options with stochastic dividend yield. *Journal of Finance*, **33**, 617–25

Harpaz, G. (1988) The non-optimality of the over-the-counter options dividend protection. *Economics Letters*, **27**, 55–59

Hilliard, J.E. and Reis, J. (1998) Valuation of commodity futures and options under stochastic convenience yields, interest rates and jump diffusions in the spot. *Journal of Financial and Quantitative Analysis*, **33**, 61–86

Hua, P. (1997) Modelling stock market crashes. Dissertation, Imperial College, London

Hull, J. (1999) *Options, Futures and Other Derivatives*, 4th edn. Prentice Hall

Kaplanis, C.P. (1986) Options, taxes and ex-dividend day behaviour. *Journal of Finance*, **41**, 411–24

Lakonishok, J. and Vermaelen, T. (1983) Tax reform and ex-dividend day behaviour. *Journal of Finance*, **38**, 1157–79

Lyons, T.J. (1995) Uncertain volatility and the risk-free synthesis of derivatives. *Applied Mathematical Finance*, **2**, 117–33

Merton, R.C. (1976) Option pricing when underlying stock returns are discontinuous. *Journal of Financial Economics*, **3**, 125–144

Miller, M.H. and Modigliani, F. (1961) Dividend policy, growth and the valuation of shares. *Journal of Business*, **34**, 411–33

Miltersen, K.R. and Schwartz, E.S. (1998) Pricing of options on commodity futures with stochastic term structures of convenience yields and interest rates. *Journal of Financial and Quantitative Analysis*, **33**, 33–59

Musiela, M. and Rutkowski, M. (1998) *Martingale Methods in Financial Modelling*. Springer

Øksendal, B. (1998) *Stochastic Differential Equations*. Springer

Shaw, W. (1998) *Modelling Financial Derivatives with Mathematica*. Cambridge University Press

Shiller, R.J. (1981) Do stock prices move too much to be justified by subsequent changes in dividends? *American Economic Review*, **71**, 421–36

Vasicek, O.A. (1977) An equilibrium characterisation of the term structure. *Journal of Financial Economics*, **5**, 177–88

Wilmott, P. (1998) *Derivatives: The Theory and Practice of Financial Engineering*. Wiley

Wilmott, P., Dewynne, J. and Howison, S.D. (1993) Option Pricing: *Mathematical Models and Computation*. Oxford Financial Press

6

Isoperimetry, log-concavity and elasticity of option prices

Christer Borell

INTRODUCTION

The classical isoperimetric inequality states that of all simple closed curves in the plane with a fixed finite length, the circle encloses the largest area. This inequality, already known to the Greeks, has been a source of inspiration for generations of mathematicians and has created its own area in mathematics. Interestingly enough, there are lots of isoperimetric inequalities in mathematical physics, too [13]. Since option pricing is closely linked to measure theory and partial differential equations, it is thus natural and tempting to seek geometric inequalities in mathematical finance. This background motivates my paper [4] and my main concern here will be to review parts of this paper and to make improvements at several points. I will give a more illuminating study of log-concavity in option pricing than in [4] and include applications to barrier options and certain bond options. I also derive the important Prékopa theorem on log-concave measures, with the aid of the Girsanov transformation theorem of Wiener measure; this is slightly more detailed than in my paper [5]. To put this chapter in a broader context, I will also recall some isoperimetric inequalities in option pricing.

A BRIEF REVIEW OF ISOPERIMETRY IN OPTION PRICING

A basic tool in proving isoperimetric inequalities in geometry and mathematical physics is the so-called Brunn–Minkowski inequality. If A and B are measurable subsets of a vector space, the Minkowski sum $A + B$ of A and B is defined by the equation

$$A + B = \{x + y; \ x \in A \text{ and } y \in B\}.$$

Moreover, for any $\lambda \geqslant 0$,

$$\lambda A = \{\lambda x; \ x \in A\}.$$

The volume of a Borel set A in $\mathbf{R}^n$ is denoted by $|A|$.

Now suppose A and B are non-empty Borel sets in $\mathbf{R}^n$. The Brunn–Minkowski inequality then says that

$$|A + B|^{1/n} \geqslant |A|^{1/n} + |B|^{1/n}. \tag{6.1}$$

Note that equality occurs in (6.1) if A is convex and $B = x + \lambda A$, where $x \in \mathbf{R}^n$ and $\lambda \geqslant 0$.

The classical isoperimetric inequality in $\mathbf{R}^n$ is immediate from (6.1). Indeed, let $\bar{B}(0; r) = \{x \in \mathbf{R}^n; \ |x| \leqslant r\}$ be the closed Euclidean ball of centre 0 and radius $r > 0$

and write $|\bar{B}(0; r)| = c_n r^n$. It follows from (6.1) that

$$|A| = c_n a^n \Rightarrow |A + \bar{B}(0; r)| \geqslant c_n (a + r)^n \tag{6.2}$$

and accordingly from this, defining the surface area $\sigma(A)$ of A by the equation

$$\sigma(A) = \lim_{\rho \to 0} \inf_{0 < r \leqslant \rho} \frac{1}{r}(|A + \bar{B}(0; r)| - |A|)$$

we get the classical isoperimetric inequality in $\mathbf{R}^n$, that is

$$\sigma(A) \geqslant n c_n^{1/n} |A|^{(n-1)/n}.$$

Unfortunately, the inequalities (6.1) and (6.2) seem less appropriate for proving isoperimetric inequalities in option pricing. However, there is a natural analogue of (6.2) for the distribution law of Brownian motion which fits well in this context. To explain this let, as usual,

$$N(x) = \int_{-\infty}^{x} e^{-y^2/2} \frac{dy}{\sqrt{2\pi}}, \quad -\infty \leqslant x \leqslant \infty.$$

Moreover, let $C([0, T]; \mathbf{R}^n)$ denote the vector space of all continuous functions of $[0, T]$ into $\mathbf{R}^n$ equipped with the topology of uniform convergence and let $W = (W(t))_{0 \leqslant t \leqslant T}$ be a normalized Brownian motion in $\mathbf{R}^n$ with time set $[0, T]$ possessing continuous sample paths. Below W will be viewed as a random vector in $C([0, T]; \mathbf{R}^n)$. Finally, denote by O the class of all functions $h = (h_1, \ldots, h_n) \in C([0, T]; \mathbf{R}^n)$ such that the functions $h_1, \ldots, h_n$ are absolutely continuous and

$$\int_0^T ((h'_1(t))^2 + \cdots + (h'_n(t))^2)\, dt \leqslant 1.$$

Then, for any Borel set A in $C([0, T]; \mathbf{R}^n)$ and $r > 0$,

$$P[W \in A] = N(a) \Rightarrow P[W \in A + rO] \geqslant N(a + r). \tag{6.3}$$

Here equality occurs if A is an affine half-space. The inequality (6.3) is called the isoperimetric inequality of Brownian motion or the isoperimetric inequality of Wiener measure, the distribution law of normalized Brownian motion. Actually, there is a similar inequality for any Gaussian Radon measure on any locally convex space. For example, if γ_n denotes the canonical Gaussian measure in $\mathbf{R}^n$, the implication of (6.3) is that

$$\gamma_n(A) = N(a) \Rightarrow \gamma_n(A + \bar{B}(0; r)) \geqslant N(a + r). \tag{6.4}$$

The isoperimetric inequality of Gaussian measure was discovered independently by Sudakov, Tsirelson and the author. The original proofs were based on geometric methods. Today there are at least two well-known analytic proofs of (6.3), one of which is based on Malliavin calculus [10, 7].

In [4] I proved several inequalities of isoperimetric type in option pricing using (6.4). To give some examples from this paper, assume a Black–Scholes model with n stocks and one bond. The stock log-prices

$$\ln S_1(t), \ldots, \ln S_n(t),\ 0 \leqslant t \leqslant T$$

are governed by a non-degenerate Brownian motion with a linear drift in n dimensions and the bond price is given by the equation

$$B(t) = B(0)e^{rt}, \ 0 \leqslant t \leqslant T.$$

Here $B(0)$ and r are positive constants. The risk-neutral measure is denoted by Q. If X is a random variable, we write

$$E^Q[X] = \int_\Omega X \, dQ, \text{ if } X \in L^1(Q)$$

and if $X \in L^2(Q)$,

$$\text{Var}^Q(X) = E^Q\left[(X - E^Q[X])^2\right].$$

Moreover, the volatility of the kth stock price $(S_k(t))_{0 \leqslant t \leqslant T}$ is denoted by σ_k and it is assumed that

$$\sigma_n = \max_{1 \leqslant k \leqslant n} \sigma_k.$$

Finally, set $S(t) = (S_1(t), \ldots, S_n(t)), \ 0 \leqslant t \leqslant T$.

In the following discussion K is a fixed positive number and we denote by $\mathcal{C}_K$ the class of all locally Lipschitz continuous functions $g : \mathbf{R}_+^n \to [0, +\infty)$ such that

$$\sum_{i=1}^n s_i \left| \frac{\partial g(s)}{\partial s_i} \right| \leqslant K + g(s) \quad \text{a.e.}$$

Now suppose $g \in \mathcal{C}_K$ is fixed and consider a European multi-asset derivative with payoff $g(S(T))$ and time of maturity T. Then, if $a \geqslant 0$ is chosen such that

$$E^Q\left[g(S(T))\right] = E^Q\left[(aS_n(T) - K)^+\right] \tag{6.5}$$

it is proved in [4] that

$$\text{Var}^Q(g(S(T))) \leqslant \text{Var}^Q((aS_n(T) - K)^+). \tag{6.6}$$

We call this property the call comparison theorem for the class $\mathcal{C}_K$. Note that the right-hand members in (6.5) and (6.6) are simple to compute explicitly.

In what follows, $\mathcal{P}_K$ denotes the class of all locally Lipschitz continuous functions $g : \mathbf{R}_+^n \to [0, K)$ such that

$$\sum_{i=1}^n s_i \left| \frac{\partial g(s)}{\partial s_i} \right| \leqslant K - g(s) \quad \text{a.e.}$$

Then, if $g \in \mathcal{P}_K$ and $a \geqslant 0$ is chosen such that

$$E^Q\left[g(S(T))\right] = E^Q\left[(K - aS_n(T))^+\right]$$

we have

$$\text{Var}^Q(g(S(T))) \leqslant \text{Var}^Q((K - aS_n(T))^+).$$

We call this property the put comparison theorem for the class $\mathcal{P}_K$.

By considering slightly more general inequalities than here, it is possible to give an exact description of the classes of derivatives for which the corresponding comparison theorems are true [4].

There are some very concrete consequences of the comparison theorems above. As an example consider the option on the maximum of the n stock prices above with strike price zero and time of maturity T. By the Black–Scholes theory, the option price at time 0 equals

$$\Pi(0) = E^Q[X]$$

where

$$X = e^{-rT} \max_{1 \leqslant k \leqslant n} S_k(T).$$

To find an approximate value on $\Pi(0)$ we use the crude Monte Carlo method and let $X_1, \ldots, X_N$ be stochastically independent observations on X. Note that

$$\bar{X}_N = \frac{1}{N} \sum_{j=1}^{N} X_j$$

is an unbiased estimator of the option price $\Pi(0)$ relative to the underlying risk-neutral probability measure. Now by using the call comparison theorem for the class $\mathcal{C}_K$ for small $K > 0$ it is possible to control the absolute relative error

$$R = \left| \frac{\bar{X}_N - \Pi(0)}{\Pi(0)} \right|$$

using the risk-neutral measure. In fact, I proved in [4] that

$$Q[R \geqslant \varepsilon] \leqslant \frac{e^{\sigma_n^2 T} - 1}{\varepsilon^2 N}.$$

If you want to extend the comparison theorems above to path-dependent options, the isoperimetric inequality (6.3) is probably a useful tool.

LOG-CONCAVITY

This section looks at the Prékopa extension of the classical Brunn–Minkowski inequality (6.1) and discusses an approach to the theory of log-concave measures based on stochastic analysis. First, however, it is natural to give some brief motivations of log-concavity in option pricing.

Consider, for simplicity, a Black–Scholes model with just one stock and a simple European derivative with time of maturity T and strictly positive price $v(t, S(t))$ at any time $t < T$. The function $v(t, s)$ is a solution of the Black–Scholes differential equation and, in particular, $v(t, s)$ a differentiable function of s for fixed t. The elasticity of the option price (relative to the stock price) is defined by the equation

$$\Omega(s) = \frac{s v'(s)}{v(s)}, \quad s > 0$$

that is,

$$\Omega(s) = \frac{(dv)/v}{(ds)/s}, \quad s > 0.$$

Thus, roughly speaking, if the stock price increases by one percent, the option price increases by $\Omega(s)$ percent (if $\Omega(s)$ is negative this means that the option price decreases by $-\Omega(s)$ percent).

The option price $v(t, S(t)) = v(S(t))$ is said to be a log-concave function of the stock log-price $\ln S(t)$, if

$$v(s_0^{1-\lambda} s_1^{\lambda}) \geqslant v(s_0)^{1-\lambda} v(s_1)^{\lambda}$$

for all $0 < \lambda < 1$ and $s_0, s_1 > 0$. Stated otherwise, this means that the function $\ln v(e^x)$, $x \in \mathbf{R}$, is concave or, what amounts to the same thing, $\Omega(s)$ is a non-increasing function of the stock price s. Note that the Black–Scholes prices of European calls and puts possess this property (see Example 6.1).

The elasticity $\Omega(s)$ enters quite naturally in connection with so-called hedging. To see this, consider a perfect hedge of the option consisting of $h_S(t)$ shares of the stock and $h_B(t)$ shares of the bond at time t so that

$$v(t, S(t)) = h_S(t)S(t) + h_B(t)B(t)$$

$$dv(t, S(t)) = h_S(t)\,dS(t) + h_B(t)\,dB(t).$$

Then

$$1 = \frac{h_S(t)S(t)}{v(t, S(t))} + \frac{h_B(t)B(t)}{v(t, S(t))}$$

and

$$h_S(t) = \frac{\partial v}{\partial s}(t, S(t)).$$

Hence $\Omega(S(t))$ is the fraction of the portfolio value invested in the risky asset at the time point t. Accordingly, this fraction is a non-increasing function of the stock price if the option log-price is a concave function of the stock log-price.

A very important tool in the study of log-concave functions is the theory of log-concave measures initiated in the beginning of the seventies by Andras Prékopa [14]. Before going into this topic, here is some notation.

Below $\theta = (\theta_0, \theta_1)$ denotes a vector with strictly positive components such that $\theta_0 + \theta_1 = 1$. By abuse of language, a vector $\theta = (\theta_0, \theta_1)$ with these properties is called a probability vector. If $x_0, x_1 \in \mathbf{R}^n$, let

$$x_\theta = \theta_0 x_0 + \theta_1 x_1$$

and if $A_0, A_1 \subseteq \mathbf{R}^n$, let

$$A_\theta = \{x_\theta; \ x_0 \in A_0 \text{ and } x_1 \in A_1\}.$$

A σ-finite positive measure μ in $\mathbf{R}^n$ is said to be log-concave if

$$\mu(A_\theta) \geqslant \mu^{\theta_0}(A_0)\mu^{\theta_1}(A_1)$$

for all probability vectors $\theta = (\theta_0, \theta_1)$ and all Borel sets A_0, A_1 in $\mathbf{R}^n$. The Brunn–Minkowski inequality (6.1) implies that the volume measure in $\mathbf{R}^n$ is log-concave. By applying the Brunn–Minkowski inequality, Prékopa proved that a positive measure μ in $\mathbf{R}^n$ is log-concave if

$$d\mu(x) = f(x)\,dx \qquad (6.7)$$

where f is log-concave, that is f is non-negative and

$$f(x_\theta) \geqslant f^{\theta_0}(x_0) f^{\theta_1}(x_1)$$

for all $x_i \in \mathbf{R}^n$, $i = 0, 1$, and all probability vectors $\theta = (\theta_0, \theta_1)$. This example essentially exhausts the class of all log-concave measures in $\mathbf{R}^n$. More precisely, the topological support of a log-concave measure μ in $\mathbf{R}^n$ is convex. Furthermore, if this set has a non-empty interior, I proved in [3] that (6.7) holds with f log-concave.

In the paper [5], treating inequalities of heat kernels, I remarked that Prékopa's result follows from a known representation formula of solutions of certain parabolic differential equations. Next we want to make this approach more direct and complete than in [5]. Accordingly, the principal result on log-concave measures follows from standard methods in mathematical finance (like the isoperimetric inequality of Brownian motion).

Let $F : \mathbf{R}^n \to \mathbf{R}$ be a bounded Borel function. Our approach to log-concave measures is based on a nice representation formula of the Gaussian integral

$$\int_{\mathbf{R}^n} e^{-F(x)} e^{-|x|^2/2} \frac{dx}{\sqrt{2\pi}^n}$$

(see Theorem 6.1). To explain this context, let P denote Wiener measure on the Banach space Ω of all continuous functions ω of $[0, 1]$ into $\mathbf{R}^n$ with $\omega(0) = 0$. Recall that if $W(\omega) = \omega = (\omega_1(t), \dots, \omega_n(t))_{0 \leqslant t \leqslant 1}$, $\omega \in \Omega$, then W is a normalized Brownian motion in $\mathbf{R}^n$ relative to the probability measure P. Given $x \in \mathbf{R}^n$ and $t \geqslant 0$, set $W_x(\omega) = x + \omega$ and

$$v(t, x) = E\left[e^{-F(W_x(t))} \right].$$

Note that

$$\int_{\mathbf{R}^n} e^{-F(x)} e^{-|x|^2/2} \frac{dx}{\sqrt{2\pi}^n} = v(1, 0).$$

Now let $\mathcal{U}$ denote the class of all bounded, progressively measurable processes $u(t)$, $0 \leqslant t \leqslant 1$. Given $u \in \mathcal{U}$, set

$$h_u(t) = \int_0^t u(\lambda)\,d\lambda, \ 0 \leqslant t \leqslant 1,$$

$$dQ_u(\omega) = e^{-\frac{1}{2}\int_0^1 |u(t)|^2\,dt - \int_0^1 u(t)\,d\omega(t)}\,dP(\omega)$$

and

$$E^{Q_u}[\varphi] = \int_\Omega \varphi\,dQ_u, \ \text{if } \varphi \in L^1(Q_u).$$

Then, by the Girsanov theorem [12],

$$E^{Q_u}\left[\varphi(W + h_u)\right] = E\left[\varphi\right]$$

for any bounded measurable function φ on Ω and it follows that

$$v(1, 0) = E\left[e^{-F(W(1))}\right] = E^{Q_u}\left[e^{-F(W(1)+h_u(1))}\right]$$

$$= E\left[e^{-F(W(1)+h_u(1))}e^{-\frac{1}{2}\int_0^1 |u(t)|^2 dt - \int_0^1 u(t)\,d\omega(t)}\right].$$

Thus, if

$$X_u(t) = W(t) + h_u(t), \ 0 \leqslant t \leqslant 1$$

then

$$v(1, 0) = E\left[e^{-Y_u}\right]$$

where

$$Y_u = F(X_u(1)) + \frac{1}{2}\int_0^1 |u(t)|^2 dt + \int_0^1 u(t)\,d\omega(t).$$

In the following, let

$$J^F(u) = E\left[F(X_u(1)) + \frac{1}{2}\int_0^1 |u(t)|^2 dt\right]$$

and note that the Jensen inequality yields

$$\ln v(1, 0) \geqslant -E\left[Y_u\right] = -J^F(u)$$

since

$$E\left[\int_0^1 u(t)\,d\omega(t)\right] = 0.$$

Accordingly, this gives

$$\int_{\mathbf{R}^n} e^{-F(x)}e^{-|x|^2/2}\frac{dx}{\sqrt{2\pi}^n} \geqslant \exp(-J^F(u)). \tag{6.8}$$

Remarkably enough, for a large class of functions F, equality occurs in (6.8) if u is chosen in an appropriate way [8, Remark 2.1, pp. 257–58]. To see this let (for simplicity) $F \in C_0^\infty(\mathbf{R}^n)$ and note that

$$\frac{\partial v}{\partial t} = \frac{1}{2}\Delta v, \ t > 0, \ x \in \mathbf{R}^n$$

and

$$v(0, x) = e^{-F(x)}, \ x \in \mathbf{R}^n.$$

The substitution

$$V = -\ln v$$

reduces the above Cauchy problem to the Hamilton–Jacobi–Bellman (HJB) equation

$$\frac{\partial V}{\partial t} + \frac{1}{2}|\nabla V|^2 = \frac{1}{2}\Delta V, \ t > 0, x \in \mathbf{R}^n$$

with the initial condition

$$V(0, x) = F(x), \ x \in \mathbf{R}^n.$$

Moreover, the assumptions on F imply that

$$\inf_{t \geqslant 0, \ x \in \mathbf{R}^n} v(t, x) > 0$$

and

$$\sup_{t \geqslant 0, \ x \in \mathbf{R}^n} |\nabla v(t, x)| < \infty.$$

Now define

$$U(t, x) = -\nabla_x V(1 - t, x), \ 0 \leqslant t \leqslant 1.$$

The function $U(t, x)$, $0 \leqslant t \leqslant 1$, $x \in \mathbf{R}^n$, is bounded and continuous and, moreover, there exists a constant $C > 0$ such that

$$|U(t, x) - U(t, y)| \leqslant C|x - y|, \ 0 \leqslant t \leqslant 1, \quad x, y \in \mathbf{R}^n.$$

Therefore the stochastic differential equation

$$dX(t) = U(t, X(t)) \, dt + d\omega(t), \ 0 \leqslant t \leqslant 1$$

with the initial condition $X(0) = 0$ possesses a unique solution. We set $u_0(t) = U(t, X(t))$, $0 \leqslant t \leqslant 1$, and have $X(t) = \omega(t) + h_{u_0}(t) = W(t) + h_{u_0}(t) = X_{u_0}(t)$, $0 \leqslant t \leqslant 1$. Moreover, we claim that the random variable Y_{u_0} is constant with probability one. To prove this we introduce the process

$$\xi(t) = V(1 - t, X(t)) + \frac{1}{2}\int_0^t |u_0(\lambda)|^2 d\lambda + \int_0^t u_0(\lambda) \, d\omega(\lambda)$$

defined for all $0 \leqslant t \leqslant 1$ and have

$$d\xi(t) = -V_t(1 - t, X(t) \, dt + \nabla_x V(1 - t, X(t)) \cdot (u_0(t) \, dt + d\omega(t))$$

$$+ \frac{1}{2}\Delta V(1 - t, X(t)) \, dt + \frac{1}{2}|u_0(t)|^2 dt + u_0(t) \, d\omega(t).$$

Moreover, since the function V satisfies the HJB equation above, $d\xi(t) = 0$, and we conclude that $\xi = V(1,0)$. In particular, $\xi(1) = Y_{u_0}$ is constant with probability one and it follows that equality occurs in (6.8) if $u = u_0$.

We can now prove Theorems 6.1 and 6.2; we will call Theorem 6.2 Prékopa's theorem.

Theorem 6.1

Suppose F is a bounded Borel function in $\mathbf{R}^n$. Then

$$\int_{\mathbf{R}^n} e^{-F(x)} e^{-|x|^2/2} \frac{dx}{\sqrt{2\pi}^n} = \exp\left(-\inf_{u \in \mathcal{U}} J^F(u)\right).$$

Proof In view of (6.8) it is enough to show that

$$\int_{\mathbf{R}^n} e^{-F(x)} e^{-|x|^2/2} \frac{dx}{\sqrt{2\pi}^n} \leqslant \exp\left(-\inf_{u \in \mathcal{U}} J^F(u)\right). \tag{6.9}$$

To prove (6.9) we first choose a uniformly bounded sequence $F_i \in C_0^\infty(\mathbf{R}^n)$, $i \in \mathbf{N}$, such that

$$F_i(W(1)) \to F(W(1)) \quad \text{a.s.}$$

as $i \to \infty$. Without loss of generality it can be assumed that

$$E\left[e^{-F(W(1))}\right] < 2^{-i} + E\left[e^{-F_i(W(1))}\right], \quad i \in \mathbf{N}.$$

Now for every fixed $i \in \mathbf{N}$ we choose a $u_i \in \mathcal{U}$ such that

$$E\left[e^{-F(W(1))}\right] < 2^{-i} + e^{-J^{F_i}(u_i)}$$

and set

$$\varphi_i = F_i - F.$$

Then

$$E\left[e^{-F(W(1))}\right] < 2^{-i} + e^{-E[\varphi_i(W(1)+h_{u_i}(1))]} e^{-\inf_{u \in \mathcal{U}} J^F(u)}$$

and (6.9) follows if

$$\lim_{i \to \infty} E\left[\varphi_i(W(1) + h_{u_i}(1))\right] = 0. \tag{6.10}$$

To prove (6.10), suppose $|F| \leqslant M$ and $|F_i| \leqslant M$, $i \in \mathbf{N}$, where $M \in \mathbf{R}$, and use the inequality

$$E\left[e^{-F(W(1))}\right] < 2^{-i} + e^{M - \frac{1}{2}E\left[\int_0^1 |u_i(t)|^2 dt\right]}, \quad i \in \mathbf{N}$$

to conclude that

$$C = \sup_{i \in \mathbf{N}} E\left[\int_0^1 |u_i(t)|^2 dt\right] < \infty.$$

In the following, let $\lambda > 0$ and $i \in \mathbf{N}$ and introduce the event

$$A_{\lambda,i} = \left[\left| \int_0^1 u_i(t)\,d\omega(t) \right| < \lambda \quad \text{and} \quad \int_0^1 |u_i(t)|^2 dt < \lambda \right].$$

Then, by the Chebyshev inequality,

$$P\left[W \notin A_{\lambda,i}\right] \leqslant D/\lambda$$

where $D = \sqrt{C} + C$, and we get

$$\left| E\left[\varphi_i(W(1) + h_{u_i}(1))\right]\right| \leqslant \left| E\left[\varphi_i(W(1) + h_{u_i}(1)); A_{\lambda,i}\right]\right| + 2MD/\lambda.$$

Moreover

$$\left| E\left[\varphi_i(W(1) + h_{u_i}(1)); A_{\lambda,i}\right]\right|$$

$$= \left| E^{Q_{u_i}}\left[\varphi_i(W(1) + h_{u_i}(1))e^{\frac{1}{2}\int_0^1 |u_i(t)|^2 dt + \int_0^1 u_i(t)\,d\omega(t)}; A_{\lambda,i}\right]\right|$$

$$\leqslant e^{3\lambda/2} E^{Q_{u_i}}\left[|\varphi_i(W(1) + h_{u_i}(1))|\right].$$

Accordingly, by using the Girsanov theorem,

$$|E\left[\varphi_i(W(1) + h_{u_i}(1))\right]| \leqslant e^{3\lambda/2} E\left[|\varphi_i(W(1))|\right] + 2MD/\lambda.$$

From this (6.10) follows at once, which completes the proof of Theorem 6.1.

Theorem 6.2
Let

$$\theta = (\theta_0, \theta_1)$$

be a probability vector and suppose $f_j : \mathbf{R}^n \to [0, \infty)$, $j = 0, 1, \theta$ are Borel functions such that

$$f_\theta(x_\theta) \geqslant f_0^{\theta_0}(x_0) f_1^{\theta_1}(x_1)$$

for all $x_i \in \mathbf{R}^n$, $i = 0, 1$. Then

$$\int_{\mathbf{R}^n} f_\theta(x)\,dx \geqslant \left(\int_{\mathbf{R}^n} f_0(x)\,dx\right)^{\theta_0} \left(\int_{\mathbf{R}^n} f_1(x)\,dx\right)^{\theta_1}.$$

Proof We first prove that

$$E\left[f_\theta(W(1))\right] \geqslant (E\left[f_0(W(1))\right])^{\theta_0} (E\left[f_1(W(1))\right]^{\theta_1}. \tag{6.11}$$

To this end, there is no loss of generality to assume that

$$0 < \inf f_j \leqslant \sup f_j < \infty, \quad j = 0, 1, \theta$$

and set

$$F_j = -\ln f_j, \quad j = 0, 1, \theta.$$

Furthermore, choose $u_0, u_1 \in \mathcal{U}$ arbitrarily and define

$$u_\theta(t) = \theta_0 u_0(t) + \theta_1 u_1(t), \quad 0 \leqslant t \leqslant 1.$$

Then

$$W(t) + h_{u_\theta}(t) = \theta_0(W(t) + h_{u_0}(t)) + \theta_1(W(t) + h_{u_1}(t))$$

for all $0 \leqslant t \leqslant 1$ and every fixed $\omega = W(\omega)$. Moreover

$$F_\theta(W(1) + h_{u_\theta}(1)) + \frac{1}{2}\int_0^1 |u_\theta(t)|^2 dt$$

$$\leqslant \theta_0\left(F_0(W(1) + h_{u_0}(t)) + \frac{1}{2}\int_0^1 |u_0(t)|^2 dt\right)$$

$$+ \theta_1\left(F_1(W(1) + h_{u_1}(1)) + \frac{1}{2}\int_0^1 |u_1(t)|^2 dt\right)$$

hence

$$E\left[F_\theta(W(1) + h_{u_\theta}(1)) + \frac{1}{2}\int_0^1 |u_\theta(t)|^2 dt\right]$$

$$\leqslant \theta_0 E\left[F_0(W(1) + h_{u_0}(t)) + \frac{1}{2}\int_0^1 |u_0(t)|^2 dt\right]$$

$$+ \theta_1 E\left[F_1(W(1) + h_{u_1}(1)) + \frac{1}{2}\int_0^1 |u_1(t)|^2 dt\right]$$

that is,

$$J^{F_\theta}(u_\theta) \leqslant \theta_0 J^{F_{\theta_0}}(u_0) + \theta_1 J^{F_{\theta_1}}(u_1).$$

From this the inequality (6.11) is an immediate consequence of Theorem 6.1.

Replacing each $f_j(x)$ by $f_j(\sigma x)$, where $\sigma > 0$, we get

$$\int_{\mathbf{R}^n} f_\theta(x) e^{-|x|^2/2\sigma^2} \frac{dx}{\sqrt{2\pi}^n}$$

$$\geqslant \left(\int_{\mathbf{R}^n} f_0(x) e^{-|x|^2/2\sigma^2} \frac{dx}{\sqrt{2\pi}^n}\right)^{\theta_0} \left(\int_{\mathbf{R}^n} f_1(x) e^{-|x|^2/2\sigma^2} \frac{dx}{\sqrt{2\pi}^n}\right)^{\theta_1}$$

and Theorem 6.2 follows by letting σ tend to plus infinity.

Finally in this section, let us recall that Bobkov in a recent paper [2] studies isoperimetric inequalities of log-concave measures.

LOG-CONCAVITY APPLIED TO OPTION PRICING

To begin with, consider a Black–Scholes model with n stocks and one bond as before. There exist real numbers $\mu_k \in \mathbf{R}$, $\sigma_k > 0$, $k = 1, \ldots, n$, and a non-singular $n \times n$ matrix C with unit rows in Euclidean $\mathbf{R}^n$ such that for each fixed $k \in \{1, \ldots, n\}$,

$$S_k(t) = S_k(0)e^{(\mu_k - \sigma_k^2/2)t + \sigma_k c_k W(t)}, \quad 0 \leqslant t \leqslant T$$

where

$$c_k = [c_{k1} \ldots c_{kn}]$$

denotes the kth row of C and where $(W(t))_{0 \leqslant t \leqslant T}$ is a normalized Brownian motion in $\mathbf{R}^n$. Here $W(t)$ is interpreted as a column vector. Note that

$$dS_k(t) = \mu_k \, dt + \sigma_k c_k \, dW(t).$$

Below we find it convenient to choose Brownian motion in its first canonical representation. Therefore, let P be Wiener measure on the Banach space Ω of all continuous functions ω of $[0, T]$ into $\mathbf{R}^n$ with $\omega(0) = 0$. If $W(\omega) = \omega = (\omega_1(t), \ldots, \omega_n(t))_{0 \leqslant t \leqslant T}$, $\omega \in \Omega$, then W is a normalized Brownian motion in $\mathbf{R}^n$ relative to the probability measure P. The risk-neutral measure is denoted by Q.

Now define $S(t) = (S_1(t), \ldots, S_n(t))$, $0 \leqslant t \leqslant T$, and consider to begin with a simple derivative security of European type, which pays $g(S(T))$ to its owner at maturity T. Here the payoff function g is a non-negative Borel function and, moreover, below it is always assumed that

$$g(e^x) \leqslant Ae^{\alpha|x|}, \quad x \in \mathbf{R}^n$$

for appropriate positive constants A and α. If $t \leqslant T$ is fixed, then the theoretic price of the derivative security at the time point $t \leqslant T$ equals $v(t, S(t); g) = v(t, S(t))$, where

$$v(t, S(t)) = e^{-r\tau} E^Q \left[g(S(T)) | S(\lambda), \lambda \leqslant t \right]$$

and $\tau = T - t$. Defining $s = (s_1, \ldots, s_n)$ and

$$M(t, T) = \left(e^{-\sigma_1^2 \tau/2 + \sigma_1 c_1(W(T) - W(t))}, \ldots, e^{-\sigma_n^2 \tau/2 + \sigma_n c_n(W(T) - W(t))} \right)$$

we have

$$v(t, s) = e^{-r\tau} E \left[g \left(s_1 e^{(r - \sigma_1^2/2)\tau + \sigma_1 c_1 W(\tau)}, \ldots, s_n e^{(r - \sigma_n^2/2)\tau + \sigma_n c_n W(\tau)} \right) \right]$$

$$= e^{-r\tau} E \left[g(se^{r\tau} M(t, T)) \right]$$

here using the convention that $xy = (x_1 y_1, \ldots, x_n y_n)$ for vectors $x = (x_1, \ldots, x_n)$ and $y = (y_1, \ldots, y_n)$ in $\mathbf{R}^n$. Below, for brevity, we will also use the notation $\ln s = (\ln s_1, \ldots, \ln s_n)$.

Next we introduce

$$h_S(t) = \left[h_{S,1}(t) \ldots h_{S,n}(t) \right]$$

$$= \left[\frac{\partial v}{\partial s_1}(t, S(t)) \ldots \frac{\partial v}{\partial s_n}(t, S(t)) \right]$$

and

$$h_B(t) = (v(t, S(t)) - h_S(t)S(t))/B(t)$$

where $S(t)$ is interpreted as a column vector. Then

$$v(t, S(t)) = h_S(t)S(t) + h_B(t)B(t)$$

and, moreover, the Itô lemma yields

$$dv(t, S(t)) = h_S(t)\, dS(t) + h_B(t)\, dB(t).$$

A portfolio consisting of $h_{S,k}(t)$ shares of the kth stock for $k = 1, \ldots, n$ and $h_B(t)$ shares of the bond at each point of time $t < T$ yields a self-financing strategy. If we assume that $P\big[g(S(T)) > 0\big] > 0$, then the risky part of the corresponding relative portfolio can be represented by the vector

$$\left(\frac{s_1}{v(t, s)} \frac{\partial v(t, s)}{\partial s_1}, \ldots, \frac{s_n}{v(t, s)} \frac{\partial v(t, s)}{\partial s_n} \right) \bigg|_{s=S(t)}$$

at the time t. Here for fixed $k \in \{1, \ldots, n\}$, the quantity $\Omega_k(t, S(t); g)$, where

$$\Omega_k(t, s; g) = \frac{s_k}{v(t, s)} \frac{\partial v(t, s)}{\partial s_k} = \frac{\partial v(t, s)/v(t, s)}{\partial s_k/s_k}$$

is called the elasticity of the option price relative to the kth asset price. Note that the maps $s_k \to v(t, s)$ and $s_k \to \Omega_k(t, s; g)$ are real analytic functions [9]. Moreover, if

$$s = (e^{\xi_1}, \ldots, e^{\xi_n}) = e^{\xi}$$

then

$$\Omega_k(t, s; g) = \frac{\partial}{\partial \xi_k} \ln v(t, e^{\xi}).$$

Now let $\theta = (\theta_0, \theta_1)$ be a probability vector and suppose $g_j : \mathbf{R}_+^n \to [0, \infty)$, $j = 0, 1, \theta$ are payoff functions such that

$$g_\theta(s(0)^{\theta_0} s(1)^{\theta_1}) \geqslant g_0^{\theta_0}(s(0)) g_1^{\theta_1}(s(1))$$

for all $s(i) \in \mathbf{R}_+^n$, $i = 0, 1$. Then the Prékopa theorem yields

$$v(t, s(0)^{\theta_0} s(1)^{\theta_1}; g_\theta) \geqslant (v(t, s(0); g_0))^{\theta_0} (v(t, s(1); g_1))^{\theta_1} \tag{6.12}$$

for all $s(i) \in \mathbf{R}_+^n$, $i = 0, 1$. Thus we have proved Theorem 6.3

Theorem 6.3

A simple derivative security of European type pays $g(S(T))$ to its owner at maturity T. Here the payoff function g is non-negative,

$$P\big[g(S(T)) > 0\big] > 0$$

and $g(s)$ is a log-concave function of $\ln s$.

Let $t < T$ and $s = S(t)$. Then the option price $v(t, s; g)$ is a log-concave function of the log-price vector $\ln s$ for any fixed t. Moreover, for fixed k and t, the elasticity function $\Omega_k(t, s; g)$ is a non-increasing function of the kth stock price s_k if all other prices are held fixed. If $\Omega_k(t, s; g)$ is a non-constant function of s_k, it is strictly decreasing.

Example 6.1: Suppose $n = 1$ and write $\sigma_1 = \sigma$. Consider a call with strike price $K > 0$ and time of maturity T. By definition, the call has the payoff function

$$g(s) = \max(0, s - K)$$

and, as is well known, the corresponding option price at time $t < T$ equals $c(t, S(t), K) = c(S(t))$, where

$$c(s) = sN(d_1) - Ke^{-r\tau}N(d_2)$$

and where

$$d_1 = \frac{1}{\sigma\sqrt{\tau}}\left\{\ln\frac{s}{K} + \left(r + \frac{\sigma^2}{2}\right)\tau\right\}$$

and $d_2 = d_1 - \sigma\sqrt{\tau}$. The payoff function g is a log-concave function of $\ln s$. To see this, set $x = \ln s$ and

$$f(x) = \ln g(e^x) = \ln(e^x - K), \quad x > \ln K. \tag{6.13}$$

Then

$$f'(x) = \frac{e^x}{e^x - K} = 1 + \frac{K}{e^x - K}$$

is non-increasing so that f is concave. Accordingly, from Theorem 6.1, the call log-price is a concave function of the stock log-price and

$$\Omega(t, s; g) = \frac{sN(d_1)}{sN(d_1) - Ke^{-r\tau}N(d_2)}$$

is a strictly decreasing function of the stock price s (see Figure 5-22 in [6]). This conclusion can also be derived by far more direct means.

The function

$$h(x) = \ln(K - e^x), \quad x < \ln K$$

is a concave function of x since

$$\ln(K - e^x) = \ln K + x + \ln(e^{-x} - K^{-1}).$$

Therefore, by Theorem 6.1, we conclude that a European put log-price is a concave function of the stock log-price as well. However, we do not know if an American put possesses the same property or not. Note that a Bermudan put log-price, in general, is not a concave function of the stock log-price (an option which may be exercised early, but only on predetermined dates, is called a Bermudan option).

There is a slightly more general formulation of the above properties of European calls and puts. Indeed, as is readily seen, the function

$$f(x, y) = \max(0, e^x - e^y), \quad (x, y) \in \mathbf{R}^2 \tag{6.14}$$

is log-concave. Therefore, in fact, by (6.12) a call (or a European put) is a log-concave function of the log-price and strike log-price. In particular, if $\theta = (\theta_0, \theta_1)$ is a probability vector

$$c\left(t, s, K_0^{\theta_0} K_1^{\theta_1}\right) \geqslant c^{\theta_0}(t, s, K_0) c^{\theta_1}(t, s, K_1).$$

Note that if $u(t, S(t), K_0, K_1, \theta_0, \theta_1)$ stands for the theoretic price at time t of a European derivative security with payoff

$$(\max(0, S(T) - K_0))^{\theta_0} (\max(0, S(T) - K_1))^{\theta_1}$$

at maturity T, then by the Hölder inequality,

$$u(t, s, K_0, K_1, \theta_0, \theta_1) \leqslant c^{\theta_0}(t, s, K_0) c^{\theta_1}(t, s, K_1).$$

Example 6.2:   Consider the European option on the minimum of n stocks with strike price $K \geqslant 0$ and time of maturity T. Here the payoff function equals

$$g(s) = \max(0, \min_{1 \leqslant k \leqslant n} s_k - K)$$

that is

$$g(s) = \min_{1 \leqslant k \leqslant n} \max(0, s_k - K).$$

If the strike price equals zero, we have the so-called quality option, which appears in connection with a future contract, when the short has some flexibility with regard to what will be delivered. Since the function in (6.13) is concave it follows that the function g is a log-concave function of $\ln s$, hence Theorem 6.1 applies.
    Set

$$\rho_{12} = \sum_{k=1}^{n} c_{k1} c_{k2}$$

and

$$\sigma_0 = \sqrt{\sigma_1^2 - 2\rho_{12}\sigma_1\sigma_2 + \sigma_2^2}.$$

If $n = 2$ the price of the quality option at time t equals $v_{\min}(S_1(t), S_2(t))$, where

$$v_{\min}(s_1, s_2) = s_1 N\left(\frac{\ln(s_2/s_1) - \sigma_0^2 \tau/2}{\sigma_0 \sqrt{\tau}}\right) + s_2 N\left(\frac{\ln(s_1/s_2) - \sigma_0^2 \tau/2}{\sigma_0 \sqrt{\tau}}\right).$$

The option to exchange the first stock for the second stock at maturity T, introduced by Margrabe [11], has the value $v_{1\to 2}(S_1(t), S_2(t))$ at time t, where

$$v_{1\to 2}(s_1, s_2) = s_2 N\left(\frac{\ln(s_2/s_1) + \sigma_0^2\tau/2}{\sigma_0\sqrt{\tau}}\right) - s_1 N\left(\frac{\ln(s_2/s_1) - \sigma_0^2\tau/2}{\sigma_0\sqrt{\tau}}\right)$$

since

$$\max(0, s_2 - s_1) = s_2 - \min(s_1, s_2).$$

Remembering that the function in (6.14) is log-concave, it follows from Theorem 6.1 that the function $v_{1\to 2}(s_1, s_2)$ is a log-concave function of $\ln s$. Given $b > 0$, we conclude that the function

$$F_b(s) = s_2 N\left(\frac{\ln(s_2/s_1) + b^2/2}{b}\right) - s_1 N\left(\frac{\ln(s_2/s_1) - b^2/2}{b}\right), \quad s_1, s_2 > 0$$

is a log-concave function of $\ln s$. This property of F_b has applications to certain bond options.

Consider the Gaussian Hull–White model of the term structure of interest rates (for exact definitions see [1]) and a European call on the $\tilde{T}$-bond with strike price K and time of maturity T, where $T < \tilde{T}$. The theoretic price $c(p(t, \tilde{T}), p(t, T))$ of this bond option at time $t < T$ equals

$$p(t, \tilde{T})N(d) - Kp(t, T)N(d - \sigma_p)$$

where

$$d = \frac{1}{\sigma_p}\ln\frac{p(t, \tilde{T})}{Kp(t, T)} + \frac{1}{2}\sigma_p$$

and

$$\sigma_p = \frac{1}{a}\left\{1 - e^{-a(\tilde{T}-T)}\right\}\sqrt{\frac{\sigma^2}{2a}(1 - e^{-2a(T-t)})}.$$

Here a and σ are positive model parameters. Note that

$$c(p(t, \tilde{T}), p(t, T)) = F_{\sigma_p}(Kp(t, T), p(t, \tilde{T})),$$

hence the call price is a log-concave function of $\ln(p(t, \tilde{T}), p(t, T))$. By applying the call/put parity relation, it follows that a European put price on the $\tilde{T}$-bond possesses the same property.

Assuming the general Gaussian model of the term structure of interest rates [1, pp. 294–95], the above conclusions are the same and they can be proved in a similar way.

In the following assume $0 = T_0 < T_1 < T_2 < \cdots < T_m$ and consider a derivative security of European type with the payoff $g(S(T_1), \ldots, S(T_m))$ at the expiry date T_m.

Here the payoff function g is a non-negative Borel function and, moreover, below it is always assumed that

$$g(e^{x_1}, \dots, e^{x_m}) \leqslant A e^{\alpha(|x_1| + \cdots + |x_m|)}, \quad x_1, \dots, x_m \in \mathbf{R}^n$$

for appropriate positive constants A and α. In what follows, suppose $j \in \{1, \dots, m\}$ is fixed. Then the theoretic price of the derivative security at the time point $t \in [T_{j-1}, T_j]$ equals $v(t, S(T_1), \dots, S(T_{j-1}), S(t); g)$, where

$$v(t, s^{(1)}, \dots, s^{(j-1)}, s; g) = e^{-r(T-t)} E \Big[g(s^{(1)}, \dots, s^{(j-1)},$$

$$s e^{r(T_j - t)} M(t, T_j), \dots, s e^{r(T_m - t)} M(t, T_m)) \Big].$$

Now, in addition, let $T_{j-1} < t < T_j$ and $s^{(1)}, \dots, s^{(j-1)} \in \mathbf{R}_+^n$ be fixed and suppose

$$P \Big[g(s^{(1)}, \dots, s^{(j-1)}, S(T_j), \dots, S(T_m)) > 0 \Big] > 0. \tag{6.15}$$

Then $v(t, s^{(1)}, \dots, s^{(j-1)}, s; g) > 0$. Moreover, given $s = (s_1, \dots, s_n)$, let $\xi = \ln s$ and

$$\Omega_k(t, s^{(1)}, \dots, s^{(j-1)}, s; g) = \frac{\partial}{\partial \xi_k} v(t, s^{(1)}, \dots, s^{(j-1)}, e^\xi; g), \quad k = 1, \dots, n.$$

For fixed $k \in \{1, \dots, n\}$ the quantity $\Omega_k(t, S(T_1), \dots, S(T_{j-1}), S(t); g)$ is called the elasticity of the option price $v(t, S(T_1), \dots, S(T_{j-1}), S(t); g)$ relative to the kth current stock price $S_k(t)$. The maps $s_k \rightarrow v(t, s^{(1)}, \dots, s^{(j-1)}, s; g)$ and $s_k \rightarrow \Omega_k(t, s^{(1)}, \dots, s^{(j-1)}, s; g)$ are real analytic functions.

By applying the Prékopa theorem as above, we have Theorem 6.4.

Theorem 6.4

Consider a derivative security of European type with the payoff $g(S(T_1), \dots, S(T_m))$ at the expiry date T_m. Here the payoff function g is non-negative and $g(s^{(1)}, \dots, s^{(m)})$ is a log-concave function of the log-price vectors $\ln s^{(1)}, \dots, \ln s^{(m)}$.

Suppose $j \in \{1, \dots, m\}$ and $t \in [T_{j-1}, T_j]$. Set $s = S(t)$. Then the theoretic option price $v(t, s^{(1)}, \dots, s^{(j-1)}, s; g)$ is a log-concave function of the log-price vectors $\ln s^{(1)}, \dots, \ln s^{(j-1)}, \ln s$. If, in addition, (6.15) holds for fixed $s^{(1)}, \dots, s^{(j-1)}$, then for fixed k and $t \in [T_{j-1}, T_j]$, the elasticity function $\Omega_k(t, s^{(1)}, \dots, s^{(j-1)}, s; g)$ is a non-increasing function of the kth current stock price s_k if all other prices are held fixed. If $\Omega_k(t, s^{(1)}, \dots, s^{(j-1)}, s; g)$ is a non-constant function of s_k, it is strictly decreasing.

In the following examples we suppose $n = 1$.

Example 6.3: Theorem 6.4 applies to a discrete down-and-out European call with strike price K and barrier L. Here the payoff is of the type

$$g(S(T_1), \dots, S(T_m)) = 1_{[\min_{1 \leqslant j \leqslant m-1} S(T_j) > L]} \max(0, S(T_m) - K)$$

where $T_1 < \cdots < T_m$ and T_m is time of maturity.

Theorem 6.4 also applies to a discrete up-and-out European put with strike price K and barrier L. Here the payoff is of the type

$$g(S(T_1), \ldots, S(T_m)) = 1_{[\max_{1 \leqslant j \leqslant m-1} S(T_j) < L]} \max(0, K - S(T_m))$$

where $T_1 < \cdots < T_m$ and T_m is time of maturity.

Example 6.4: Suppose $g : \mathbf{R}_+ \to [0, \infty)$. Moreover, suppose that $g(s)$ is a log-concave function of $\ln s$ and consider a derivative security of European type with time of maturity T and payoff

$$X = 1_{[\min_{0 \leqslant \lambda \leqslant T} S(\lambda) > L]} g(S(T)).$$

Let $u(t, (S(\lambda))_{0 \leqslant \lambda \leqslant t}; X)$ denote its price at time t and suppose

$$S(\lambda) > L, \ 0 \leqslant \lambda \leqslant t.$$

Conditioned on this event we write

$$u(t, (S(\lambda))_{0 \leqslant \lambda \leqslant t}; X) = u(t, S(t); X).$$

Let now $m \in \mathbf{N}_+$ and $T_i = t + i(T - t)/m$, $i = 1, \ldots, m$, and consider a derivative security of European type with payoff

$$1_{[\min_{1 \leqslant j \leqslant m-1} S(T_j) > L]} g(S(T_m))$$

at time of maturity T. By applying Theorem 6.4 to this option and letting m tend to plus infinity, it follows that the function $u(t, s; X)$ is a log-concave function of $\ln s$. Set

$$g_L(s) = g(s) 1_{[s > L]}.$$

Then

$$u(t, s; X) = v(t, s; g_L) - \left(\frac{L}{s}\right)^{2\bar{r}/\sigma^2} v\left(t, \frac{L^2}{s}; g_L\right)$$

where

$$\bar{r} = r - \frac{\sigma^2}{2};$$

see Theorem 13.8 in [1]. Recall that

$$v(t, s; g_L) = e^{-r\tau} E^Q \left[g_L(se^{r\tau} M(t, T))\right]$$

so that $u(t, s; X)$ is a real analytic function of s for any fixed $t < T$.

For example, if $0 \leqslant L < K$ and $g(s) = \max(0, s - K)$ we get, using the same notation as in Example 6.1, that

$$u(t, s; X) = c(t, s, K) - \left(\frac{L}{s}\right)^{2\bar{r}/\sigma^2} c\left(t, \frac{L^2}{s}, K\right), \ s > L.$$

Moreover, for fixed $t < T$, the elasticity of the option price $u(t, s; X)$ is a strictly decreasing function of the stock price in the domain $s > L$.

REFERENCES

1. Björk, T. (1998) *Arbitrage Theory in Continuous Time*. Oxford University Press, Oxford
2. Bobkov, S.G. (1999) Isoperimetric and analytic inequalities for log-concave probability measures. *Ann. Probab.* **27**, 1903–21
3. Borell, Ch. (1975) Convex set functions in *d*-space. *Period. Math. Hungar.* **6**, 111–36
4. Borell, Ch. (1998) *Geometric inequalities in option pricing: convex geometry*. MSRI Publications, pp. 29–51; Cambridge University Press, New York (1999)
5. Borell, Ch. (2000) Geometric inequalities in diffusion theory. *Potential Analysis* **12**, 49–71
6. Cox, J.C. and Rubinstein, M. (1985) *Options Markets*. Prentice Hall, Englewood Cliffs, NJ
7. Capitaine, M., Hsu, P. and Ledoux, M. (1997) Martingale representation and a simple proof of logarithmic Sobolev inequalities on path spaces. *Elec. Commun. in Probab.* **2**, 71–81
8. Fleming, W.H. and Soner, H.M. (1993) *Controlled Markov Processes and Viscosity Solutions*. Springer-Verlag, New York
9. John, F. (1982) *Partial Differential Equations*. Springer-Verlag, New York
10. Ledoux, M. (1998) A short proof of the Gaussian isoperimetric inequality. In *High Dimensional Probability*, (Eds E. Eberlein, M. Hahn and M. Talagrand), pp. 229–232. Birkhäuser, Basel
11. Margrabe, W. (1978) The value of an option to exchange one asset for another. *Journal of Finance* **33**, 177–86
12. Nualart, D. (1995) *The Malliavin Calculus and Related Topics*. Springer-Verlag, New York
13. Pólya, G. and Szegö, G. (1951) *Isoperimetric Inequalities in Mathematical Physics*. Princeton University Press, Princeton
14. Prékopa, A. (1995) *Stochastic Programming*. Kluwer Academic, Dordrecht

Part Two
New Directions in Interest Rate Modelling

7

Introduction

As we said earlier, interest rate modelling is much harder than equity modelling. Why is this? One reason is to do with correlation.

If you have a decent model for equities then you can find a decent model for equity derivatives. The option value depends on the value of the underlying according to some equation or formula. But that can be *your* formula, whatever formula *you* think best, and so *by definition* the option value to you and the underlying are correlated. Correlation in this case is a consequence of the modelling. You can therefore hedge away the risk in an option by exploiting this perfect correlation.

Now think what happens with interest rates. We tend to think of different interest rates applying at different maturities, each bond as being a different product. Eliminating risk, in order to arrive at a pricing methodology, requires correlation between different maturities. But this type of correlation does not depend on a model, it depends on the prices of bonds in the market. These may show some correlation some of the time, but that correlation is far from perfect and highly unstable. Perfect hedging and elimination of risk are therefore not possible.

There is another problem as well. One that is even more irritating. Suppose we could hedge perfectly, to eliminate risk. We would then find ourselves with a position that was risk-free from one moment to the next. As every equity derivative modeller knows, the next stage in arriving at a pricing equation is equating the return on the hedged portfolio with the instantaneous risk-free rate. Problem. In order to do this you must model the instantaneous, zero-maturity, interest rate. But that is not a traded quantity and can't be hedged against (Figure 7.1). Compare and contrast with equity derivative modelling.

In the equity world, you model the asset and use it for hedging. In the interest rate world, you model the short rate but cannot eliminate its risk. The conclusion is that you end up with a pricing equation containing a 'market price of risk' term. Don't worry about what this means exactly. It's another one of those ideas that are nice in theory, but in practice are not very realistic.

This is what Vasicek found, skipping all the details. Starting from a model for the short-term interest rate r such as

$$dr = \mu(r, t)\, dt + \sigma(r, t)\, dX$$

we get the following pricing equation for $V(r, t)$, a non-path-dependent interest rate contract,

$$\frac{\partial V}{\partial t} + \tfrac{1}{2}\sigma^2 \frac{\partial^2 V}{\partial r^2} + (\mu - \lambda\sigma)\frac{\partial V}{\partial r} - rV = 0.$$

Here $\lambda(r, t)$ is that market price of risk.

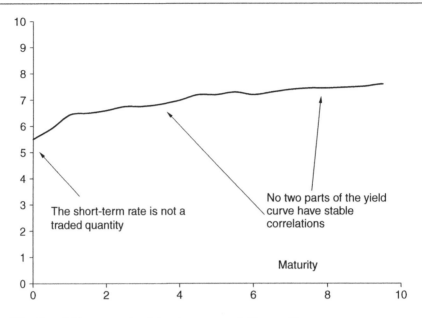

Figure 7.1 The yield curve and pointers to some modelling problems

Some people believe that λ can be found from the market prices of bonds, or equivalently from forward interest rates. This was the approach adopted by Ho and Lee originally. They derived the market price of risk, under certain assumptions about $\mu - \lambda\sigma$ and σ, from the market yield curve. Unfortunately, statistics and common sense tell us that the market response to supply and demand is more important than its response to the niceties of a mathematical model.

More sophisticated models such as Heath, Jarrow and Morton (and its successor Brace, Gatarek and Musiela), which models the evolution of the whole forward curve, also suffer from this disadvantage. The neat trick in Heath, Jarrow and Morton, though, is that its mathematical complexity very effectively hides its shortcomings.

Between them the next two chapters may give some hint of possible future directions for interest rate modelling.

CHAPTERS 8 AND 9

Dynamic, deterministic and static optimal portfolio strategies in a mean–variance framework under stochastic interest rates

Isabelle Bajeux-Besnainou and Roland Portait

People are so hung up on delta hedging because they think it can eliminate risk that they miss what's going on under their noses. Welcome to the real world, for a squillion reasons delta hedging only works approximately, in the fixed income world it's especially problematic. For reasons outlined above, one should look more broadly for hedging techniques.

Before we talk about mean–variance concepts, let's take a quick look at the whole concept of risk and return.

Broadly speaking, return is your profit, positive one hopes. Since the future is unknown one often talks about *expected* return, what you would get on average if the future consisted of lots of parallel universes all evolving differently from the same starting point. Usually the statistics of that future evolution are chosen to match the statistics of the past.

Risk is more complicated, it's a measure of the randomness or uncertainty in the future. Often we say that the standard deviation of future return is the risk. And the variance, needed for this model, is the square of that standard deviation.

Many pricing models and hedging strategies have risk elimination as a building block. Perfect hedging is possible by delta hedging, at least in theory. Then we say that every risk-free portfolio must earn the same, risk-free, rate of return. And, Bob's your uncle, you've got a pricing model.

There's another way to hedge perfectly, and that's by diversification. Invest in lots and lots of uncorrelated assets and, once you've got an infinite number of them, you'll end up with no risk.

But what if you want to take a risk? No pain, no gain. How do you decide whether taking a risk is worth the potential return? There are many frameworks for such a decision. They all fall broadly into the subject area of utility theory. And what are the roles of expected, or mean, return and variance? In a nutshell, the more variance or risk in some asset or strategy, the greater return you'd want from it.

One of the first practical uses of utility theory was in the game of blackjack. Ed Thorp showed how to win in the long run at this casino game by, among other things, betting optimally on each hand. He used a simple mean–variance strategy for money management that involved betting a fixed fraction of his wealth on each hand. That fraction depended on the mean return and the variance of returns.

In this chapter Isabelle and Roland examine mean–variance strategies in the world of randomly fluctuating interest rates. They cover a large amount of ground, discussing quite a selection of strategies in the same framework. They discuss the dynamic allocation of wealth across various fixed income instruments, as well as a stock. They discuss predetermined strategies such as buy and hold. The conclusions are not obvious, but you'll have to read the chapter to find out what they are!

Pricing bond options in a worst-case scenario

David Epstein and Paul Wilmott

The model described here could be arrived at by pure logical thought based on requirements for a mathematical model and drawbacks in common models. The logical thought would go something like this.

What does a mathematical model for interest rate products need? If we are to derive pricing equations based on the dynamics of an interest rate, several interest rates or simple traded products, then we will as a minimum requirement need a model for the short-term interest rate. After all, we will be looking at how a product will evolve in time and there is nothing simpler surely than the evolution of money in the bank. So our starting point will be a model for r.

We want a simple model that captures reality as much as possible. We want as few variables as possible. What is the minimum necessary? It must be r and time t. So let's try and build up an interest rate pricing model that only uses these two as the dependent variables. A simple contract can be represented as a function $V(r, t)$. This won't apply to products depending on the path taken by interest rates. After all, we don't expect to come up with an interest rate product model that is even simpler than the equity derivative model, and we know we need more variables to cope with path dependency there.

If every part of the yield curve is a different product and as such unreliably correlated with other parts, we cannot hope to capture the behaviour of the whole yield curve with one source of randomness. But we cannot have one random factor for each product or each point on the yield curve; that would result in a potentially infinite number of variables. We conclude that stochasticity is not the way forward.

That last bit is the revolutionary bit. We are now entering relatively uncharted territory. (Plodders, turn back now.)

If we do not have randomness, does that mean that we are left with determinacy? We don't like that because, first, it's wrong, clearly, and second, we tend to think of options having value because we don't know what the future holds.

Is there anything besides randomness that means not deterministic? Yes, the word 'uncertain' is usually used to denote unknown outcomes, but with unspecified probabilities.

Think of an integer from 1 to 10. I have no idea how likely you are to pick any particular number, but I do know that you won't pick zero or a negative number, or 11 or higher. That's uncertainty.

We are close to the model proposed by David and Paul.

When we have a probabilistic model for a financial product, we usually get a price by taking expectations (almost always a risk-neutral expectation). This is a single price and one that everyone with the same data should agree on. That price does not depend in any way on what else we have in our portfolio and the model tells us nothing about static hedging, only dynamic. To match market data, we have to go through many tortuous hoops to calibrate our model.

When we have a model with uncertainty, it is usually non-linear. We get a spread of prices. The value of a contract depends on what it is hedged with. The model tells us the optimal way to statically hedge and also fits market prices perfectly and naturally.

The model you will be seeing shortly is without doubt the best published model to date *from a scientific viewpoint*. Whether it is practical is another matter.

(Did you pick 7? No, 6? We give up then.)

MODELS NEEDED

Everything we said about the future of equity derivative modelling applies here, only in spades. The number, complexity and importance of fixed income products easily outweighs equity derivatives. Currently, this complexity in the type of products and the complexity in the models, together with the nature of the banking business, make it extremely difficult to see the wood for the trees.

The nature of the equity markets, indeed the nature of the world, is such that, barring nuclear war, global epidemics or a particularly nasty computer virus, the global economy increases in value. Whatever equity derivatives there may be, the market is net long the underlyings, the sum of all derivatives is zero, for every long there is a short. The relationship between fixed income products is more complicated, with links across currencies and all kinds of assets. Valuing interest rate products accurately is therefore more important and not just harder than valuing equity products.

BIBLIOGRAPHY

Apabhai, M.Z. (1995) *Term structure modelling and the valuation of yield curve derivative securities.* DPhil thesis, Oxford University

Apabhai, M.Z., Choe, K., Khennach, F. and Wilmott, P. (1995) Spot-on modelling. *Risk* **8** (11) 59–63 (December)

Apabhai, M.Z., Georgikopoulos, N.I., Hasnip, D., Jamie, R.K.D., Kim, M. and Wilmott, P. (1998) A model for the value of a business, some optimisation problems in its operating procedures and the valuation of its debt. *IMA Journal of Applied Mathematics* **60** 1–13

Black, F., Derman, E. and Toy, W. (1990) A one-factor model of interest rates and its application to Treasury bond options. *Financial Analysts Journal* **46** 33–39

Brace, A., Gatarek, D. and Musiela, M. (1997) The market model of interest rate dynamics. *Mathematical Finance* **7** 127–54

Brennan, M. and Schwartz, E. (1982) An equilibrium model of bond pricing and a test of market efficiency. *Journal of Financial and Quantitative Analysis* **17** 301–29

Chan, K., Karolyi, A., Longstaff, F. and Sanders, A. (1992) An empirical comparison of alternative models of the short-term interest rate. *Journal of Finance* **47** 1209–27

Cox, J., Ingersoll, J. and Ross, S. (1980) An analysis of variable loan contracts. *Journal of Finance* **35** 389–403

Cox, J., Ingersoll, J. and Ross, S. (1981) The relationship between forward prices and futures prices. *Journal of Financial Economics* **9** 321–46

Cox, J., Ingersoll, J. and Ross, S. (1985) A theory of the term structure of interest rates. *Econometrica* **53** 385–467

Cox, J.C., Ross, S. and Rubinstein, M. (1979) Option pricing: a simplified approach. *Journal of Financial Economics* **7** 229–63

Dothan, M.U. (1978) On the term structure of interest rates. *Journal of Financial Economics* **6** 59–69

Epstein, D. and Wilmott, P. (1997) Yield envelopes. *Net Exposure* **2** (August) www.netexposure.co.uk

Epstein, D. and Wilmott, P. (1998) A new model for interest rates. *International Journal of Theoretical and Applied Finance* **1** 195–226

Epstein, D. and Wilmott, P. (1999) A nonlinear non-probabilistic spot interest rate model. *Philosophical Transactions A* **357** 2109–17

Heath, D., Jarrow, R. and Morton, A. (1992) Bond pricing and the term structure of interest rates: a new methodology. *Econometrica* **60** 77–105

Ho, T. and Lee, S. (1986) Term structure movements and pricing interest rate contingent claims. *Journal of Finance* **42** 1129–42

Hull, J.C. and White, A. (1990) Pricing interest rate derivative securities. *Review of Financial Studies* **3** 573–92

Lewicki, P. and Avellaneda, M. (1996) *Pricing interest rate contingent claims in markets with uncertain volatilities.* CIMS Preprint

Longstaff, F.A. and Schwartz, E.S. (1992) A two-factor interest rate model and contingent claims valuation. *Journal of Fixed Income* **3** 16–23

Rebonato, R. (1996) *Interest-rate Option Models.* John Wiley

Vasicek, O.A. (1977) An equilibrium characterization of the term structure. *Journal of Financial Economics* **5** 177–88

8

Dynamic, deterministic and static optimal portfolio strategies in a mean–variance framework under stochastic interest rates

Isabelle Bajeux-Besnainou and Roland Portait

INTRODUCTION

Markowitz (1959) was able to set up the grounds of modern portfolio theory. More precisely, he characterized, in a one-period context, mean–variance efficient portfolios. While the Markowitz model is still a cornerstone of portfolio management, much work has been done on portfolio theory in the last 30 years. Some of it deals with dynamic portfolio optimization decisions. The most spectacular breakthrough in this area is due to Merton (1971, 1973), who solved the theoretical problem of consumption—portfolio choice in a continuous time context where security prices follow diffusion processes. However, Merton was able to derive closed-form solutions only for very particular cases of utility functions or very particular stochastic processes for the security prices.

This chapter studies the impact of continuous rebalancing on optimal portfolio selection when the investor follows the mean–variance criteria. The starting point of the analysis is the mean–variance dynamic optimization model developed initially in Bajeux-Besnainou and Portait (1998), BP, and then in Bajeux-Besnainou *et al.* (2001), BJP, which is an extension of the Richardson (1989) framework to the case of one-factor stochastic interest rates. More precisely, the interest rate follows an Ornstein–Uhlenbeck process and the stock price dynamics depend on the interest rate. The model is therefore appropriate to the analysis of the optimal allocation in three securities: stocks, bonds and cash.

We compare the evolution of the dynamic allocations through explicit formulas and simulations in three cases: (i) continuous stochastic rebalancing is allowed (full optimality); (ii) only deterministic rebalancing is allowed (most of the popular advice for asset allocation is actually given in these terms); (iii) only buy-and-hold strategies are allowed (the standard situation assumed by Markowitz). We are thus adding more constraints to the investor at each step, since he starts (i) being allowed to rebalance freely his portfolio depending on all the new information revealed by the markets (new stock prices and new value of the interest rate level), then (ii) he is constrained to use portfolio rules that are predetermined (the deterministic weights cannot depend on new information), and finally (iii) he is limited to buy-and-hold strategies only. In case (iii) the corresponding dynamic weights will be stochastic as they will actually change 'mechanically' as the new stock prices and interest rates are progressively revealed. It is not clear then how these three strategies can be compared in terms of variance reduction. Intuitively, since the stochastic strategy is unconstrained, it should allow the investor to reach a more efficient portfolio than the two constrained strategies. The strategies are then compared by assessing, through simulations, the differences of the variances of their implied terminal wealth (for a given expected value).

The chapter is organized as follows. The framework of the analysis is specified. Then we recall the results of the stochastic dynamic case as proven in BJP. Next we solve the deterministic case with predetermined weights, followed by the buy-and-hold strategy. Finally, we run simulations for the values of the variance of terminal wealth for these three cases and give our conclusions.

THE FRAMEWORK

The framework of this chapter is identical to the one used in Bajeux-Besnainou *et al.* (2001) and is briefly recalled. Markets are assumed arbitrage-free, frictionless, continuously open between 0 and T, and dynamically complete. The stochastic structure is represented by the probability space (Ω, F, P) where the filtration $F = (F_t), t \in [0, T]$ satisfies the usual conditions (e.g. Duffie 1992). Four assets are traded on these markets (one is redundant): an instantaneously riskless money market fund (cash) with price at t given by $M(t)$; a stock index fund with price $S(t)$; a \$1 par value constant-maturity, zero-coupon bond fund maturing at $t + K$ with price $B_K(t)$; and a \$1 par value zero-coupon bond maturing at date T with maturity $T - t$ and price $B_{T-t}(t)$. The bond fund is continuously rebalanced to maintain a constant maturity of K throughout the period 0 to T.[1] The $(T - t)$-maturity bond is the risk-free asset for an investor with a horizon of T and its maturity decreases as time passes. Since the term structure is driven by only one state variable, the bonds are perfectly correlated and therefore redundant. The notation M, S, B_K and B_{T-t} is also used to represent the four assets when there will be no confusion between this use of the notation and the prices of the assets.

The instantaneous riskless interest rate r follows an Ornstein–Uhlenbeck process given by

$$dr(t) = a_r(b_r - r(t))\,dt - \sigma_r\,dz_r \qquad (8.1)$$

where a_r, b_r and σ_r are positive constants and $z_r(t)$ is a standard Brownian motion. The market price of interest rate risk λ_r is assumed constant. This framework leads to a Vasicek-type bond market.

The stochastic processes for the securities are given by

$$\frac{dM(t)}{M(t)} = r(t)\,dt \qquad (8.2)$$

$$\frac{dS(t)}{S(t)} = (r(t) + \theta_s)\,dt + \sigma_1\,dz + \sigma_2\,dz_r \qquad (8.3)$$

$$\frac{dB_K(t)}{B_K(t)} = (r(t) + \theta_K)\,dt + \sigma_K\,dz_r \qquad (8.4)$$

$$\frac{dB_{T-t}(t)}{B_{T-t}(t)} = (r(t) + \theta_{T-t}(t))\,dt + \sigma_{T-t}(t)\,dz_r \qquad (8.5)$$

where θ_S and θ_K are the (constant) risk premiums of the stock fund and the bond fund, respectively; σ_1, σ_2 and σ_K are positive constants; dz is a standard Brownian motion orthogonal to dz_r; $\theta_{T-t}(t)$ is the time-dependent risk premium of the bond maturing at

T and $\sigma_{T-t}(t)$ its the time-dependent volatility. By normalization convention, the initial prices of the money market fund and the stock index fund are equal to one.

The volatility and risk premium of the bond fund are given by Vasicek's formulas:

$$\sigma_K = \frac{\sigma_r(1 - e^{-a_r K})}{a_r} \tag{8.6}$$

and

$$\theta_K = \sigma_K \lambda_r \tag{8.7}$$

The volatility and risk premium of the bond maturing at T are also given by (8.6) and (8.7) if $\sigma_{T-t}(t)$ is substituted for σ_K and $T - t$ is substituted for K. σ_K and θ_K are constant; $\theta_{T-t}(t)$ and $\sigma_{T-t}(t)$ are deterministic functions of time. The market price of stock market risk (λ) is assumed constant, hence the risk premium of the stock index fund, θ_S, is also constant and given by

$$\theta_S = \sigma_1 \lambda + \sigma_2 \lambda_r \tag{8.8}$$

The instantaneous variance–covariance matrix of stock fund and bond fund returns is then given by

$$\mathbf{\Gamma} = \begin{pmatrix} \sigma_1^2 + \sigma_2^2 & \sigma_2 \sigma_K \\ \sigma_2 \sigma_K & \sigma_K^2 \end{pmatrix} \tag{8.9}$$

Portfolio strategies can be defined by their weights on the risky assets denoted $x_i(t)$, $i = M, S, K$, and $T - t$. Initially, strategies are expressed in terms of a three-asset portfolio excluding the bond maturing at T (which is redundant), by the vector $\mathbf{x}'(t) = (x_S(t), x_K(t))$; the weight in cash is implicit and given by $x_M(t) = 1 - x_S(t) - x_K(t)$.

The weight vector $\mathbf{x}(t)$ satisfies integrability conditions and the terminal payoff (the return when initial prices are normalized to one) displays finite mean and variance (Harrison and Pliska 1981; Duffie 1992). Only self-financing strategies are considered here; the self-financing condition is

$$\frac{dX(t)}{X(t)} = x_M(t) \frac{dM(t)}{M(t)} + x_S(t) \frac{dS(t)}{S(t)} + x_K(t) \frac{dB_K(t)}{B_K(t)} \tag{8.10}$$

where $X(t)$ is the portfolio value at t.

Among the admissible self-financing strategies, one is of special interest—the numeraire portfolio (Long 1990), also known as the logarithmic or growth-optimal portfolio (Merton 1992) since it maximizes expected logarithmic utility. The weights $\mathbf{h}$ of the logarithmic portfolio are given by $\mathbf{h} = \mathbf{\Gamma}^{-1}\boldsymbol{\theta}$.

In the three-asset framework (choosing the constant-maturity, K-maturity bond fund in lieu of the $(T - t)$-maturity bond), $\mathbf{h}' = (h_S, h_K)$ is given, as shown in BJP, by the constant weights:

$$h_S = \frac{\lambda}{\sigma_1} \quad \text{and} \quad h_K = \frac{-\lambda \sigma_2 + \lambda_r \sigma_1}{\sigma_1 \sigma_K} \tag{8.11}$$

Setting its initial value $H(0)$ to unity, the price $H(t)$ of the growth-optimal portfolio is then

$$H(t) = \exp\left[\int_0^t r(s)\,ds + \frac{1}{2}(\lambda^2 + \lambda_r^2)t\right]\exp[\lambda(z(t) - z(0)) + \lambda_r(z_r(t) - z_r(0))] \tag{8.12}$$

The logarithmic portfolio has the remarkable property that all prices of self-financing portfolios or securities, relative to $H(t)$, are martingales with respect to the historical (true) probability P, e.g. $E[X(T)/H(T)] = X(0)$, where the expectation is taken at date 0), (Merton 1992). Therefore a portfolio paying $1/H(T)$ requires an initial investment (has a present value) of $E[1/H^2(T)]$.[2] The return on this portfolio, denoted $H^{\min}(T)$, is then given by

$$H^{\min}(T) = \frac{1/H(T)}{E[1/H^2(T)]} \tag{8.13}$$

$H^{\min}(T)$ is called the minimum norm return since it can be characterized as the admissible return with the minimum second moment; see BP. The value of $H^{\min}(t)$ is explicitly derived in Appendix A of BJP.

MEAN–VARIANCE EFFICIENT STRATEGIES WHEN STOCHASTIC REBALANCING IS ALLOWED

A complete development and presentation of this case can be found in BP or BJP. We summarize here the main results, without providing any proofs.

The notation $D[x_M(t), x_S(t), x_K(t), x_{T-t}(t)]$ defines a dynamic portfolio strategy by specifying the four allocations $x_M(t), x_S(t), x_K(t), x_{T-t}(t)$ in securities M, S, B_K, and B_{T-t} at date t (the four weights sum to one). Note that there is no unique specification of strategy D because of the redundancy of securities B_K and B_{T-t}. Indeed, \$1 invested in B_{T-t}, denoted $D[0, 0, 0, 1]$, is equivalent to $\sigma_{T-t}(t)/\sigma_K$ invested in B_K and the complement $(1 - \sigma_{T-t}(t)/\sigma_K)$ in M, or $D[1 - \sigma_{T-t}(t)/\sigma_K, 0, \sigma_{T-t}(t)/\sigma_K, 0]$. In this notation the weights of the logarithmic portfolio strategy can be written $D[1 - h_S - h_K, h_S, h_K, 0]$ which is equivalent to the previously used more compact notation (h_S, h_K). We use the transformation of the dynamic optimization problem into a static problem as developed in Pliska (1982, 1986), Karatzas *et al.* (1987), and Cox and Huang (1989). Following this approach, we first obtain the equation of the optimal portfolio value and then the optimal strategy (weights) yielding the optimal portfolio value.

The problem is a mean–variance optimization program for a target expected return μ:

$$\min_{\mathbf{x}(t)} \text{variance}[X(T)]$$

$$\text{s.t.}\quad X_0 = 1; \quad E[X(T)] = e^{\mu T}; \quad E\left[\frac{X(T)}{H(T)}\right] = 1 \tag{P_1}$$

with the technical condition $e^{\mu T} \geqslant 1/B_T(0)$; the required return must be at least equal to the period 0–T risk-free rate. The solution $X^*(T)$ of this program, derived in BP, is the following function of $H(T)$:

$$X^*(T) = q - q' \frac{1}{H(T)} \tag{8.14}$$

with

$$q' = \frac{B_T(0)\exp(\mu T) - 1}{\text{var}(1/H(T))}; \quad q = \exp(\mu T) + q' B_T(0)$$

The conditions $q \geqslant 1/B_T(0)$, $\exp(\mu T) \geqslant 1/B_T(0)$ and $q' \geqslant 0$ are equivalent. They mean that the investor seeks an expected return higher than the risk-free rate and thus saturates the budget constraint.

The optimal terminal wealth, $X^*(T)$, in (8.14) is bounded from above by q (since $H(T)$ and q' are positive).

Equation (8.14) shows that the optimal strategy consists of a static (buy-and-hold) position, long q zero-coupon bonds maturing at T (and paying \$1) and short q' units of a portfolio with a payoff at T of $1/H(T)$ (the minimum norm fund).[3] This static combination will result in stochastic weights in the minimum norm fund $H^{\min}(T)$ and in B_{T-t}.

BP shows that, in this framework, the minimum norm portfolio is generated by a dynamic strategy consisting of short \$1 in the logarithmic portfolio and long \$2 in B_{T-t}, or $D[-1 + h_S + h_K, -h_S, -h_K, 2]$. This last strategy exhibits constant weights (requiring continuous rebalancing).[4] The corresponding variance of optimal terminal wealth is then derived from equation (8.14):

$$\text{var}(X^*(T)) = \frac{(B_T(0)e^{\mu T} - 1)^2}{\text{var}(1/H(T))}$$

where

$$E\left[\frac{1}{H_T}\right] = B_T(0) = \exp\left[-(\alpha(0) - \frac{1}{2}\gamma^2(0)\sigma_r^2 + \lambda_r\delta(0)\sigma_r)T\right]$$

and

$$E\left[\frac{1}{H(T)^2}\right] = \exp\left[(\lambda_r^2 + \lambda^2 - 2\alpha(0) - 4\lambda_r\delta(0)\sigma_r + 2\gamma(0)^2\sigma_r^2)T\right]$$

the coefficients $\alpha(0)$, $\gamma(0)$ and $\delta(0)$ being defined in the lemma of Appendix A.

PREDETERMINED WEIGHTS: DETERMINISTIC MEAN–VARIANCE DYNAMIC EFFICIENCY

A mean–variance efficient strategy with deterministic weights is defined as the solution to the following program:

$$\min_{\mathbf{x}(t)} \text{ variance } [X(T)]$$

$$\text{s.t. } X(0) = 1$$

$$E[X(T)] = \exp(\mu T) \tag{P_2}$$

$$\mathbf{x}(t) \text{ deterministic and self-financing}$$

where μ is the continuously compounded target rate of return.

The solution of (P_2), derived in Appendix A, is

$$x_S^* = w(\mu)h_S$$

$$x_K^*(t) = [1 - w(\mu)]\frac{\sigma_{T-t}}{\sigma_K} + w(\mu)h_K \tag{8.15}$$

where $w(\mu)$ is a constant weight for a given target expected return μ.[5] The closed-form expression of $w(\mu)$ is quite complex and is provided by equation (A.10). The weight in the money market fund, x_M^*, is the complement $1 - x_S^* - x_K^*$.

These results can be interpreted as follows. Call $\mathbf{b}_{T-t}'(t)$ the deterministic dynamic strategy $(0, \sigma_{T-t}/\sigma_K)$ involving B_K and M that replicates the zero-coupon bond B_{T-t} maturing at T.[6] Then (8.15) can be rewritten

$$\mathbf{x}^* = w(\mu)\mathbf{h} + [1 - w(\mu)]\mathbf{b}_{T-t}(t) \tag{8.16}$$

The efficient deterministic strategies are then constant-weight combinations of the growth-optimal portfolio $\mathbf{h}$ and the zero-coupon bond maturing at the investor's horizon, which is the risk-free asset for the investor. This result resembles static two-fund separation involving buy-and-hold combinations of the risk-free asset and an efficient portfolio; however, continuous rebalancing is required to maintain the constant weights of this dynamic two-fund strategy. The variance of optimal terminal wealth is derived in Appendix A and given by

$$\mathrm{var}(X_T) = \exp[2(E(Y_T) + \mathrm{var}(Y_T))] - \exp[2(E(Y_T) + \tfrac{1}{2}\mathrm{var}(Y_T))]$$

where

$$E(Y_T) = \alpha_0 T + \boldsymbol{\theta}\int_0^T \mathbf{x}(t)\,dt - \frac{1}{2}\int_0^T \mathbf{x}'(t)\boldsymbol{\Gamma}\mathbf{x}'(t)\,dt$$

and

$$\mathrm{var}(Y_T) = \gamma^2\sigma_r^2 T + \int_0^T \mathbf{x}'(t)\boldsymbol{\Gamma}x(t)\,dt - 2\int_0^T \sigma_{t-t}(t)\mathbf{x}'(t)\boldsymbol{\Sigma}_2\,dt$$

BUY-AND-HOLD STRATEGIES

We consider now buy-and-hold portfolio strategies (the positions are taken at time 0 and no transactions are allowed between 0 and T) and three securities: cash M, the stock S and a zero-coupon bond B_{T-t}. The last security is risk-free for the given horizon since its maturity matches the investor horizon; the stock and the cash are risky.

The buy-and-hold optimization program is as follows:

$$\min_{\mathbf{x}(t)} \text{variance } X(T)$$

$$X(T) = x_1 M(T) + x_2 S(T) + (1 - x_1 - x_2)\frac{1}{B_T(0)} \tag{P$_3$}$$

$$E[X(T)] = \exp(\mu T)$$

Using the standard derivation, it is proved in Appendix B that the solution of (P$_3$) is the vector of weights $\mathbf{x} = (x_1, x_2)$ satisfying

$$\mathbf{x}^* = \frac{e^{\mu T} - 1/B_T(0)}{(\mathbf{E} - [1/B_T(0)]\mathbf{1})'\mathbf{\Gamma}^{-1}(\mathbf{E} - [1/B_T(0)]\mathbf{1})}\mathbf{\Gamma}^{-1}(\mathbf{E} - [1/B_T(0)]\mathbf{1}) \qquad (8.17)$$

where the matrix $\mathbf{\Gamma}$ and the vector $\mathbf{E}$ coefficients are defined as

$$\Gamma_{11} = \text{var}(M(T)), \ \Gamma_{22} = \text{var}(S(T))$$

$$\Gamma_{12} = \text{cov}(M(T), S(T)), \ E_1 = E(M(T)), \ E_2 = E(S(T))$$

and $\mathbf{1}$ is the unit vector.

The explicit derivation of these coefficients is provided in Appendix B; these coefficients are

$$E_1 = \exp[(\alpha + \tfrac{1}{2}\gamma^2\sigma_2^2)T] \ E_2 = \exp[(\theta_S + \alpha + \tfrac{1}{2}\gamma^2\sigma_r^2 - \delta\sigma_r\sigma_2)T]$$

$$\Gamma_{11} = E_1^2[\exp(\gamma^2\sigma_r^2 T - 1)] \ \Gamma_{22} = E_2^2[\exp\{(\sigma_1^2 + \sigma_1^2 + \gamma^2\sigma_r^2 - 2\sigma_2\sigma_r\delta)T\} - 1]$$

$$\Gamma_{12} = E_1 E_2[\exp\{(\gamma^2\sigma_r^2 - \sigma_2\sigma_r\delta)T\} - 1]$$

Then the variance of the optimal terminal wealth $X^*(T)$ is given by

$$\text{var}(X^*(T)) = x_1^{*2}\Gamma_{11} + x_2^{*2}\Gamma_{22} + 2x_1^*x_2^*\Gamma_{12}$$

SIMULATIONS AND COMPARISON OF THE DIFFERENT CASES

We can now compare, for a given target expected return μ, the variance of terminal wealth obtained from the optimal solutions of these three different portfolio strategies using the closed-form expressions obtained for these variances. Table 8.1 is a summary of simulations for different investor horizons and a set of assumed parameters.

As the stochastic strategy takes full advantage of the information revealed on the markets, stock prices and interest levels, it always dominates the other two strategies. We see in the simulations of Table 8.1 that the gain of the stochastic strategy over the deterministic and buy-and-hold strategies increases dramatically with the investor horizon. However, this gain appears to be quite significant even for relatively short horizons like five years.

We also observe that for shorter horizons the deterministic strategy dominates the buy-and-hold strategy, whereas for longer horizons the opposite is true. This may seem quite surprising. In general, there is no direct theoretical dominance of one strategy over the other. Indeed, when considering buy-and-hold strategies, the investor puts on very strong constraints in the optimization program. These constraints imply stochastic weights that are 'mechanically' driven by the realization of stock prices and interest rate levels. It is then possible to find a buy-and-hold strategy dominating the deterministic strategies.

Table 8.1 Standard deviations of terminal wealth obtained from the optimal solutions of the three different portfolio strategies

T (years)	Stochastic (%)	Deterministic (%)	Buy and hold (%)
1	9.820	9.823	10.759
2	13.97	14.48	16.38
3	17.30	18.55	21.37
4	20.29	22.49	26.05
5	23.13	26.47	30.52
10	37.32	49.85	52.56
15	53.81	83.76	82.20
20	74.07	134.69	129.03
25	99.20	211.41	203.93
30	130.34	326.72	322.81

Assumed parameters:

$a_r = 18.00\%$	$\sigma_1 = 19.00\%$	$\lambda_r = 16.00\%$	$r_0 = 4.00\%$
$b_r = 4.00\%$	$\sigma_2 = 6.00\%$	$K = 10$ years	
$\sigma_r = 2.00\%$	$\lambda = 26.00\%$	$\mu = 7.00\%$	

APPENDIX A

Technical lemma

Consider the Ornstein–Uhlenbeck process

$$dr = a_r(b_r - r)\,dt - \sigma_r\,dz_r$$

$$\Leftrightarrow r(s) = (r_0 - b_r)\exp(-a_r s) + b_r - \sigma_r \exp(-a_r s)\int_0^s \exp(a_r u)\,dz_r(u)$$

The following relations hold for $\int_t^T r(s)\,ds$:

$$\int_t^T r(s)\,ds = \alpha(t)(T - t) - \int_t^T \sigma_{T-s}(s)\,dz_r(S)$$

$$\text{hence}\quad \int_t^T r(s)\,ds \sim N[\alpha(t)(T - t), \gamma^2(t)\sigma_r^2(T - t)]$$

where

$$\begin{aligned}
\alpha(t) &= b_r + (r(t) - b_r)\frac{\sigma_{T-t}}{\sigma_r(T - t)} \\
\gamma^2(t) &= \frac{1}{a_r^2}\left[1 - 2\frac{\sigma_{T-t}}{(T - t)\sigma_r} + \frac{\sigma_{2(T-t)}}{2(T - t)\sigma_r}\right]
\end{aligned} \qquad (A.1)$$

Also

$$E\left\{[z_r(T) - z_r(t)]\int_t^T r(s)\,ds\right\} = -\delta(t)\sigma_r(T - t)$$

$$\text{where}\quad \delta(t) = \frac{1}{a_r}\left(1 - \frac{\sigma_{T-t}}{(T - t)\sigma_r}\right) \qquad (A.2)$$

The proof is available on request from the authors; see also BP and BJP.

Deterministic weights

To derive the deterministic weights, we start form the dynamics of the portfolio value $X(t)$:

$$\frac{dX(t)}{X(t)} = r(t)\,dt + x_s(t)\left[\frac{dS(t)}{S(t)} - r(t)\,dt\right] + x_K(t)\left[\frac{dB_K(t)}{B_K(t)} - r(t)\,dt\right] \tag{A.3}$$

which can be written as

$$\frac{dX(t)}{X(t)} = [r(t) + \mathbf{x}'(t)\,\boldsymbol{\theta}]\,dt + \mathbf{x}'(t)\boldsymbol{\Sigma}\,d\mathbf{z}$$

where

$$d\mathbf{z} = \left(\begin{array}{c} dz \\ dz_r \end{array}\right), \boldsymbol{\Sigma} = \left(\begin{array}{cc} \sigma_1 & \sigma_2 \\ 0 & \sigma_K \end{array}\right), \mathbf{x} = \left(\begin{array}{c} x_S \\ x_K \end{array}\right), \boldsymbol{\theta} = \left(\begin{array}{c} \theta_S \\ \theta_K \end{array}\right), \tag{A.4}$$

and

$$\boldsymbol{\Gamma} = \boldsymbol{\Sigma}\boldsymbol{\Sigma}' = \left(\begin{array}{cc} \sigma_1^2 + \sigma_2^2 & \sigma_2\sigma_K \\ \sigma_2\sigma_K & \sigma_K^2 \end{array}\right)$$

The portfolio value at T is given by $X_T = e^{Y_T}$ with

$$Y_T = \int_0^T [r(t) + \mathbf{x}'(t)\,\boldsymbol{\theta}]\,dt - \frac{1}{2}\int_0^T \mathbf{x}'(t)\boldsymbol{\Gamma}\mathbf{x}(t)\,dt + \int_0^T \mathbf{x}'(t)\boldsymbol{\Sigma}\,d\mathbf{z} \tag{A.5}$$

Then, since Y_T follows a normal distribution, the first two moments of X_T are

$$E(X_T) = E(e^{Y_T}) = \exp[E(Y_T) + \tfrac{1}{2}\,\mathrm{var}(Y_T)]$$

$$E(X_T^2) = E(e^{2Y_T}) = \exp 2[E(Y_T) + \mathrm{var}(Y_T)]$$

The optimization problem yielding the efficient strategies can be written

$$\min_{\mathbf{x}} E(X_T^2) \text{ s.t. } E(X_T) = e^{\mu T}$$

which is equivalent to

$$\min_{\mathbf{x}}\{E(Y_T) + \mathrm{var}\ (Y_T)\} \text{ s.t. } E(Y_T) + \tfrac{1}{2}(\mathrm{var}Y_T) = \mu T$$

Using the Lagrangian we obtain

$$\min_{\mathbf{x}}\{(1 - w(\mu))\mathrm{var}(Y_T) - 2w(\mu)E(Y_T\} \tag{A.6}$$

where $2w(\mu)$ stands for the Lagrange multiplier of the goal constraint and may be interpreted as a risk tolerance parameter.

Computation of $E(Y_T)$

Using (A.5) and the technical lemma $\left(E \int_0^T r(t)\,dt = \alpha T\right)$

$$E(Y_T) = \alpha T + \boldsymbol{\theta}'\int_0^T \mathbf{x}(t)\,dt - \frac{1}{2}\int_0^T \mathbf{x}'(t)\boldsymbol{\Gamma}\mathbf{x}(t)\,dt \tag{A.7}$$

where for brevity $\alpha(0)$ is denoted α.

Computation of $var(Y_T)$

It follows from (A.5) that

$$\text{var } (Y_T) = \text{var} \left\{ \int_0^T r(t)\,dt + \int_0^T \mathbf{x}'(t)\mathbf{\Sigma}\,\mathbf{dz} \right\}$$

$$\text{var } (Y_T) = \text{var} \left\{ \int_0^T r(t)\,dt \right\} + \text{var} \left\{ \int_0^T \mathbf{x}'(t)\mathbf{\Sigma}\,\mathbf{dz} \right\} + 2\,\text{cov} \left\{ \int_0^T r(t)\,dt, \int_0^T \mathbf{x}'(t)\mathbf{\Sigma}\,\mathbf{dz} \right\}$$

Three points to note:

- $\text{var} \left\{ \int_0^T r(t)\,dt \right\} = \gamma^2 \sigma_r^2 T$ (from lemma; for brevity $\gamma(0)$ is denoted γ)

- $\text{var} \left\{ \int_0^T \mathbf{x}'(t)\mathbf{\Sigma}\,\mathbf{dz} \right\} = \int_0^T \mathbf{x}'(t)\mathbf{\Gamma}\mathbf{x}(t)\,dt$

- $\text{cov} \left\{ \int_0^T r(t)\,dt, \int_0^T \mathbf{x}'(t)\mathbf{\Sigma}\,\mathbf{dz} \right\} = \text{cov} \left\{ \int_0^T -\sigma_{T-t}(t)\,dz_r, \int_0^T \mathbf{x}'(t)\mathbf{\Sigma}\,\mathbf{dz} \right\}$

$$= \text{cov} \left\{ \int_0^T -\sigma_{T-t}(t)\,dz_r, \int_0^T [\mathbf{x}'(t)\mathbf{\Sigma}_1\,\mathbf{dz} + \mathbf{x}'(t)\mathbf{\Sigma}_2\,\mathbf{dz}_r] \right\}$$

where $\mathbf{\Sigma}_1$ and $\mathbf{\Sigma}_2$ are respectively the first and second columns of $\mathbf{\Sigma}$.

Hence

$$\text{cov} \left\{ \int_0^T r(t)\,dt, \int_0^T \mathbf{x}'(t)\mathbf{\Sigma}\,\mathbf{dz} \right\} = -\int_0^T \sigma_{T-t}(t)\mathbf{x}'(t)\mathbf{\Sigma}_2\,dt$$

Therefore

$$\text{var}(Y_T) = \gamma^2 \sigma_r^2 T + \int_0^T \mathbf{x}'(t)\mathbf{\Gamma}\mathbf{x}(t)\,dt - 2\int_0^T \sigma_{T-t}(t)\mathbf{x}'(t)\mathbf{\Sigma}_2\,dt \qquad (A.8)$$

Then, the first-order conditions stem from (A.6):

$$(1 - w(\mu))\frac{\partial\,\text{var}(Y_T)}{\partial\mathbf{x}(t)} + 2w(\mu)\frac{\partial E(Y_T)}{\partial\mathbf{x}(t)} = 0$$

with

$$\frac{\partial\,\text{var}(Y_T)}{\partial\mathbf{x}(t)} = 2[\mathbf{\Gamma}\mathbf{x}(t) - \sigma_{T-t}(t)\mathbf{\Sigma}_2] \quad \text{(from A.8)}$$

$$\frac{\partial E(Y_T)}{\partial\mathbf{x}(t)} = \boldsymbol{\theta} - \mathbf{\Gamma}\mathbf{x}(t) \quad \text{(from A.7)}$$

And the first-order condition can be written

$$(1 - w(\mu))[\mathbf{\Gamma}\mathbf{x}^*(t) - \sigma_{T-t}(t)\mathbf{\Sigma}_2] - w(\mu)[\boldsymbol{\theta} - \mathbf{\Gamma}\mathbf{x}^*(t)] = 0$$

$$\mathbf{\Gamma}\mathbf{x}^*(t) = (1 - w(\mu))\sigma_{T-t}(t)\mathbf{\Sigma}_2 + w(\mu)\,\boldsymbol{\theta}$$

$$\mathbf{x}^*(t) = (1 - w(\mu))\sigma_{T-t}(t)\mathbf{\Gamma}^{-1}\mathbf{\Sigma}_2 + w(\mu)\mathbf{\Gamma}^{-1}\boldsymbol{\theta} \qquad (A.9)$$

On the one hand, $\mathbf{\Gamma}^{-1}\boldsymbol{\theta} = \mathbf{h}$.

On the other hand,

$$\boldsymbol{\Gamma}^{-1} = \frac{1}{\sigma_1^2 \sigma_K^2} \begin{pmatrix} \sigma_K^2 & -\sigma_2 \sigma_K \\ -\sigma_2 \sigma_K & \sigma_1^2 + \sigma_2^2 \end{pmatrix}$$

$$\boldsymbol{\Gamma}^{-1}\boldsymbol{\Sigma}_2 = \boldsymbol{\Gamma}^{-1} \begin{pmatrix} \sigma_2 \\ \sigma_K \end{pmatrix} = \begin{pmatrix} 0 \\ 1/\sigma_K \end{pmatrix}$$

Let

$$\mathbf{b}_{T-t} = \sigma_{T-t} \boldsymbol{\Gamma}^{-1}\boldsymbol{\Sigma}_2 = \begin{pmatrix} 0 \\ \sigma_{T-t}/\sigma_K \end{pmatrix}$$

be the dynamic strategy involving B_K and M that duplicates B_{T-t}. Then (A.9) implies $\mathbf{x}^*(t) = (1 - w(\mu))\mathbf{b}_{T-t} + w(\mu)\mathbf{h}$, and since $\mathbf{b}_{T-t}$ implies no weight in stock and a weight of σ_{T-t}/σ_K in the bond fund B_K, we get (8.15).

The value of the Lagrange parameter $2w(\mu)$ still needs to be determined. The goal constraint $(E(Y_T) + \frac{1}{2} \operatorname{var} Y_T = \mu T)$ can be written

$$\alpha T + \boldsymbol{\theta}' \int_0^T \mathbf{x}(t)\, dt + \frac{1}{2}\gamma^2 \sigma_r^2 T - \int_0^T \sigma_{T-t} \mathbf{x}'(t) \boldsymbol{\Sigma}_2\, dt = \mu T$$

$$\Leftrightarrow \boldsymbol{\theta}' \int_0^T \mathbf{x}(t)\, dt - \int_0^T \sigma_{T-t} \mathbf{x}'(t) \boldsymbol{\Sigma}_2\, dt = \left(\mu - \alpha - \frac{1}{2}\gamma^2 \sigma_2^2\right) T$$

First we compute the value of $\boldsymbol{\theta}' \int_0^T \mathbf{x}(t)\, dt$ using (8.15) and our lemma:

$$\boldsymbol{\theta}' \int_0^T \mathbf{x}(t)\, dt = w(\mu)\, \boldsymbol{\theta}'\mathbf{h}T + (1 - w(\mu))\frac{\theta_K}{\sigma_K} \int_0^T \sigma_{T-t}\, dt$$

$$= w(\mu)(\boldsymbol{\theta}'\mathbf{h})T + (1 - w(\mu))\frac{\theta_K}{\sigma_K}\delta_T \sigma_r T$$

$$= T\left\{ w(\mu)\left(\boldsymbol{\theta}'\mathbf{h} - \frac{\theta_K}{\sigma_K}\delta_T \sigma_r\right) + \frac{\theta_K}{\sigma_K}\delta_T \sigma_r\right\}$$

$$\text{where}\quad \delta_T = \frac{1}{a_r}\left(1 - \frac{\sigma_T}{T\sigma_r}\right)$$

Then we compute $\int_0^T \sigma_{T-t}\mathbf{x}'(t)\boldsymbol{\Sigma}_2\, dt$ using $\mathbf{x}'(t)\boldsymbol{\Sigma}_2 = w(\mathbf{h}'\boldsymbol{\Sigma}_2) + (1 - w)\sigma_{T-t}$ and our lemma:

$$\int_0^T \sigma_{T-t}\mathbf{x}'(t)\boldsymbol{\Sigma}_2\, dt = w(\mu)(\mathbf{h}'\boldsymbol{\Sigma}_2)\int_0^T \sigma_{T-t}\, dt + (1 - w(\mu))\int_0^T (\sigma_{T-t})^2\, dt$$

$$= w(\mu)(\mathbf{h}'\boldsymbol{\Sigma}_2)\delta_T \sigma_r T + (1 - w(\mu))\gamma^2 \sigma_r^2 T$$

$$= w(\mu)\left[(\mathbf{h}'\boldsymbol{\Sigma}_2)\delta_T \sigma_r - \gamma^2 \sigma_r^2\right]T + \gamma^2 \sigma_r^2 T$$

This implies that the constraint can be written

$$w(\mu)\left\{\boldsymbol{\theta}'\mathbf{h} - \frac{\theta_K}{\sigma_K}\delta_T \sigma_r + \gamma^2 \sigma_r^2 - (\mathbf{h}'\boldsymbol{\Sigma}_2)\delta_T \sigma_r\right\} + \frac{\theta_K}{\sigma_K}\delta_T \sigma_r - \gamma^2 \sigma_r^2$$

$$= w(\mu)\left\{\boldsymbol{\theta}'\mathbf{h} + \gamma^2 \sigma_r^2 - \delta_T \sigma_r\left(\frac{\theta_K}{\sigma_K} + \mathbf{h}'\boldsymbol{\Sigma}_2\right)\right\} + \frac{\theta_K}{\sigma_K}\delta_T \sigma_r - \gamma^2 \sigma_r^2$$

$$= \mu - \alpha - \frac{1}{2}\gamma^2 \sigma_r^2$$

which implies

$$\omega(\mu) = \frac{\mu - \alpha - (\theta_K/\sigma_K)\delta_T\sigma_r + \frac{1}{2}\gamma^2\sigma_r^2}{\theta_S h_S + \theta_K h_K + \gamma^2\sigma_r^2 - \delta_T\sigma_r[(\theta_K/\sigma_K) + h_S\sigma_2 + h_K\sigma_K]} \tag{A.10}$$

Calculation of variance in the deterministic case

From the notation and the calculations of the previous section, we have

$$X_T = \exp(Y_T)$$

$$E(X_T) = \exp[E(Y_T) + \tfrac{1}{2}\operatorname{var}(Y_T)]$$

$$E(X_T{}^2) = \exp[2(E(Y_T) + \operatorname{var}(Y_T))]$$

where

$$E(Y_T) = \alpha_0 T + \boldsymbol{\theta} \int_0^T \mathbf{x}(t)\,dt - \tfrac{1}{2}\int_0^T \mathbf{x}'(t)\boldsymbol{\Gamma}\mathbf{x}'(t)\,dt$$

$$\operatorname{var}(Y_T) = \gamma^2\sigma_r^2 T + \int_0^T \mathbf{x}'(t)\boldsymbol{\Gamma}\mathbf{x}(t)\,dt - 2\int_0^T \sigma_{t-t}(t)\mathbf{x}'(t)\boldsymbol{\Sigma}_2\,dt$$

$$\boldsymbol{\Sigma}_2 = \begin{pmatrix} \sigma_2 \\ \sigma_k \end{pmatrix} \qquad \mathbf{x}(t) = \begin{pmatrix} x_s \\ x_k(t) \end{pmatrix}$$

Then $\displaystyle \int_0^T \mathbf{x}(t)\,dt = \begin{pmatrix} x_s T \\ \frac{1-w(\mu)}{\sigma_k}\int_0^T \sigma_{T-t}\,dt + w(\mu)h_k T \end{pmatrix}$

From our lemma:

$$\int_0^T \sigma_{T-t}\,dt = \frac{\sigma_r}{a_r}\int_0^T (1-\exp[-a_r(T-t)])\,dt = \frac{\sigma_r}{a_r}\left[T - \frac{1}{a_r}\left[1-\exp(-a_r T)\right]\right]$$

$$\mathbf{x}'(t)\boldsymbol{\Gamma}\mathbf{x}(t) = x_s^2(\sigma_1^2 + \sigma_2^2) + 2\sigma_2\sigma_k x_s \int_0^T x_k(t)\,dt + \sigma_k^2 \int_0^T x_k^2(t)\,dt$$

$$\int_0^T x_k^2\,dt = w(\mu)^2 h_k^2 T + 2h_k w(\mu)(1-w(\mu))\frac{1}{\sigma_k}\int_0^T \sigma_{T-t}\,dt$$

$$+ (1-w(\mu))^2\frac{1}{\sigma_k^2}\int_0^T \sigma_{T-t}^2\,dt$$

$$\int_0^T \sigma_{T-t}^2\,dt = \frac{\sigma_r^2}{a_r^2}\left[T - \frac{2}{a_r}\left(1-e^{-a_r T}\right) + \frac{1}{2a_r}\left(1-e^{-2a_r T}\right)\right]$$

$$\int_0^T \sigma_{T-t}(t)\mathbf{x}'(t)\boldsymbol{\Sigma}_2\,dt = \int_0^T \sigma_{T-t}(t)(\sigma_2 x_s + \sigma_k x_k(t))\,dt$$

$$\int_0^T \sigma_{T-t}(t)x_k(t)\,dt = (1-w(\mu))\frac{1}{\sigma_k}\int_0^T \sigma_{T-t}^2(t)\,dt + w(\mu)h_k \int_0^T \sigma_{T-t}(t)\,dt$$

Then $\operatorname{var}(X_T) = \exp[2(E(Y_T) + \operatorname{var}(Y_T))] - \exp[2(E(Y_T) + \tfrac{1}{2}\operatorname{var}(Y_T))]$

APPENDIX B

To obtain the coefficients of the investment opportunity set in the static case, we start from the terminal values (returns) of the two risky securities:

$$M(T) = \exp\left(\int_0^T r(t)\,dt\right)$$

$$S(T) = \exp\left(\int_0^T r(t)\,dt + \left[\theta_S - \frac{1}{2}(\sigma_1^2 + \sigma_2^2)\right]T + \int_0^T \sigma_1\,dz(t) + \sigma_2\,dz_r(t)\right)$$

We let $\gamma = \gamma(0)$, $\alpha = \alpha(0)$ and $\delta = \delta(0)$, and we use our lemma from Appendix A:

$$E_1 = E[M(T)] = E\left[\exp\left(\int_0^T r(t)\,dt\right)\right], \quad \text{and from (A.1) we have } E_1 = \exp\left(\left(\alpha + \frac{1}{2}\gamma^2\sigma_r^2\right)T\right)$$

$$E_2 = E[S(T)] = E\left\{\exp\left(\int_0^T r(t)\,dt + \left(\theta_S\frac{1}{2}(\sigma_1^2 + \sigma_2^2)\right)T + \int_0^T \sigma_1\,dz(t) + \sigma_2\,dz_r(t)\right)\right\}$$

$$= \exp\left(\theta_s - \frac{1}{2}\sigma_2^2\right)E\left[\exp\left(\int_0^T r(t)dt + \sigma_2[z_r(T) - z_r(0)]\right)\right]$$

and using equations (A.1) and (A.2), we have

$$E_2 = \exp\left(\left(\theta_S + \alpha + \tfrac{1}{2}\gamma^2\sigma_r^2 - \delta\sigma_r\sigma_2\right)T\right)$$

$$\Gamma_{11} = \mathrm{var}\left[\exp\left(\int_0^T r(t)\,dt\right)\right] = E\left[\exp\left(2\int_0^T r(t)\,dt\right)\right] - E_1^2$$

And from our lemma:

$$\Gamma_{11} = \exp\left(2(\alpha + \gamma^2\sigma_r^2)T\right) - E_1^2 = E_1^2\left(e^{\gamma^2\sigma_r^2 T} - 1\right)$$

$$\Gamma_{22} = \mathrm{var}(S(T))$$

Then

$$\Gamma_{22} = E\left[\exp\left(2\int_0^T r(t) + [2\theta_S - (\sigma_1^2 + \sigma_2^2)]T + 2\int_0^T \sigma_1\,dz(t) + \sigma_2\,dz_r(t)\right)\right] - E_2^2$$

$$= \exp\left([2\theta_S - (\sigma_1^2 + \sigma_2^2)]T\right)E\left[\exp\left(2\int_0^T \sigma_1\,dz(t)\right)\right]$$

$$\times E\left[\exp\left(2\left[\int_0^T r(t)\,dt + \sigma_2\,dz_r(t)\right]\right)\right] - E_2^2$$

$$= E_2^2\left[\exp\left((\sigma_1^2 + \sigma_2^2 + \gamma^2\sigma_r^2 - 2\sigma_2\sigma_r\delta)T\right) - 1\right]$$

The same kind of calculations yields

$$\Gamma_{12} = \mathrm{cov}[M(T), S(T)] = E_1 E_2\left[\exp((r^2\sigma_r^2 - \sigma_2\sigma_r\delta)T)\right]$$

Let's calculate the optimal weights for an annualized return goal equal to μ. Standard calculation provides the tangent portfolio as

$$\mathbf{t} = \frac{\mathbf{\Gamma}^{-1}(\mathbf{E} - [1/B_T(0)]\mathbf{1})}{\mathbf{1}'\mathbf{\Gamma}^{-1}(\mathbf{E} - [1/B_T(0)]\mathbf{1})}$$

Any efficient portfolio $\mathbf{x}^*$ is homothetical to $\mathbf{t}$, hence

$$\mathbf{x}^* = \alpha \mathbf{t}$$

And its expected return can be written

$$(1 - \alpha\mathbf{1}'\mathbf{t})\frac{1}{B_T(0)} + \alpha\mathbf{E}'\mathbf{t} = e^{\mu T}$$

thus

$$\alpha = \frac{e^{\mu T} - 1/B_T(0)}{(\mathbf{E} - [1/B_T(0)]\mathbf{1})\mathbf{t}}$$

Then the optimal portfolio $\mathbf{x}^*$ is given by

$$\mathbf{x}^* = \frac{e^{\mu T} - 1/B_T(0)}{(\mathbf{E} - [1/B_T(0)]\mathbf{1})'\mathbf{\Gamma}^{-1}(\mathbf{E} - [1/B_T(0)]\mathbf{1})}\mathbf{\Gamma}^{-1}(\mathbf{E} - [1/B_T(0)]\mathbf{1})$$

NOTES

1. In theory, at time t the bond fund manager can sell all bonds (with time to maturity $K - dt$) and use the proceeds to buy bonds with a time to maturity K. This operation is repeated at $t + dt$, and so on; then at each moment, this self-financing fund contains only bonds with time to maturity K and constant volatility σ_K. In practice the bond fund might include different non-zero-coupon bonds and be managed to maintain approximately a constant duration K. In this case the price dynamics of the fund would only approximate the constant-maturity zero-coupon bond fund dynamics (8.4).

2. The present value is the expected value of the payoff relative to the value of the logarithmic portfolio, $E\left[\frac{1/H(T)}{H(T)}\right] = E\left[\frac{1}{H^2(T)}\right]$.

3. This static combination of two funds can be viewed as a Black two-fund separation result in which the dynamic strategies are considered as traded securities (which are infinite in number).

4. Note that if only one of the two bonds is used, the minimum norm portfolio does not have constant weights. For example, using only the K-period bond fund, we have $D[-1 + h_S + h_K - 2\sigma_T(t)/\sigma_K, -h_S, -h_K + 2\sigma_T(t)/\sigma_K, 0]$.

5. $w(\mu)$ is increasing in μ and depends on T but not on t.

6. The dynamic stategy replicating bond B_{T-t} (using the bond B_K and the money market M) is characterized by a weight y in B_K (and $1 - y$ in M) that must satisfy $y\sigma_K = \sigma_{T-t}$, using (8.4) and (8.5).

REFERENCES

Bajeux-Besnainou, I. and Portait, R. (1998) Dynamic asset allocation in a mean–variance framework. *Management Science*, November.

Bajeux-Besnainou, I., Jordan, J. and Portait, R. (2001) Dynamic asset allocation for stocks, bonds and cash. *Journal of Business*, forthcoming.

Cox, J. and Huang, C.F. (1989) Optimal consumption and portfolio policies when asset prices follow a diffusion process. *Journal of Economic Theory*, **49**, 33–83.

Duffie, D. (1992) *Dynamic Asset Pricing Models*. Princeton: Princeton University Press.

Harrison, J.M. and Pliska, S. (1981) Martingales and the stochastic integrals in the theory of continuous trading. *Stochastic Processes and Their Applications*, **11**, 215–60.

Karatzas, I., Lehoczky, J. and Shreve, S. (1987) Optimal portfolio and consumption decisions for a 'small investor' on a finite horizon. *SIAM Journal of Control and Optimization*, **25**, 1157–86.

Long, J.B. (1990) The numeraire portfolio. *Journal of Financial Economics*, **26**, 29–69.

Markowitz, H. (1959) *Portfolio Selection: Efficient Diversification of Investments*. New York: Wiley.

Merton, R. (1971) Optimum consumption and portfolio rules in a continuous time model. *Journal of Economic Theory*, **3**, 373–413.

Merton, R. (1973) An intertemporal capital asset pricing model. *Econometrica*, **41**, 867–88.

Merton, R. (1992) *Continuous Time Finance*. Oxford: Basil Blackwell.

Pliska, S.R. (1982) A discrete time stochastic decision model. In *Advances in Filtering and Optimal Stochastic Control* (Eds W.H. Fleming and L.G. Gorostiza), pp. 290–304. New York: Springer.

Pliska, S.R. (1986) A stochastic calculus model of continuous trading: optimal portfolios. *Mathematics of Operations Research*, **11**, 371–84.

Richardson, H. (1989) A minimum variance result in continuous trading portfolio optimization. *Management Science*, **35**, 1045–55.

9

Pricing bond options in a worst-case scenario

David Epstein and Paul Wilmott

INTRODUCTION

In contrast to the asset price world, there is no commonly accepted model for the movement of the underlying in the interest rate world. Consequently, there are a number of different approaches to the pricing of fixed-income products. The simplest approach is to price a product off a yield curve. This method is effective for simple contracts, bonds for instance. However, for more complex products, where optionality or convexity play a role, the precise nature of the interest rate movements is significant and so the method does not give accurate results.

The 'traditional' approach to pricing these more complicated products is to introduce stochastic variables to model a number of 'unknown' factors, on which we believe the interest rate movements depend [7, 17, 19, 20]. These models can be single- or multifactor models for the movement of the short-term interest rate, or models for the movement of the whole yield curve (the Heath, Jarrow and Morton approach). All of these methods rely on the estimation of parameters. Not only are these parameters (e.g. volatility) difficult to estimate, but they can also be unstable [1]. The single- and multifactor models have the additional disadvantages that they can require fitting to the current yield curve, again in an unstable fashion, and that they can assume an equally difficult to estimate and unstable correlation between yields of different maturities.

In the following work, we present an alternative approach to the pricing of fixed-income products. We introduce a non-stochastic non-probabilistic model for the short-term interest rate. This work has, in part, been inspired by the work on uncertain volatility in equity derivatives by Avellaneda, Levy and Parás [2, 3] and Lyons [18]. However, the ideas cannot be directly translated into the interest rate world, because the underlying that we consider is not a traded quantity.

Rather than specify how the short rate evolves, we will just constrain the possible movements. We will make no probabilistic statements whatsoever, solely stating what is possible and what is not. Clearly, there are going to be a number of possible paths that the short rate could take. For each path, when we use the short rate as a discount rate, the contract in question could have a different value (where we consider the position of the holder of the contract). We will consequently find a range of possible values for the price of a contract. We identify the lowest of these as the 'worst-case scenario value'.

The analysis of this worst-case valuation problem leads to a non-linear, first-order, hyperbolic partial differential equation. We can solve this equation either analytically or via numerical methods. The results motivate us to investigate whether there is any role for hedging. Rather than dynamic hedging, we find there is an optimal static hedge for a product [5–9]. This form of hedging mirrors the yield curve fitting that is often applied to stochastic interest rate models, but has none of the associated problems with inconsistency.

There are a number of practical applications for this model. Clearly, it can be used to find price ranges for instruments and spot potential arbitrage opportunities in the market [10, 12, 13]. If we have an over-the-counter (OTC) contract—one that is not listed in the market—then we can use the uncertain interest rate model to construct an optimal static hedge of market-traded products and reduce the inherent interest rate risk [14, 15]. Finally, we can use the model as a risk management tool. With a sensible choice of parameters, it is possible to show that the model is completely consistent with past interest rate history. In this case the worst-case scenario value is a definitive lower bound for the value of a portfolio. The same consistency cannot easily be shown for any other model [11,16].

In this chapter, we show how to apply the model to the pricing and hedging of bond options. This is a problem of note because optionality must be carefully dealt with to ensure a consistent approach to pricing under an uncertain regime. We first demonstrate how to price a European option on a zero-coupon bond. This approach will still be appropriate when we hedge the option with the underlying bond. However, if we wish to hedge with a different instrument, or price the American option, we will need to modify our approach to ensure that we have a consistent and optimal worst- or best-case interest rate path. This will be a more general method of solution and, consequently, computationally more intensive.

A WORST-CASE SCENARIO VALUATION

We first review the uncertain interest rate model and the general pricing problem: we propose a model for a short-term interest rate, r, which we will use as a discount rate for all cashflows. We do not give a probabilistic description for the possible interest rate movements, but solely place bounds on them:

$$r^- \leqslant r \leqslant r^+,$$

and

$$c^-(r) \leqslant \frac{dr}{dt} \leqslant c^+(r).$$

These constraints ensure that the spot rate lies within the region (r^-, r^+) and grows at a speed within the range (c^-, c^+).

Under this model, we find that a simple fixed-income contract has worst-case value $V(r, t)$, where V satisfies the first-order non-linear hyperbolic partial differential equation

$$V_t + c(r, V_r)V_r - rV = 0, \tag{9.1}$$

where

$$c(r, X) = \begin{cases} c^+(r) & \text{if } X < 0 \\ c^-(r) & \text{if } X > 0, \end{cases}$$

with appropriate final and jump conditions. (For instance, a zero-coupon bond with maturity at time T and principal P would have the final condition $V(r, T) = P$.)

Similarly, we can derive the equation for the best-case scenario value,

$$V_t + \bar{c}(r, V_r)V_r - rV = 0, \tag{9.2}$$

where

$$\bar{c}(r, X) = \begin{cases} c^+ & \text{if } X > 0 \\ c^- & \text{if } X < 0 \end{cases} = c(r, -X).$$

Note that we can view the best-case scenario valuation as equivalent to a worst-case scenario valuation in which we hold the contract short instead of long. The financial reasoning behind this is that the best-case scenario for the holder of a contract will always be the worst-case scenario for the writer, and vice versa. Consequently, we find

$$V_{\text{best case}} = -(-V)_{\text{worst case}}. \tag{9.3}$$

Since these problems are non-linear, we find that the value of a contract depends on what it is hedged with [12]. The marginal value in question may be different from the value of the unhedged contract. By changing the quantities of each of the hedging instruments, and revaluing the portfolio, it is possible to alter the marginal value of the hedged contract. Using an optimisation routine, we can therefore find a maximum worst-case value or a minimum best-case value for the hedged contract along with the associated optimal static hedges.

THE PRICING PROBLEM WITH OPTIONALITY

We now consider the application of the model to the pricing of contracts which include some form of optionality. We begin with the simplest problem, the unhedged European bond option.

Pricing a European option on a zero-coupon bond

We consider a European option with a zero-coupon bond as the underlying. The bond has a principal payment of P at time T_Z. The option expires at time $T_O < T_Z$ and has payoff $\Lambda(Z)$. For a long call option, we have

$$\Lambda(Z) = \max(Z - E, 0),$$

where E is the exercise price of the option.

We will consider the option value in a worst-case scenario and price the option in two stages. We first ascertain the spread for the zero-coupon bond price at expiry of the option.

Consider a fixed value of r, r^* say. For this value of r, we find the worst-case scenario price, $Z^-(r^*, T_O)$, and the best-case scenario price, $Z^+(r^*, T_O)$, for the zero-coupon bond, at time T_O. We then know that at T_O the actual bond price, $Z(r^*, T_O)$, lies between these two values, i.e.

$$Z^-(r^*, T_O) \leqslant Z(r^*, T_O) \leqslant Z^+(r^*, T_O).$$

We can thus find the spread in price for the zero-coupon bond for each value of r between r^- and r^+, at time T_O. Figure 9.1 shows the form that these results take.

We then consider the value of the option at expiry, for this fixed value of r, r^*. In general, this is $\Lambda(Z(r^*, T_O))$. Figure 9.2 shows the extremal possible values for a long call option.

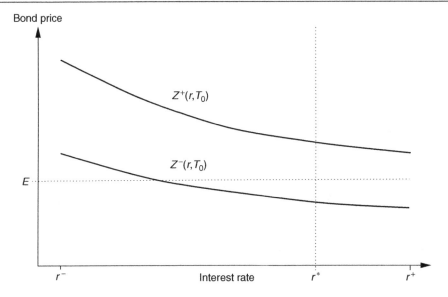

Figure 9.1   Worst-case and best-case prices for the underlying zero-coupon bond

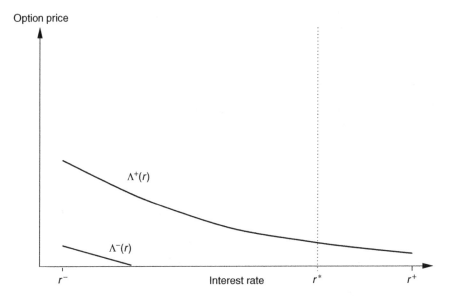

Figure 9.2   Value of the call option

To find the option value in a worst-case scenario, we determine the minimum possible value of $\Lambda(Z(r^*, T_O))$, when $Z(r^*, T_O)$ can vary between $Z^-(r^*, T_O)$ and $Z^+(r^*, T_O)$. This minimum value is $\Lambda^-(r^*)$, say, where

$$\Lambda^-(r^*) = \min_{Z(r^*, T_O)} \left(\Lambda(Z(r^*, T_O))\right),$$

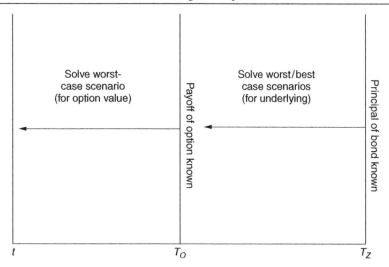

Figure 9.3   Pricing a bond option in a worst-case scenario

For a long call option, we have

$$\Lambda^-(r^*) = \min_{Z(r^*,T_O)} \left(\max(Z(r^*, T_O) - E, 0) \right).$$

The minimum value will occur, for this call option, when the bond price $Z(r^*, T_O)$ is as low as possible. We therefore take $Z(r^*, T_O) = Z^-(r^*, T_O)$ and find that

$$\Lambda^-(r^*) = \max(Z^-(r^*, T_O) - E, 0).$$

This holds for each possible value of r^* between r^- and r^+. We have therefore determined the worst-case scenario value of the option, $\Lambda^-(r)$, at its expiry, for all possible r.

We solve (9.1) with $\Lambda^-(r)$ as our final data, to determine the worst-case value of the option, $V^-(r, t)$ say, at earlier times $t \leqslant T_O$. The method of solution is shown schematically in Figure 9.3.

We can also value the option in a best-case scenario. Here we find the maximum possible value of $\Lambda(Z(r, T_O))$, $\Lambda^+(r)$ say, where

$$\Lambda^+(r^*) = \max_{Z(r^*,T_O)} \left(\Lambda(Z(r^*, T_O)) \right),$$

and solve (9.2) with this as our final data to determine the best-case value of the option, $V^+(r, t)$, at earlier times.

Hedging the European option with the underlying zero-coupon bond

We can hedge our option with the underlying bond to reduce the spread between the worst-case and best-case prices. We will buy λ of the bond, which has a current market price of Z_M and price the resulting portfolio in a worst-case scenario.

The first stage of the pricing process remains the same. For each possible fixed value of r, r^*, we find the worst-case and best-case prices for the zero-coupon bond at time

T_O, $Z^-(r^*, T_O)$ and $Z^+(r^*, T_O)$ respectively. We then value our combined portfolio of the option and the hedging bond, Π, at expiry of the option. The portfolio is worth

$$\Pi(Z(r^*, T_O), T_O) = \Lambda(Z(r^*, T_O)) + \lambda Z(r^*, T_O).$$

We want to value this portfolio in a worst-case scenario. We therefore determine the minimum possible value of the portfolio, when $Z(r^*, T_O)$ can vary between $Z^-(r^*, T_O)$ and $Z^+(r^*, T_O)$. This value is $\Pi^-(r^*, T_O)$, say, where

$$\Pi^-(r^*, T_O) = \min_{Z(r^*, T_O)} \left(\Lambda(Z(r^*, T_O)) + \lambda Z(r, T_O) \right).$$

We perform this calculation for each value of r^* between r^- and r^+. We then have the minimum possible value of the portfolio, $\Pi^-(r, T_O)$, for all r at time T_O. This is the worst-case value of the portfolio at expiry of the option.

We solve (9.1) with $\Pi^-(r, T_O)$ as final data to find the value of the portfolio in a worst-case scenario at earlier times, $\Pi^-(r, t)$. This is our minimum possible value for the portfolio when we hedge with λ of the bond.

To find the marginal worst-case value of the option, $V^-(r, t)$, we must subtract the cost of the static hedge, λZ_M, to obtain

$$V^-(r, t) = \Pi^-(r, t) - \lambda Z_M.$$

We can maximise the worst-case value of the option, with respect to λ, to find the optimal static hedge of the underlying bond, λ, and the best worst-case value,

$$V^-(r, t) = \max_{\lambda} \left(\Pi^-(r, t) - \lambda Z_M \right).$$

This is the minimum possible value for the optimally hedged bond option.

We can also value the hedged option in a best-case scenario. Here we find the maximum possible value of the portfolio at expiry of the option, $\Pi^+(r, T_O)$ say, where

$$\Pi^+(r^*, T_O) = \max_{Z(r^*, T_O)} \left(\Lambda(Z(r^*, T_O)) + \lambda Z(r, T_O) \right).$$

We can then work out the current value of the portfolio in a best-case scenario, by solving (9.2) with $\Pi^+(r, T_O)$ as final data. To determine the optimal static hedge and the minimal best-case value for the bond option, we minimise with respect to λ to find

$$V^+(r, t) = \min_{\lambda} \left(\Pi^+(r, t) - \lambda Z_M \right).$$

This is the maximum possible value for the optimally hedged bond option.

Example 9.1: We price vanilla European call and put options with expiry in 1 year and exercise price E, on a zero-coupon bond with principal 1 and maturity in 5 years. The current market price of the bond is 0.687. The spot short-term interest rate is 6% and the parameters of our model are

$$r^- = 3\%, \ r^+ = 20\%, \ c^- = -4\% \text{ p.a. and } c^+ = 4\% \text{ p.a.}$$

Tables 9.1 and 9.2 show results for the option valuation, without hedging and with the optimal static hedges for both worst-case and best-case valuations. We see that hedging

Table 9.1 Value of a European call option hedged with the underlying

	Worst case	Best case	Hedge quantity
$E = 0.4$			
No hedge	0.102	0.468	–
Optimal hedge on worst case	0.303	0.318	−0.993
Optimal hedge on best case	0.303	0.318	−0.996
$E = 0.5$			
No hedge	0.009	0.372	–
Optimal hedge on worst case	0.207	0.226	−0.993
Optimal hedge on best case	0.207	0.226	−0.996
$E = 0.6$			
No hedge	0.000	0.276	–
Optimal hedge on worst case	0.111	0.215	−0.993
Optimal hedge on best case	0.077	0.161	−0.743

Table 9.2 Value of a European put option hedged with the underlying

	Worst case	Best case	Hedge quantity
$E = 0.8$			
No hedge	0.000	0.268	–
Optimal hedge on worst case	0.052	0.164	0.996
Optimal hedge on best case	0.021	0.117	0.710
$E = 0.9$			
No hedge	0.012	0.361	–
Optimal hedge on worst case	0.144	0.177	0.996
Optimal hedge on best case	0.144	0.177	0.993
$E = 1.0$			
No hedge	0.108	0.453	–
Optimal hedge on worst case	0.237	0.273	0.996
Optimal hedge on best case	0.237	0.273	0.993

significantly reduces the spread in price and that the optimal hedges for both worst-case and best-case valuations are similar. When the option is significantly in the money, the hedge is almost exactly one of the underlying (short for the call, or long for the put). To reduce the spread further, however, we will need to hedge the option with contracts other than the underlying bond.

Hedging the European option with other instruments

Unfortunately, this approach to option pricing is no longer appropriate when we try to hedge the option with a contract that is not the underlying. This is because there will now be two quantities that we need to determine at expiry of the option. The first of these is the spread for prices for the underlying zero-coupon bond. Without this spread, we cannot determine the worst-case payoff for the option. The second quantity of interest is the value of the hedging instruments in a worst-case scenario. The worst-case value of the overall portfolio at expiry of the option will be the sum of the value of these instruments and the worst-case value of the option payoff.

We could perform two separate valuations to find these two quantities. To achieve this we would solve (9.1) for the underlying bond price and then resolve the same equation, with different final data and jump conditions, to find the value of the hedging instruments, at expiry of the option. However, there is no guarantee that these two solutions would have the same interest rate path. This is because of the non-linearity of the pricing equation. If the interest rate paths were different, then there would be an inconsistency in our pricing methodology.

There are several ways in which this could manifest itself. Our spread for the underlying bond price may be too large—the presence of the hedging bonds should narrow the spread in zero-coupon bond price at expiry of the option. Alternatively, our worst-case value for the portfolio of hedging instruments may be too low. In either occurrence, our eventual option price will not be optimal. It will be lower than the actual worst-case value (hence it will still be a valid lower bound, just not the best one).

We will develop a more general approach to the pricing of contracts with optionality by considering the cases in which we exercise and do not exercise the option separately, i.e. we consider all of our options individually and then choose the appropriate course of action. The drawback to this approach will be that for each instance of either/or optionality, we double the number of cases to be considered. Let Π_0 be the overall portfolio of cashflows that we would have if we chose to exercise the option at expiry. This consists of the cashflows due to the hedging instruments plus the cashflows that we would receive if we were to exercise the option. In the case of a call option, the latter cashflows would be those of the underlying bond (for a put option, they would be the cashflows for the short bond). We also let Π_1 be the portfolio of cashflows that we would have if we did not exercise the option (i.e. just those from the hedging instruments).

We solve (9.1) with the appropriate final and jump conditions (dependent on the nature of the hedging instruments and option payoff) to find the value of the portfolio in a worst-case scenario at expiry, when we do exercise the option. This is $\Pi_0^-(r, T_0)$. We also solve (9.1) with the appropriate final and jump conditions to find the value of the portfolio in a worst-case scenario at expiry, when we do not exercise the option. This is $\Pi_1^-(r, T_0)$.

Since we are long the option, we have control over whether or not to exercise, and so we set the value of the portfolio at expiry to be the more valuable of the two courses of action, where we take the exercise price into account. For a call option, this is the maximum of the value of the portfolio when we do exercise minus the exercise price and the value when we do not exercise, i.e.

$$\Pi^-(r, T_O) = \max\left(\Pi_0^-(r, T_0) - E, \Pi_1^-(r, T_0)\right).$$

(For a put option, we add the exercise price, since the holder of the option receives the exercise price at expiry.)

We then solve (9.1) with $\Pi^-(r, T_O)$ as final data and apply appropriate jump conditions (for the hedging instruments) to find the current worst-case scenario value of the portfolio. This method is shown schematically in Figure 9.4. To find the marginal worst-case value of the option, we then subtract the cost of the static hedge. Finally, we can maximise the marginal option value with respect to the hedge quantities to find the optimal worst-case scenario value for the option.

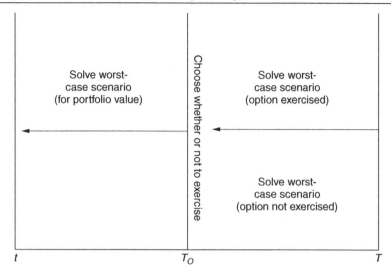

Figure 9.4   A more general approach to option pricing

We can also find the value of the option in a best-case scenario. We solve (9.2) with appropriate final and jump conditions to find the best-case values of Π_0 and Π_1 at expiry of the option, $\Pi_0^+(r, T_0)$ and $\Pi_1^+(r, T_0)$ respectively. We then set the value of the portfolio at expiry of the option to be the most valuable course of action. For a call option,

$$\Pi^+(r, T_O) = \max \left(\Pi_0^+(r, T_0) - E, \Pi_1^+(r, T_0) \right).$$

We solve (9.2) with $\Pi^+(r, T_O)$ as final data and appropriate jump conditions to find the current best-case scenario value of the portfolio. We then subtract the cost of the static hedge to find the marginal best-case value of the option. Again, we can optimise the result and minimise with respect to the hedge quantities to find the optimal best-case value.

Example 9.2:   We price vanilla European call and put options with expiry in 1 year, on a zero-coupon bond with principal 1 and maturity in 5 years. The current market price of the bond is 0.687. The spot short-term interest rate is 6% and the parameters of our model are

$$r^- = 3\%, r^+ = 20\%, c^- = -4\% \text{ p.a. and } c^+ = 4\% \text{ p.a.}$$

We hedge with the hedging bonds of Table 9.3. The results when we price a call option, with exercise price 0.5, are shown in Tables 9.4 and 9.5 and those when we price a put option, with exercise price 0.9, are shown in Tables 9.6 and 9.7. Figure 9.5 show the value of the put option in a worst-case scenario under the various hedging strategies. We can see that although the extra hedging instruments have not had a particularly noticeable effect in raising the worst-case price at the spot short rate (over and above that when we

Table 9.3 The zero-coupon bonds with which we hedge

Hedging bond	Maturity (yrs)	Market price
Z_1	0.5	0.970
Z_2	1	0.933
Z_3	2	0.868
Z_4	3	0.805
Z_5	5	0.687
Z_6	7	0.579
Z_7	10	0.449

Table 9.4 Value of the optimally hedged European call option

Call, $E = 0.5$	Worst case	Best case
No hedge	0.009	0.372
Optimal hedge on worst case	0.220	0.221
Optimal hedge on best case	0.220	0.221

Table 9.5 The optimal static hedges for the European call option

Hedging bond	Maturity (yrs)	Worst-case hedge quantity	Best-case hedge quantity
Z_1	0.5	0.012	0.082
Z_2	1	0.488	0.456
Z_3	2	0.001	0.002
Z_4	3	−0.002	−0.008
Z_5	5	−1.004	−0.994
Z_6	7	0.006	0.000
Z_7	10	0.000	0.000

hedged with the underlying), they have flattened out the curve and this must correspond to a significant decrease in the interest rate risk in the portfolio.

If we examine the static hedges, we see that they still include approximately one of the underlying bond (short for the call, long for the put) although the specific quantities of this bond have altered slightly. The hedges also include sizable amounts of the 1 year bond. This bond matures at the same time as the option expires and is consequently an effective hedging tool for the option payoff. With the extra hedging instruments it has been possible to reduce the option price spread to a level which is of the same magnitude as the bid/offer spread seen in practice.

Finally, we remark that if we were to construct the yield curve from the hedging instruments and then price the options off this, the call would be worth

$$0.687 - 0.5 \times 0.933 = 0.2205,$$

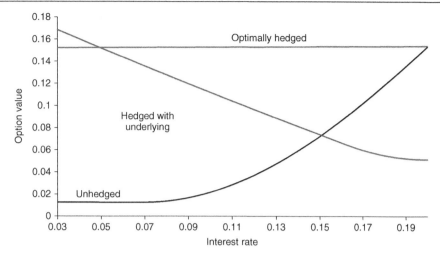

Figure 9.5   European put option value in a worst-case scenario

Table 9.6   Value of the optimally hedged European put option

Put, $E = 0.9$	Worst case	Best case
No hedge	0.012	0.361
Optimal hedge on worst case	0.152	0.154
Optimal hedge on best case	0.152	0.153

Table 9.7   The optimal static hedges for the European put

Hedging bond	Maturity (yrs)	Worst-case hedge quantity	Best-case hedge quantity
Z_1	0.5	−0.136	−0.034
Z_2	1	−0.826	−0.874
Z_3	2	−0.003	−0.003
Z_4	3	0.008	0.008
Z_5	5	0.996	0.995
Z_6	7	−0.001	−0.001
Z_7	10	0.000	0.000

and the put would be worth

$$0.9 \times 0.933 - 0.687 = 0.1527.$$

Both of these values are contained within their respective spreads for the prices.

Alternatively, we could use the Black approximation to the bond option value, an approach popular with practitioners [4]. We value the bond option using the Black–Scholes equity option pricing methodology, where we have assumed that the bond price behaves in a lognormal fashion. The price of a European call option, expiring at time T_1, on a bond maturing at time T_2, is then given by

$$Z(t;T_1)(FN(d_1) - EN(d_2)),$$

where the forward price of the bond at expiry of the option, F, is

$$F = \frac{Z(t;T_2)}{Z(t;T_1)},$$

$$d_1 = \frac{\log(F/E) + \frac{1}{2}\sigma^2(T - t)}{\sigma\sqrt{T - t}},$$

and

$$d_2 = d_1 - \sigma\sqrt{T - t}.$$

The corresponding put option has value

$$Z(t;T_1)(EN(-d_2) - FN(-d_1)).$$

In our example, with a volatility of 8%, the call option is then worth 0.2205 and the put option 0.1528. Again, both of these prices are contained within the spreads predicted.

Pricing and hedging American options

For the European option, we compared the value of two portfolios at expiry of the option and just picked the course of action that had the higher value. However, for the American option, we may also exercise at earlier times. We must therefore be aware that at any time before expiry, it may be optimal to exercise rather than hold the option. This presents itself as a constraint on the value of the portfolio in which we continue to hold the option.

We again consider two portfolios—one containing the cashflows we would have if we were to exercise the option, the other containing those we would have if we continued to hold the option. We consider an option with the same specification as before, with the one exception that the holder now has the right to exercise the option at any time before T_O. We let $\Pi_0(r, t)$ be the overall portfolio of cashflows that we would have at time t if we were to exercise the option at time t and $\Pi_1(r, t)$ be the portfolio of cashflows that we would have if we continued to hold the option at time t (this does not include any cashflow due to the option payoff at expiry). We remark that when $t = T_O$, these are the same portfolios as for the European option in the previous section.

We solve (9.1) with the appropriate final data and jump conditions to find the worst-case value of the portfolio when we do exercise at time t, $\Pi_0^-(r, t)$. This tells us what our portfolio payoff would be if we decided to exercise at time t. We then solve (9.1) with the appropriate final data and jump conditions to find the worst-case value of the portfolio when we continue to hold the option at time t, $\Pi_1^-(r, t)$. In the absence of arbitrage, we would exercise the option if the value of the consequent portfolio, with the exercise price taken into account, were greater than the current value of the portfolio when we continue to hold the option. For the call option, this gives us the additional constraint

$$\Pi_1^-(r, t) \geqslant \Pi_0^-(r, t) - E,$$

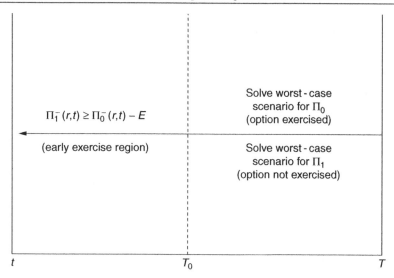

Figure 9.6   Pricing American options

during the period in which we are allowed to exercise the option (in this case, for $t \leqslant T_0$). We show this method schematically in Figure 9.6. For a put option, the constraint is

$$\Pi_1^-(r, t) \geqslant \Pi_0^-(r, t) + E.$$

The marginal worst-case value of the option at time t is then the value of the portfolio in which we still hold the option, $\Pi_1^-(r, t)$, minus the cost of the static hedge. We can maximise with respect to the hedge quantities to find the optimal marginal value.

We can also find the best-case scenario value of the option. We solve (9.2) with the appropriate final data and jump conditions to find the best-case value of the portfolio in which we still hold the option, $\Pi_1^+(r, t)$, with a suitable constraint whilst we are allowed to exercise the option. For a call option,

$$\Pi_1^+(r, t) \geqslant \Pi_0^+(r, t) - E,$$

where $\Pi_0^+(r, t)$ is the solution of (9.2) for the portfolio value when we exercise the option at time t.

Example 9.3:   We price the vanilla American put option with expiry in 1 year and exercise price E, on a zero-coupon bond with principal 1 and maturity in 5 years. The current market price of the bond is 0.687. The spot short-term interest rate is 6% and the parameters of our model are

$$r^- = 3\%, \ r^+ = 20\%, \ c^- = -4\% \text{ p.a. and } c^+ = 4\% \text{ p.a.}$$

Initially, we solely hedge with the underlying zero-coupon bond. The results for the option valuation, without hedging and with the optimal static hedges for both worst-case and best-case valuations, are shown in Table 9.8.

Table 9.8 Value of an American put option hedged with the underlying

	Worst case	Best case	Hedge quantity
$E = 0.8$			
No hedge	0.000	0.328	–
Optimal hedge on worst case	0.112	0.164	0.998
Optimal hedge on best case	0.090	0.142	0.862
$E = 0.9$			
No hedge	0.048	0.428	–
Optimal hedge on worst case	0.212	0.213	0.998
Optimal hedge on best case	0.211	0.213	1.000
$E = 1.0$			
No hedge	0.148	0.528	–
Optimal hedge on worst case	0.312	0.313	0.998
Optimal hedge on best case	0.311	0.313	1.000

Table 9.9 Value of the optimally hedged American put option

Put, $E = 0.9$	Worst case	Best case
No hedge	0.048	0.428
Optimal hedge on worst case	0.212	0.213
Optimal hedge on best case	0.212	0.213

Table 9.10 The optimal static hedges for the American put

Hedging bond	Maturity (yrs)	Worst-case hedge quantity	Best-case hedge quantity
Z_1	0.5	−0.002	−0.036
Z_2	1	0.002	−0.001
Z_3	2	−0.002	−0.003
Z_4	3	0.008	0.009
Z_5	5	0.994	0.994
Z_6	7	0.000	−0.001
Z_7	10	0.000	0.000

We then hedge the option with the bonds of Table 9.3. The results when we price a put option, with exercise price 0.9, are shown in Tables 9.9 and 9.10. Figure 9.7 shows the value of the unhedged option in a worst-case scenario.

The further an option is in the money (whether American or European), the more likely it is to be exercised and the nearer the quantity of the underlying, in the static hedge, is to unity. The spread in price also decreases because we are effectively valuing the exercised option and we can hedge this very efficiently with the underlying bond.

The spreads for the American option are therefore smaller than those for the European option and the hedge quantities of the underlying are larger. This is because the American option has more exercise opportunities and is consequently more likely to be exercised. We note that if we were to immediately exercise the option with exercise price 0.9, it

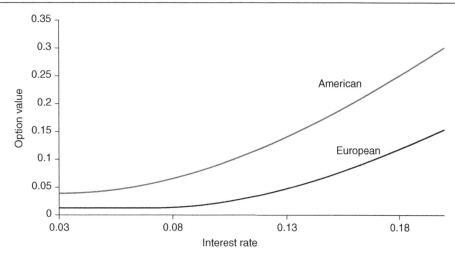

Figure 9.7   American put option value in a worst-case scenario

would be worth

$$0.9 - 0.687 = 0.213,$$

which is contained within our spread for prices and is the optimally hedged best-case price. (In this best-case scenario the optimal strategy is therefore to exercise imme-diately.)

If we were to price the American call option then we would find that it had the same value as the European call option. This is because the underlying is a zero-coupon bond. It is an equivalent result to the equality of American and European call options on equities which do not pay a dividend [21]. If we were to price a call option on a coupon bond (where the coupon was paid before expiry of the option) then the American option would be worth more than the European, since the holder of the option would not receive the coupon, whereas the holder of the bond would. We remark that we can also use this approach to value Bermudan options (options with exercise allowed only on or between specified dates). To value such an option, we proceed as for the American option. However, when we come to solve our partial differential equation for Π_1, we only include the relevant constraint at (or between) times when exercise is allowed.

CONCLUSION

We have developed two different approaches to pricing options under an uncertain interest rate model. The first approach is simple to implement but only appropriate for European options hedged with no more than the underlying. The second approach is more general and can be used to value European and American options with no such constraint on the choice of hedging instrument. Unfortunately, there is a drawback to this approach. For each instance of either/or optionality, we must double the number of cases to be considered. This means that to value a portfolio which includes n instances of optionality (e.g. n vanilla options), we must price 2^n separate portfolios. This can quickly become computationally intensive.

In this work, we have only discussed the pricing of options on zero-coupon bonds. However, both methodologies are still valid for other underlying contracts. The first approach is still appropriate for any underlying contract that we can price using our model, as long as all of the cashflows of the contract are after the expiry date of the option (since all we have to do is to find the spread in price for the underlying at this date).

However, if we want to hedge the option with anything but the underlying, or with an underlying which has cashflows before expiry of the option, then we must use the second approach. This methodology is still valid for any underlying contract, as long as the contract can be expressed as a set of cashflows which are either fixed or only dependent on our short-term interest rate, r. We can then include them as jump conditions when we solve the partial differential equation for the portfolio value when we exercise the option, Π_0.

Finally, we remark on the existence of a static hedging strategy for bond options under this model. Although it is unlikely that such a static method could ever be considered as effective as the more common dynamic hedging strategies for bond options (as found through stochastic models for interest rates), the use of a static hedge should decrease the interest rate risk in a position, in some general sense. The static hedge should therefore be of use in minimising the interest rate risk left to be hedged dynamically. Since dynamic hedging is not perfect, this approach may result in a more effective hedge overall.

REFERENCES

1. Apabhai, M.Z., Choe, K., Khennach, K. and Wilmott, P. (1995) Spot-on modelling. *Risk*, **8**(11):59–63
2. Avellaneda, M., Levy, A. and Parás, A. (1995) Pricing and hedging derivative securities in markets with uncertain volatilities. *Applied Mathematical Finance*, **2**:73–88
3. Avellaneda, M. and Parás, A. (1996) Managing the volatility risk of portfolios of derivative securities: the Lagrangian uncertain volatility model. *Applied Mathematical Finance*, **3**:21–52
4. Black, F. (1976) The pricing of commodity contracts. *Journal of Financial Economics*, **3**:167–79
5. Bowie, J. and Carr, P. (1994) Static simplicity. *Risk*, **7**:45–49
6. Carr, P. and Chou, A. (1997) Breaking barriers. *Risk*, **10**:139–44
7. Cox, J.C., Ingersoll, J.E. and Ross, S.A. (1985) A theory of the term structure of interest rates. *Econometrica*, **53**:385–407
8. Dembo, R. (1992) The art of the optimum. In *From Black–Scholes to Black Holes: New Frontiers in Options*. Risk/Finex
9. Derman, E., Ergener, D. and Kani, I. (1997) Static options replication. In *Frontiers in Derivatives*. Irwin
10. Epstein, D. (1996) Fixed income security valuation in a worst case scenario. DPhil transfer thesis
11. Epstein, D. (1998) *Instructors Manual for Derivatives: The Theory and Practice of Financial Engineering*. Wiley
12. Epstein, D. and Wilmott, P. (1997) The yield envelope: price ranges for fixed income products. *NetExposure*, **1**(2)
13. Epstein, D. and Wilmott, P. (1998) A new model for interest rates. *International Journal of Theoretical and Applied Finance*, **1**(2):195–226
14. Epstein, D. and Wilmott, P. (1998) A note on the pricing of index amortising rate swaps in a worst-case scenario. *International Journal of Theoretical and Applied Finance*, forthcoming.

15. Epstein, D., Haber, R. and Wilmott, P. (2000) Pricing and hedging convertible bonds under non-probabilistic interest rates. *Journal of Derivatives*, **7**(4)

16. Epstein, D. and Wilmott, P. (1999) A nonlinear non-probabilistic spot interest rate model. *Philosophical Transactions of the Royal Society*, **357**:2109–17

17. Heath, D., Jarrow, R. and Morton, A. (1992) Bond pricing and the term structure of interest rates: a new methodology for contingent claims valuation. *Econometrica*, **60**:77–105

18. Lyons, T.J. (1995) Uncertain volatility and the risk-free synthesis of derivatives. *Applied Mathematical Finance*, **2**:117–33

19. Strickland, C. (1996) A comparison of diffusion models of the term structure. *European Journal of Finance*, **2**:103–23

20. Vasicek, O.A. (1977) An equilibrium characterization of the term structure. *Journal of Financial Economics*, **5**:177–88

21. Wilmott, P., Dewynne, J.N. and Howison, S.D. (1993) *Option Pricing: Mathematical Models and Computation*. Oxford Financial Press

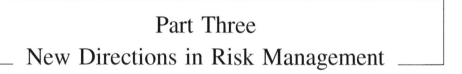

Part Three
New Directions in Risk Management

10

Introduction

Risk management didn't seem to exist prior to the mid 1990s. There'd previously been plenty of big, headline-making losses but these had all been due to stock market crashes. When the markets plummet, everyone suffers, no one is held responsible for the drop and no one held accountable for the fallout. But then derivatives became really big news. Everyone started to invest in fancy products. With these fancy products you could make a dramatic profit or a dramatic loss on more modest market behaviour. And this is what happened in the early to mid 1990s. Many of these 'fiascos', as they are often called, were non-financial corporates fooling around on the derivatives markets when they should have been concentrating on making widgets. They'd made some cash supposedly hedging and fooled themselves into thinking they were infallible and so started to take a punt.

Once the idea of risk management or Risk Management, as it now is, had appeared, so the pedlars of new-fangled ideas and software crawled out from under the rocks. And it was only a matter of time before the regulators stuck their noses in.

We won't go into the details of Risk Management much. It is a very time-consuming and inaccurate process currently, and it is still not clear what benefits it yields. Many of the early models, such as RiskMetrics and CreditMetrics, have been criticised for their simplicity and tendency to errors. Most of the early methods make such incredible assumptions that it is hard to believe they were ever taken seriously. One of the craziest notions is that we can assume market returns are normally distributed and correlations across products are stable. Hello? Earth to Risk Management, can you hear us?

Maybe, just maybe, we could get away with such assumptions during the less exciting days on the trading floor. But then who cares? What about the exciting days, when the markets are taking a tumble, you're on the phone trying to offload your positions until you find there's no answer on the other end?

We are now going to see three chapters on completely different aspects of the Risk Management problem.

CHAPTERS 11 TO 13

Implementing VaR by historical simulation

Aldo Nassigh, Andrea Piazzetta and Ferdinando Samaria

Updating your estimate of Value at Risk is a lengthy process, often run overnight by banks, with a brief document going to managers the next morning after the calculation is complete. In order to be able to speed up this process, some approximation technique is required. Aldo, Andrea and Ferdinando suggest a technique they call 'partial revaluation'. The methodology is based on using a Taylor series approximation to the portfolio profit and loss. Because of this simplicity they can cope with very many risk factors. A probabilistic analysis of risk is then just a simple matter of linear algebra.

CrashMetrics

Philip Hua and Paul Wilmott

Few approaches to Risk Management take as bold an approach as Philip and Paul's CrashMetrics. Most Risk Management methodologies worry about what happens on average, or in a certain percentage of cases. Some of the more sophisticated ones concern themselves with exotic distributions, normal being too 'thin-tailed' compared with reality. But CrashMetrics goes the whole nine yards. 'What is the worst that can happen to your portfolio?' ask Philip and Paul. Not only do they ask the question, they also answer it, and as an added bonus they tell you exactly what to do to insure yourself against that worst case. As we've said before, the sum of all derivatives is zero, so if using derivatives helps you in times of a market crash, then somebody else is going to suffer even more. Hard cheese. That's life.

Herding in financial markets: a role for psychology in explaining investor behaviour?

Henriëtte Prast

There are many possible reasons for extreme market movements. Occasionally an earthquake or outbreak of war gives a genuine reason for sudden, sharp 'corrections'. But the vast majority of the dramatic moves, as opposed to the slower bull markets, are caused by nothing more than panic. Selling begets selling begets chaos. Henriëtte, in this thought-provoking, entertaining and highly learned chapter, gives us an account of various experiments, theories and conjectures from the world of behavioural finance. It is Henriëtte who coined the phrase 'emotionomics' as the study of irrational economic behaviour. A refreshing blast of common sense, a perfect end to this book. But it does make one wonder whether the taxpayer is still funding those economists who believe in the rational investor. Now, how irrational is that?

MODELS NEEDED

From a VaR model we need several things:

- *Speed*: we must be able to estimate risk much faster than currently.
- *Contracts*: we must be able to incorporate all the new-fangled products that are constantly being invented.
- *Liquidity*: it's no good marking to a market that may well not be there.
- *Robustness*: ideally parameters used should be stable, but then that's a problem for the whole subject of quantitative finance.
- *Utility*: a confidence percentage may be too risky, worst cases too conservative. How should banks measure the risk? Is this a job for regulators or should banks be left alone?
- *Tails*: the distribution of returns cannot be assumed to be normal.

Are we there yet? We don't think so.

(Can people please stop inventing new types of risk, before we've had a chance to allow adequately for the old ones.)

BIBLIOGRAPHY

Artzner, P., Delbaen, F., Eber, J.-M. and Heath, D. (1997) Thinking coherently. *Risk* **10**(11) 68–72 (November)

Eberlein, E. and Keller, U. (1995) Hyperbolic distributions in finance. *Bernoulli* **1** 281–99

Embrechts, P., Klüppelberg, C. and Mikosch, T. (1997) *Modelling Extremal Events*. Springer-Verlag

Hua, P. (1997) Modelling stock market crashes. *Dissertation*, Imperial College, London

Hua, P. and Wilmott, P. *(1997) Crash courses. Risk* **10**(6) 64–67 (June)

Jorion, P. (1997) *Value at Risk*. Irwin

Jorion, P. (1999) *Risk management lessons from Long-Term Capital Management*. Working Paper, University of California at Irvine

Kolman, J. (1999) LTCM speaks. *Derivatives Strategy*, April, pp. 12–17

Lawrence, D. (1996) *Measuring and Managing Derivative Market Risk*. International Thompson Business Press

Partnoy, F. (1998) *F.I.A.S.C.O.* Profile Books

Prast, H. (2000a) Herding and financial panics: a role for cognitive psychology? De Nederlandische Bank Report

Prast, H. (2000b) A cognitive dissonance model of financial market behaviour. De Nederlandische Bank Report

Thomson, R. (1998) *Apocalypse Roulette: The Lethal World of Derivatives*. Pan

Vose, D. (1997) *Quantitative Risk Analysis: A Guide to Monte Carlo Simulation Modelling*. John Wiley

11

Implementing VaR by historical simulation

Aldo Nassigh, Andrea Piazzetta and Ferdinando Samaria

INTRODUCTION

Historical simulation is a simple method that allows us to calculate Value at Risk (VaR) without making any assumptions about the a priori statistical distribution of the portfolio value movements. This approach involves the construction of the hypothetical distribution of the yields (profit and losses) of a portfolio of financial instruments directly by means of the historical fluctuations of the market prices. Once the hypothetical distribution has been calculated, the VaR is given by the percentile evaluation with the selected confidence interval. One of the more popular approaches to VaR is based on the application of parametric methods like *RiskMetrics* [1]. Historical simulation, however, is becoming more widespread since in most cases it offers the optimal trade-off between accuracy and ease of implementation.

An exhaustive discussion of the historical simulation technique and its comparison to other methodologies can be found in the literature [2, 3]. In this chapter we focus on implementation of historical simulation based on *partial revaluation*. Our aim is to present this technique from the practitioner viewpoint. We are interested in the discussion of the technical aspects of the implementation and in the process of data aggregation and disaggregation. The chapter is organised as follows. The next section contains a short description of the mathematics of the *partial revaluation* approach. Then we look at the reliability of the results depending on the *quality* of the historical market data. This topic is discussed through a practical example which allows us to introduce several aspects of the day-to-day work in a risk management department: reporting risks arising from different sources and netting, back-testing of the model and constructing a daily VaR and P&L plot. The chapter ends with a conclusion.

HISTORICAL SIMULATION: THE PARTIAL REVALUATION APPROACH

The method of historical simulation can be summarised in the following four steps:

1. Identification of the model to be used for calculating the prices of the instruments that make up the portfolio and, among the different parameters of the pricing formulas, selection of the risk factors.

2. Collection of the historical values of the risk factors observed in the most recent N periods. We stress here that the sampling frequency should coincide with the holding period adopted for VaR calculation. A daily sampling is the most efficient since it can be used with any longer time horizon.

3. Revaluation of the portfolio on the basis of the set of data relative to the N periods and calculation of the hypothetical profit and loss (P&L) compared to the current value of the portfolio.

4. Evaluation of the percentile of the empirical profit and loss distribution.

Let us assume that, in first step, M different risk factors have been selected for the simulation. These could be the values of a set of market variables.

We denote with $\mathbf{S}^t$ the vector in 3^M containing the values of the risk factors at time t. The corresponding value Π^t of a portfolio is therefore expressed as

$$\Pi^t = \Pi(t, \mathbf{S}^t) \qquad (11.1)$$

The historical data collection results in a set of M time series sampled at constant frequency. We shall denote with t_j the sampling time stamps and with $S_{ij}(i = 1, \ldots, M; j = 1, \ldots, N + 1)$ the sample of the ith element of $\mathbf{S}$ taken at the jth time stamp.

We evaluate a set of $M \times N$ simulated risk factor fluctuations ΔS_{ij}. The technique used to estimate the set ΔS_{ij} derives from the theoretical assumptions on the distribution of the ith risk factor values. Under the *lognormality* hypothesis, the fluctuation at time t of the ith risk factor corresponding to the jth time stamp is given by

$$\Delta S_{ij} = S_i^t \ln \left(\frac{S_{i,j+1}}{S_{ij}} \right) \qquad (11.2)$$

The third step is to evaluate a vector in 3^N containing the simulated portfolio profit and losses. We shall identify this vector as the P&L strip. For the required holding period Δt, we calculate a set of N simulated portfolio values as follows:

$$\Pi_j^{t+\Delta t} = \Pi(t + \Delta t, \mathbf{S}^t + \Delta \mathbf{S}_j) \quad j = 1, \ldots, N \qquad (11.3)$$

where $\Delta \mathbf{S}_j$ denotes the vector in 3^M containing the simulated fluctuations of the risk factors at time t_j. The portfolio P&L strip is then given by

$$\Delta \Pi_j = \Pi_j^{t+\Delta t} - \Pi^t \qquad j = 1, \ldots, N \qquad (11.4)$$

The procedure described above calculates the P&L strip by means of the *full revaluation* method, since it is assumed that the function which determines the value of the portfolio is known and can be evaluated according to the specified inputs. In practice this can be difficult since there are cases where the function is not known in the risk management system or requires too much time to be calculated.

Here we define an alternative method—*partial revaluation*. It simplifies the calculation through an approximation of the portfolio profit and loss computation based on the Taylor expansion of the portfolio pricing function $\Pi(t, \mathbf{S})$:

$$\Pi^{t+\Delta t} = \Pi^t + \frac{\partial \Pi}{\partial t} \Delta t + \sum_{i=1}^{M} \frac{\partial \Pi}{\partial S_i} \Delta S_i + \frac{1}{2} \sum_{i,k=1}^{M} \Delta S_i \frac{\partial^2 \Pi}{\partial S_i \partial S_k} \Delta S_k + o(\Delta S^2) \qquad (11.5)$$

where $o(\Delta S^2)$ is used to denote terms greater than or equal to third order in the risk factor fluctuations ΔS_i.

From a theoretical viewpoint there is no difference between different risk factors. However, we distinguish between the risk factors that are already linked to quoted market prices or rates and those that represent volatility:

- δ (delta) is defined as the vector of the first-order partial derivatives with respect to risk factors directly linked to prices or rates
- γ (gamma) is defined as the matrix of the second-order partial derivatives (Hessian) with respect to the same risk factors
- v (vega) is defined as the vector of the first-order partial derivatives with respect to the risk factors that represent the volatility of prices or rates
- θ (theta) is defined as the partial derivative with respect to time

It is also assumed that the second-order terms with respect to volatility are of the same order as the third-order terms with respect to the prices or rates and are therefore negligible. Through these definitions it is possible to express a fluctuation of the portfolio value in synthetic form:

$$\Delta \Pi^t = \Pi^{t+\Delta t} - \Pi^t = \theta \, \Delta t + \sum_{i=1}^{M} \delta_i \, \Delta S_i + \sum_{i=1}^{M} v_i \, \Delta \sigma_i + \frac{1}{2} \sum_{i,k=1}^{M} \gamma_{ik} \Delta S_i \Delta S_k + o(\Delta S^2)$$

(11.6)

where $\Delta \sigma_i$ is the variation of volatility of the ith risk factor. The required portfolio P&L strip is evaluated by replacing in (11.6) the set of simulated risk factor fluctuations ΔS_{ij}.

Equation (11.6) shows the advantages of the partial revaluation approach in the VaR calculation with the historical simulation. They can be summarised as follows:

- Once the Greeks of the portfolio and the fluctuations of the risk factors are known, the calculation of the distribution of the portfolio value is reduced to a simple algebraic operation.
- Taking into account the volatility and second-order terms in the Taylor expansion, historical simulation gives a more accurate estimate of VaR compared to the commonly used *delta-normal* method, regardless of any consideration about the analytical form of the distribution of the risk factors.
- No constraints are placed on the linear independence of the time series S_{ij}, therefore the number of risk factors included in the simulation can be large at the discretion of the risk manager.
- The portfolio is divided into synthetic *assets*: a delta asset, a vega asset and a gamma-theta asset, each one corresponding to a different risk source. This allows us to split the VaR into different components.

The delta P&L strip is given by

$$\Delta \Pi_j^\delta = \sum_{i=1}^{M} \delta_i \Delta S_{ij} \quad j = 1, \dots, N$$

(11.7)

The vega P&L strip is given by

$$\Delta \Pi_j^v = \sum_{i=1}^{M} v_i \Delta \sigma_{ij} \quad j = 1, \dots, N$$

(11.8)

The gamma-theta P&L strip is given by

$$\Delta \Pi_j^\gamma = \theta \, \Delta t + \frac{1}{2} \sum_{i,k=1}^M \gamma_{ik} \Delta S_{ij} \Delta S_{kj} \quad j = 1, \dots, N \qquad (11.9)$$

Another advantage of the partial revaluation approach is that, by itself, evaluation of the Greeks (δ, γ, ν) gives the sensitivity analysis of the portfolio, and especially for portfolios with only a few risk factors, this is an effective way of sharing the risk perception between risk manager and traders.

In deriving (11.6) we took advantage of a Taylor expansion. This approximation works for a small perturbation of the risk factors and when the third-order terms neglected in (11.6) are not significant. The approximation can therefore become inexact in the face of notable market variations, which is when the full revaluation technique becomes necessary.

The fourth step of the VaR evaluation requires the evaluation of the percentile corresponding to the selected confidence interval. This is simply achieved by ordering the P&L strip for increasing values and identifying the sample that corresponds to the chosen percentile. If the portfolio is composed of several subportfolios, or if it has been split into synthetic assets—see (11.7) to (11.9)—the aggregated P&L strip can be determined by simple vector addiction of the different P&L strips, and VaR is evaluated accordingly.

IMPLEMENTING VALUE AT RISK: A PRACTICAL EXAMPLE

One of the concerns about the reliability of historical simulation is that the chosen historical period is short, in order to be indicative of present market conditions. Typical values are normally one or two years, i.e. a few hundred daily observations. Therefore the statistics of the fluctuations of the portfolio value are not particularly varied with only a handful of samples in the *tails* of the distribution. This means that lack of accuracy in the time series can have strong consequences on the reliability of the VaR evaluation. The possible sources of inaccuracy in a time series are several and we shall not discuss them in detail. We focus on the consequence of a time lag in the sampling across different markets.

Any VaR calculation method requires that the time series sampling is *synchronous*. In practice it is not possible to avoid a small time lag, but through the implementation *in house* of a market price collection system it can be reduced to a few minutes. From a practical viewpoint, the time series set obtained in this way can be regarded as synchronous. However, it is a demanding task to populate and maintain a synchronous time series database. On the other hand, the time series of the official closing prices are generally very accurate and can be easily obtained by a *data provider*. These series are *non-synchronous*: the time lag can be several hours, due to the differences in the closing time of the various markets. A key issue for the risk manager seeking the optimal trade-off between accuracy of results and ease of implementation is therefore to estimate the impact of the error induced by a time lag of this kind on the accuracy of VaR.

A complete analysis of the impact of a time lag on the VaR calculation with a parametric approach is found in the literature [1, 4]. Here we prefer to deal with this topic through a practical example.

Let us assume that a euro-based investor owns a portfolio composed of *high-tech stocks* in the euro market, as outlined in Table 11.1. The portfolio is chosen in such a way that the weight of each component is approximately 33% and all the stocks are positively

Table 11.1 Stock portfolio components and relative weights on 26 May 2000

Stock	Market	Mid price (€) on 26/05/00	Position	Mark to market (€m)	Relative weight (%)
Nokia	Helsinki	51.97	420 000	21.8	32.8
Terra Network	Madrid	47.65	470 000	22.4	33.7
ST Microelectronics	Paris	61.78	360 000	22.2	33.5

Table 11.2 Volatility (annualised) and correlation

Stock	Volatility (%)	Correlation		
		Nokia	Terra N.	ST M.
Nokia	68	1.00	0.46	0.49
Terra N.	85	0.46	1.00	0.41
ST M.	115	0.49	0.41	1.00

correlated, as shown in Table 11.2. The VaR calculation for the portfolio is performed on 26 May 2000 and is based on a *holding period* of one business day and a *confidence interval* of 95%. Given the high volatility of the stocks, the sampling period will be limited to 75 days. This period is adopted for all statistical measures (volatility, correlation and beta) reported in this section.

In our example we assume that the investor takes the equity portfolio introduced above and adds a short position in an equity index future for hedging purposes. The most suitable contracts for this purpose are the futures on the DJ Euro STOXX 50 index and the Nasdaq 100 index. The first is the most significant cross-market index for the euro market and the second is a standard benchmark for US high-tech stocks.

Table 11.3 shows the result of the beta analysis of the portfolio into the two indexes. The stock portfolio is positively correlated with both indexes, as shown in Table 11.4, but regression analysis gives poor results. Figure 11.1 shows a plot of the regression which confirms the low R^2 outcome.

Although the regression results are so poor, a popular choice among investors is to hedge high-tech portfolios with a short position in the Nasdaq 100 future. The short position required to hedge the equity portfolio is 1000 contracts of the June 2000 expiry, with a contract size of 20 USD per index point. The market price of this future contract, on 26 May 2000, is 3087 USD and the FX euro/USD rate on the same day is 0.93. The

Table 11.3 Regression analysis: stock portfolio vs. the two most significant market indexes

	Nasdaq 100	DJ Euro STOXX 50
β	0.66	1.9
Intercept	0.10%	−0.60%
R^2	0.46	0.43
Standard error	3.2%	3.4%
Observations	75	75

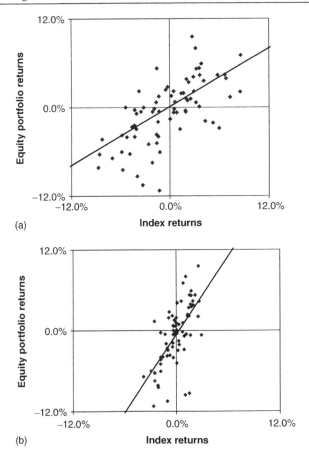

Figure 11.1   Scatterplot of the stock portfolio returns versus (a) Nasdaq index returns and (b) DJ Euro STOXX 50 index

Table 11.4   Volatility (annualised) and correlation between stock portfolio and the two most significant market indexes

	Volatility (%)	Correlation		
		Stock portfolio	Nasdaq 100	DJ Euro STOXX 50
Stock portfolio	70	1.00	0.68	0.65
Nasdaq 100	68	0.68	1.00	0.55
DJ Euro STOXX 50	24	0.65	0.55	1.00

future notional value is therefore 66.3 million euro. The stock portfolio market value at the same date (Table 11.1) is 66.5 million euro.

Implementing the VaR calculation for the hedged portfolio is fairly simple. We select four risk factors: the three stock prices and the Nasdaq 100 value. Basis risk of the future contract can be neglected, as well as FX risk, since only margins have to be cleared in

USD. With this choice of the risk factors all the instruments are linear, so that only the evaluation of the portfolio delta P&L strip (11.7) is needed. The delta of the portfolio value with respect to each risk factor is simply the stock position for the three equities and the contract number times the contract size divided by the spot FX rate euro/USD for the future position.

The time series lag problem arises since the official closing prices of the European stocks correspond to prices observed on the market at around 1730 Central European Time (CET); the official *last* of the Nasdaq 100 corresponds to the index value at 2200 CET. To estimate the impact of sampling lag on the calculation accuracy, we compare the VaR evaluation with the non-synchronous time series against the results obtained by means of a set of synchronous time series sampled daily exactly at 1700 CET. To obtain the maximum possible accuracy, we collect the *mid prices* (mean between asked and offered prices) for the single stocks.

Clearly, there is no significant discrepancy between the synchronous time series and the official data for the European stocks. The discrepancy is evident for the Nasdaq 100 data. In Figure 11.2 we compare the bar chart of the official data with the outcome of the snapshot at 1700 CET. The time series trend and volatility are similar, as displayed in Table 11.5, but the series correlations with the stock portfolio are different.

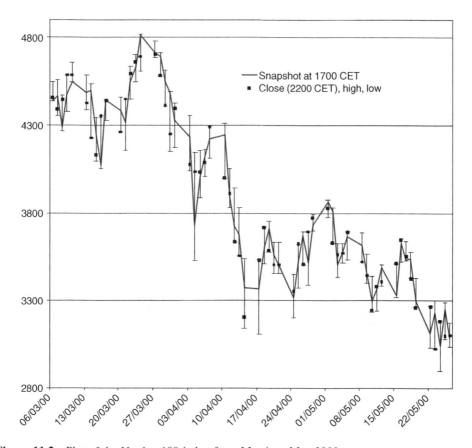

Figure 11.2   Plot of the Nasdaq 100 index from March to May 2000

Table 11.5 Comparison between statistical parameters of the synchronous and non-synchronous time series of the Nasdaq 100 index displayed in Figure 11.2

	Daily trend (%)	Annualised volatility (%)	Correlation with stock portfolio
Synchronous data	−0.35	68	0.68
Non-synchronous data	−0.34	61	0.20

Table 11.6 VaR on 26 May 2000: historical simulation with 1 day holding period, 95% confidence interval and 75 observations

	Stocks VaR (€m)	Future VaR (€m)	Stocks + future VaR (€m)
Synchronous data	5.5	4.5	4.1
Non-synchronous data	5.3	3.4	4.7

We present in Table 11.6 the comparison between the VaR of the test portfolio obtained by means of the synchronous and non-synchronous time series. The VaR of the stock portfolio is indicated in the first column. It does not depend significantly on the time series set. The VaR of the future position (indicated in the second column) is 30% larger with our time series than with the official data, even if the volatility of our time series is only 11% higher than the volatility of the official data. If both the time series are lognormal, the VaR should be proportional to the volatility, so this discrepancy could be an indicator

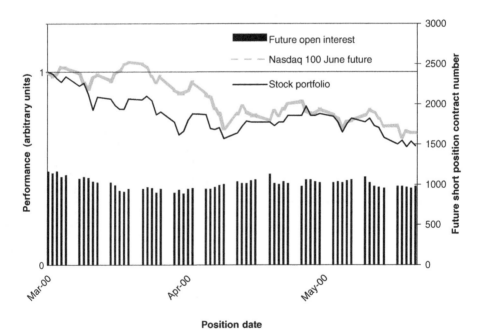

Figure 11.3 Dynamic hedging of the stock portfolio in Table 11.1

of the presence of anomalous tails in one or both of the time series. The small number of samples used in our simulation, however, does not allow us to draw any firm conclusions.

The aggregated VaR of the position composed by the stocks and the future is indicated in the third column of Table 11.6. The difference between this value and the VaR of the stock portfolio is a measure of the effectiveness of the hedging position in reducing market risk. The VaR decrease due to the hedging is more significant with the synchronous time series, in agreement with the correlation discrepancy in Table 11.5. As a consequence, the use of the synchronous time series results in a decrease of the aggregated VaR of 13%.

A *back-test* of the VaR calculation is the best method to check whether the error induced by the use of the non-synchronous time series set is systematic. To accomplish this task, we simulate a dynamic hedging strategy in the following way: the portfolio is monitored for 60 business days, from 6 March 2000 to 26 May 2000. During this period the portfolio is hedged by a short position in the Nasdaq 100 June 2000 future. Each day at 1700 CET, the short position is balanced in such a way that the mark to market of the future notional position matches the mark to market of the stock portfolio.

The outcome of this dynamic hedging strategy is shown in Figure 11.3. The solid line represents the relative performance of the stock portfolio during the back-testing period.

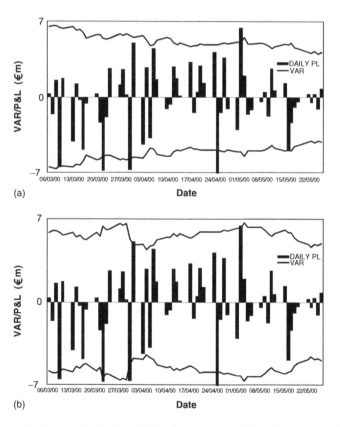

Figure 11.4 Back-testing results: VaR and P&L plot of the portfolio daily profit and loss compared to the daily VaR. The VaR is calculated using (a) the synchronous time series set and (b) the non-synchronous time series set

The portfolio value is normalised on its value on the first day of the period. The dashed line represents the relative performance (normalised as the stock portfolio) of a unit position in the Nasdaq 100 June 2000 future contract. Bars on the bottom are the amount of futures contracts (short) of the hedging.

The back-testing results are shown in Figure 11.4. For each of the 60 business days in the observation period we calculate the day-to-day profit/loss of the test portfolio, which is represented by bars. The VaR is evaluated daily, on the basis of the position and the time series of the preceding business day. Figure 11.4 shows the *VaR and P&L plot*. The two solid lines represent the VaR with plus/minus sign respectively. The plot emphasises that, for *linear portfolios* like our test portfolio, the VaR represents the expected loss and the expected profit with the same probability (in this case 95%). In the VaR and P&L plot the event given by a profit/loss exceeding the VaR is indicated by a bar which lies outside the channel formed by the two solid lines. In our example this should happen approximately six times (10% of 60 days). Figure 11.4(a), synchronous, and Figure 11.4(b), non-synchronous, show that despite the small number of days in the sample, the back-testing confirms the accuracy of the historic simulation, with six events of profit/loss exceeding the expected values in both cases.

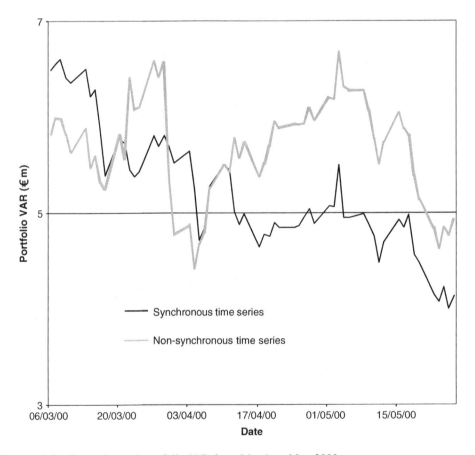

Figure 11.5 Comparison of portfolio VaR from March to May 2000

Figure 11.5 compares the VaR from the synchronous time series with the VaR from the non-synchronous time series. The VaR from the non-synchronous set is not systematically higher than the VaR from the synchronous set. The VaR value averaged on the back-testing period is 5.7 million euro with the non-synchronous set and 5.2 million euro with the synchronous set. The difference between the two averages, approximately 10% of the average VaR, is a measure of the amount of error induced by the time lag of the official time series, which in our example is of the order of 5 hours.

CONCLUSION

The conceptual simplicity of historical simulation makes it particularly easy to implement. Aggregation across several portfolios is elementary, since it is reduced to a vector addition between P&L strips, with no explicit calculation of the correlation matrix. Moreover, as long as the time series for the risk factors are the same, a different technique can be exploited for each portfolio. Therefore, in a large financial institution, one can adopt full revaluation for portfolios containing complex exotic options and partial revaluation for the other, simpler portfolios. For books composed only of linear instruments, we need only evaluate the delta P&L strip.

The small number of samples in the time series is one of the critical issues of the methodology. In the preceding section we discussed one of the most relevant consequences of this issue, namely the impact of an approximation in the time series sampling on the reliability of the results. Through the discussion we showed how to overcome this problem by using synchronous sampling and how to control the reliability of the results by back-testing the VaR values with the actual profit and loss values.

REFERENCES

1. Morgan Guaranty Trust Company (1996) *RiskMetrics—Technical Document*. New York
2. Linsmeier, T.J. and Pearson, N.D. (1996) Risk Measurement: An Introduction to Value at Risk. Working Paper, University of Illinois at Urbana-Champaign
3. Duffie, D. and Pan, J. (1997) An overview of value at risk. *Journal of Derivatives* **4**, 7–49
4. Shanken, J. (1997) Nonsynchronous data and covariance-factor structure of returns. *Journal of Finance* **42**, 221–31

12

CrashMetrics

Philip Hua and Paul Wilmott

INTRODUCTION

This chapter contains new research beyond that contained in *Paul Wilmott on Quantitative Finance*. If Value at Risk is about normal market conditions then CrashMetrics is the opposite side of the coin, it is about 'fire sale' conditions and the far from orderly liquidation of assets in far from normal conditions. CrashMetrics is a dataset and methodology for estimating the exposure of a portfolio to extreme market movements or crashes. It assumes that the crash is unhedgeable and then finds the worst outcome for the value of the portfolio. The method then shows how to mitigate the effects of the crash by the purchase or sales of derivatives in an optimal fashion, so-called Platinum Hedging. Derivatives have sometimes been thought of as being a dangerous component in a portfolio, in the CrashMetrics methodology they are put to a benign use.

WHY DO BANKS GO BROKE?

There are two main reasons why banks get into serious trouble. The first reason is the lack of suitable or sufficient control over the traders. Through misfortune, negligence or dishonesty, large and unmanageable positions can be entered into. The consequences are either that the trader concerned becomes a hero and the bank makes a fortune, or the bank loses a fortune, the trader makes a run for it and the bank goes under. The odds are fifty-fifty. The second causes of disaster are the extreme, unexpected and unhedgeable moves in the stock market, the crashes.

MARKET CRASHES

In typical market conditions one's portfolio will fluctuate rapidly, but not dramatically. That is, it will rise and fall, minute by minute, day by day, but will not collapse. There are times, say once a year on average, when that fluctuation is dramatic ... and usually in the downward direction. These are extreme market movements or market crashes. VaR can tell us nothing about these and they must be analysed separately.

What's special about a crash? Two things spring to mind. Obviously a crash is a sudden fall in market prices, too rapid for the liquidation of a portfolio. But a crash isn't just a rise in volatility. It is also characterised by a special relationship between individual assets. During a crash, all assets fall together. There is no such thing as a crash where half the stocks fall and the rest stay put. Technically this means that all assets become perfectly correlated. In normal market conditions there may be some relationship between stocks, especially those in the same sector, but this connection may not be that strong. Indeed, it is the weakness of these relationships that allows diversification. A small insurance

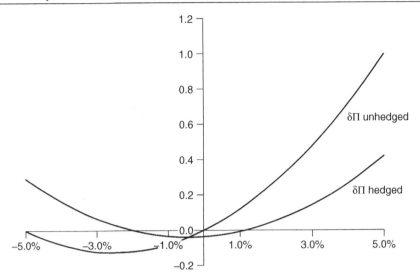

Figure 12.1 The correlation between several assets for a few days before and after the 1987 crash. When the correlation is close to 1, all assets move in the same direction

company will happily insure your car, because they can diversify across individuals. Insuring against an earthquake is a different matter. A high degree of correlation makes diversification impossible. This is where traditional VaR falls down, at exactly the time when it is needed most. Figure 12.1 shows the behaviour of the correlation of several constituents of the S&P 500 around the time of the 1987 stock market crash.

All is not lost. VaR is a very recent concept, created during the 1990s and fast becoming a market standard, with known drawbacks. Many researchers in universities and in banks are turning their thoughts to analysing and protecting against crashes. Some of these researchers are physicists who concern themselves with examining the tails of returns distributions; are crashes more likely than traditional theory predicts? The answer is a definite yes.

Our personal preference though is for models that don't make any assumptions about the likelihood of a crash. One line of work is that of 'worst-case scenarios'. Given that a crash could wipe out your portfolio, wouldn't you like to know what is the worst that could realistically happen, or would you be happy knowing what you would lose on average? CrashMetrics is used to analyse worst cases, and provide advice about how to hedge or insure against a crash.

CRASHMETRICS

CrashMetrics is a methodology for evaluating portfolio performance in the event of extreme movements in financial markets. It is not part of the JP Morgan family of performance measures. The only assumptions made are that the market move, the 'crash', is limited in size and that the number of such crashes is limited in some way. There are no assumptions about the probability distribution of the size of the crash or its timing.

This simple method, used for day-to-day portfolio protection, is concerned with the extreme market movements that may occur when we are not watching, or that cannot be hedged away. These are the fire sale conditions. There are many nice things about the method such as its simplicity and ease of generalisation, and no explicit dependence on the annoying parameters volatility and correlation.

CRASHMETRICS FOR ONE STOCK

To introduce the ideas, let's consider a portfolio of options on a single underlying asset. For the moment, think in terms of a stock, although we could equally well talk about currencies, commodities or interest rate products.

If the stock changes dramatically by an amount δS, how much does the portfolio of options on that stock behave? There will be a relationship between the change in the portfolio value $\delta \Pi$ and δS:

$$\delta \Pi = F(\delta S).$$

The function $F(\cdot)$ will simply be the sum of all the formulae, expressions, numerical solutions, etc., for each of the individual contracts in the portfolio. Think of it as the sum of lots of Black–Scholes formulae with lots of different strikes, expiries, payoffs. If there is no change in the asset price, there will be no change in the portfolio, so $F(0) = 0$. (There will be a small time decay, which we'll come back to later.) Figure 12.2 shows a possible portfolio change against underlying change.

If we are lucky, and we are not too near to the expiries and strikes of the options then we could approximate the portfolio by the Taylor series in the change in the underlying asset:

$$\delta \Pi = \Delta \, \delta S + \tfrac{1}{2} \Gamma \, \delta S^2. \tag{12.1}$$

In practice this won't be a good enough approximation. Imagine having some knockout options in the portfolio, we really will have to use the relevant formula or numerical

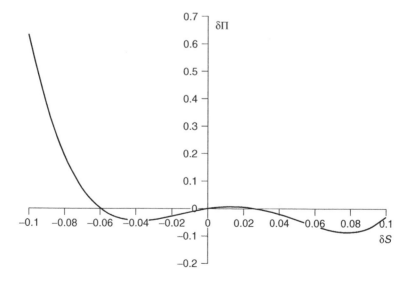

Figure 12.2   Size of portfolio change against change in the underlying

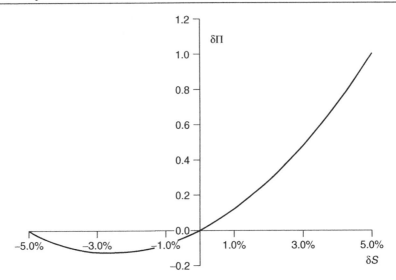

Figure 12.3 Size of portfolio change against change in the underlying: Taylor approximation

method to capture the sudden drop in value of this contract at the barrier. A simple delta-gamma approximation is not going to work.

However, as far as the math is concerned, we're going to show you both the general CrashMetrics methodology and the simple Taylor series version.

Now let's ask what is the worst that could happen to the portfolio overnight say? We want to find the minimum of $F(\delta S)$.

In Figure 12.3 we see a plot of the change in the portfolio against δS assuming for the moment that a Taylor approximation is valid. Note that it is zero at $\delta S = 0$. If the gamma is positive, the portfolio change (12.1) has a minimum at

$$\delta S = -\frac{\Delta}{\Gamma}.$$

The portfolio change in this worst-case scenario is

$$\delta \Pi_{\text{worst}} = -\frac{\Delta^2}{2\Gamma}.$$

This is the worst case given an arbitrary move in the underlying. If the gamma is small or negative, the worst case will be a fall to zero or a rise to infinity, both far too unrealistic. For this reason we may want to constrain the move in the underlying by

$$-\delta S^- < \delta S < \delta S^+.$$

Now the portfolio fall is restricted.

If we can't use the Greek approximation (Taylor series) then we're looking for

$$\min_{-\delta S^- < \delta S < \delta S^+} F(\delta S).$$

Figure 12.2 shows an example where there is one local minimum as well as a global one; it's the global one we want.

Portfolio optimisation and the Platinum Hedge

Having found a technique for finding out what could happen in the worst case, it is natural to ask how to make that worst case not so bad. This can be done by optimal static hedging. To start with, we'll assume the Taylor expansion and then generalise.

Suppose there is a contract available with which to hedge our portfolio. This contract has a bid/offer spread, a delta and a gamma. I will call the delta of the hedging contract Δ^*, meaning the sensitivity of the hedging contract to the underlying asset. The gamma is similarly Γ^*. Denote the bid/offer spread by $C > 0$, meaning that if we buy (sell) the contract and immediately sell (buy) it back, we lose this amount.

Imagine that we add a number λ of the hedging contract to our original position. Our portfolio now has a first-order exposure to the crash of

$$\delta S \left(\Delta + \lambda \Delta^* \right)$$

and a second-order exposure of

$$\tfrac{1}{2} \delta S^2 \left(\Gamma + \lambda \Gamma^* \right).$$

Not only does the portfolio change by these amounts for a crash of size δS but also it loses a *guaranteed* amount $|\lambda| C$ just because we cannot close our new position without losing out on the bid/offer spread.

The total change in the portfolio with the static hedge in place is now

$$\delta \Pi = \delta S \left(\Delta + \lambda \Delta^* \right) + \tfrac{1}{2} \delta S^2 \left(\Gamma + \lambda \Gamma^* \right) - |\lambda| C.$$

In general, the optimal choice of λ is such that the worst value of this expression for $-\delta S^- \leqslant \delta S \leqslant \delta S^+$ is as high as possible. Thus we are exchanging a guaranteed loss (due to bid/offer spread) for a reduced worst-case loss. This is simply insurance and the optimal choice gives the *Platinum Hedge*, named after the plastic card that follows green and gold. For the optimal choice of λ, Figure 12.4 shows the change in the portfolio value as a function of δS. Note that it no longer goes through $(0, 0)$.

If we can't use the Taylor approximation, as will generally be the case, we must look for the worst case of

$$F(\delta S) + \lambda F^*(\delta S) - |\lambda| C.$$

Here $F^*(\cdot)$ is the 'formula' for the change in value of the hedging contract. Having found the worst case, we just make this as painless as possible by optimising over the hedge ratio λ.

Of course, there won't just be the one option with which to statically hedge, there will be many. How does this change the optimisation? We'll find out soon.

THE MULTI-ASSET/SINGLE-INDEX MODEL

A bank's portfolio has many underlyings, not just the one. How does CrashMetrics handle them? This is done via an index or benchmark.

We can measure the performance of a portfolio of assets and options on these assets by relating the magnitude of extreme movements in any one asset to one or more *benchmarks*

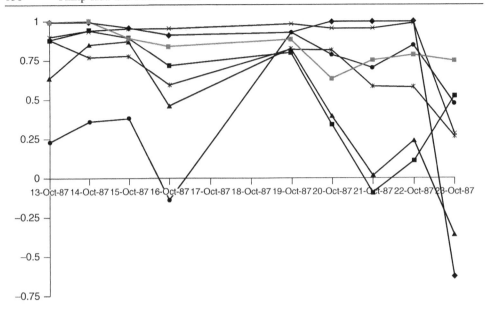

Figure 12.4   Size of portfolio change against δS after optimal hedging: Taylor approximation

such as the S&P 500. The relative magnitude of these movements is measured by the *crash coefficient* for each asset relative to the benchmark. If the benchmark moves by $x\%$ then the ith asset moves by $\kappa_i x\%$. Estimates of the κ_i for the constituents of the S&P 500, with that index as the benchmark, may be downloaded free of charge from www.crashmetrics.com. Note that the benchmark need not be an index containing the assets, but can be any representative quantity. Unlike the RiskMetrics and CreditMetrics datasets, the CrashMetrics dataset does not have to be updated frequently because of the rarity of extreme market movements.

The following tables give the crash coefficients for a few constituents of major indices in several countries. The crash coefficients have been estimated using the tails of the daily returns distributions from the beginning of 1985 until the end of 1997, and so include the Black Monday crash of October 1987 and the rice/dragon/sake/Asian 'flu' effect starting in October 1997. For example, in Table 12.1 we see the 10 largest positive and negative daily returns in the S&P 500 during that period. It also shows the returns on the same days for several constituents of the index.

Figure 12.5 shows the returns data for Disney. The fine line in this figure has slope CAPM β. The bold line is the line with zero intercept that fits the largest 20 rises and falls in the S&P 500.

Figure 12.6 shows the returns on the Hong Kong and Shanghai Hotel group versus returns on the Hang Seng and Figure 12.7 shows the 40 extreme moves in Daimler-Benz versus returns on the Dax. Note here that the crash coefficient is not the same as the asset's beta with respect to the index. Not only is the number different, but preliminary results suggest that the crash coefficient is more stable than the beta. Moreover, for large moves in the index, the stock and the index are far more closely correlated than under normal market conditions. In other words, when there is a crash all stocks move together.

Table 12.1 The 10 largest positive and negative moves in several constituents of the S&P 500 against the moves in the S&P 500 on the same days

Date	S&P 500	Change (%)	Abbott Labs	Adobe Systems	AMD	Aeroequip Vickers	AETNA	Ahmanson (H.F.)
19-Oct-87	225	−20.4	−10.5	−22.2	−36.1	−36.6	−15.3	−20.8
26-Oct-87	228	−8.3	−7.3	−20.0	−14.3	−15.2	−4.5	−4.3
27-Oct-97	877	−6.9	−5.3	−6.1	−19.8	−6.7	−8.5	−6.5
08-Jan-88	243	−6.8	−3.8	−14.3	−6.8	−13.5	−7.1	−6.2
13-Oct-89	334	−6.1	−8.2	−12.5	−5.8	−9.3	−5.5	−3.7
16-Oct-87	283	−5.2	−4.6	0.0	−5.3	−6.4	−1.5	−1.3
11-Sep-86	235	−4.8	−5.2	−50.0	−4.7	−5.3	−3.3	−2.9
14-Apr-88	260	−4.4	−4.0	−12.5	−5.6	−2.6	−4.4	−4.8
30-Nov-87	230	−4.2	−6.7	−16.7	−1.4	−9.8	−2.7	−6.1
22-Oct-87	248	−3.9	−4.6	0.0	−5.9	−6.5	−1.9	−1.4
21-Oct-87	258	9.1	4.3	0.0	4.1	11.5	8.0	9.5
20-Oct-87	236	5.3	−0.6	−14.3	6.5	14.3	−3.7	3.3
28-Oct-97	921	5.1	5.2	4.3	19.0	−0.6	4.3	7.4
29-Oct-87	244	4.9	2.4	33.3	10.3	15.5	−1.9	3.2
17-Jan-91	327	3.7	4.3	0.0	4.6	8.0	2.8	3.0
04-Jan-88	255	3.6	0.8	0.0	7.6	−0.4	1.9	−0.7
31-May-88	262	3.4	2.7	0.0	5.3	0.9	3.9	2.5
27-Aug-90	321	3.2	5.4	8.3	4.5	2.2	1.4	3.1
02-Sep-97	927	3.1	3.8	2.6	3.3	0.1	2.5	2.3
21-Aug-91	391	2.9	3.1	4.2	3.5	0.0	−3.3	2.6

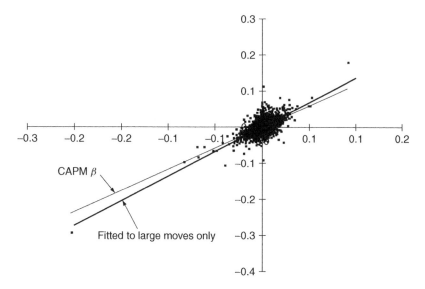

Figure 12.5 The returns on Disney versus returns on the S&P 500. Also shown are the line with slope β, fitted to all points, and the line with slope κ fitted to the 40 extreme moves and having zero intercept

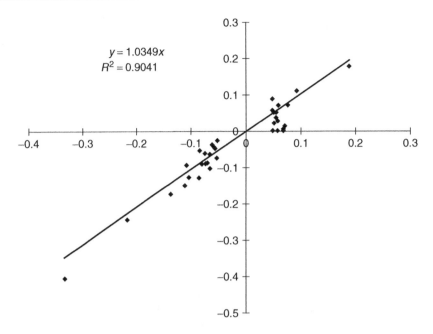

Figure 12.6   The returns on the Hong Kong and Shanghai Hotel group versus returns on the Hang Seng. Also shown is the line with slope κ fitted to the 40 extreme moves and having zero intercept

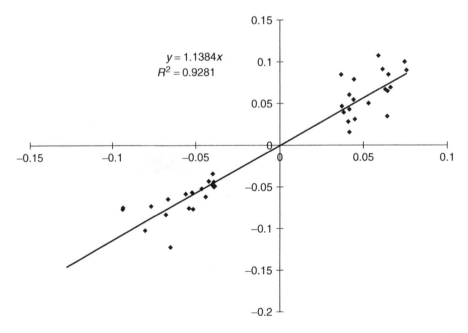

Figure 12.7   The returns on Daimler-Benz versus returns on the Dax. Also shown is the line with slope κ fitted to the 40 extreme moves and having zero intercept

Let's use these ideas, first assuming a Taylor expansion for the portfolio change. In the single-index, multi-asset model we can write the change in the value of the portfolio as

$$\delta\Pi = \sum_{i=1}^{N} \Delta_i \, \delta S_i + \tfrac{1}{2} \sum_{i=1}^{N} \sum_{j=1}^{N} \Gamma_{ij} \, \delta S_i \, \delta S_j \qquad (12.2)$$

with the obvious notation. (In particular, observe the cross gammas.) We assume that the percentage change in each asset can be related to the percentage change in the benchmark, x, when there is an extreme move:

$$\delta S_i = \kappa_i x S_i.$$

This simplifies (12.2) to

$$\delta\Pi = x \sum_{i=1}^{N} \Delta_i \kappa_i S_i + \tfrac{1}{2} x^2 \sum_{i=1}^{N} \sum_{j=1}^{N} \Gamma_{ij} \kappa_i S_i \kappa_j S_j$$

$$= xD + \tfrac{1}{2} x^2 G.$$

Observe how this contains a first- and a second-order exposure to the crash. The first-order coefficient D is the *crash delta* and the second-order coefficient G is the *crash gamma*.

Now we constrain the change in the benchmark by

$$-x^- \leqslant x \leqslant x^+.$$

The worst-case portfolio change occurs at one of the endpoints of this range or at the internal point

$$x = -\frac{D}{G}.$$

In this last case the extreme portfolio change is

$$\delta\Pi_{\text{worst}} = -\frac{D^2}{2G}.$$

We can also calculate the crash delta and gamma at this worst point.

All of the ideas contained in the single-asset model described above carry over to the multi-asset model; we just use x instead of δS to determine the worst that can happen to our portfolio.

If we can't use the delta-gamma Taylor series expansion then we must look for the worst case of an expression such as

$$\delta\Pi = F(\delta S_1, \dots, \delta S_N) = F(\kappa_1 x S_1, \dots, \kappa_N x S_N).$$

This is not hard, or even time-consuming, as long as we have formulae for the options in our portfolio.

Portfolio optimisation and the Platinum Hedge in the multi-asset model

Suppose there are M contracts available with which to hedge our portfolio. Let us call the deltas of the kth hedging contract Δ_i^k, meaning the sensitivity of the contract to the

ith asset, $k = 1, \ldots, M$. The gammas are similarly Γ^k_{ij}. Denote the bid/offer spread by $C_k > 0$, meaning that if we buy (sell) the contract and immediately sell (buy) it back we lose this amount.

Imagine that we add a number λ_k of each of the available hedging contracts to our original position. Our portfolio now has a first-order exposure to the crash of

$$x \left(D + \sum_{k=1}^{M} \lambda_k \sum_{i=1}^{N} \Delta^k_i \kappa_i S_i \right)$$

and a second-order exposure of

$$\tfrac{1}{2} x^2 \left(G + \sum_{k=1}^{M} \lambda_k \sum_{i=1}^{N} \sum_{j=1}^{N} \Gamma^k_{ij} \kappa_i S_i \kappa_j S_j \right).$$

Not only does the portfolio change by these amounts for a crash of size x but also it loses a guaranteed amount

$$\sum_{k=1}^{M} |\lambda_k| C_k$$

just because we cannot close our new positions without losing out on the bid/offer spread.

The total change in the portfolio with the static hedge in place is now

$$\delta \Pi = x \left(D + \sum_{k=1}^{M} \lambda_k \sum_{i=1}^{N} \Delta^k_i \kappa_i S_i \right)$$
$$+ \tfrac{1}{2} x^2 \left(G + \sum_{k=1}^{M} \lambda_k \sum_{i=1}^{N} \sum_{j=1}^{N} \Gamma^k_{ij} \kappa_i S_i \kappa_j S_j \right) - \sum_{k=1}^{M} |\lambda_k| C_k.$$

And if we can't use the Taylor series expansion? We must examine

$$\delta \Pi = F(\kappa_1 x S_1, \ldots, \kappa_N x S_N) + \sum_{k=1}^{M} \lambda_k F_k(\kappa_1 x S_1, \ldots, \kappa_N x S_N) - \sum_{k=1}^{M} |\lambda_k| C_k.$$

Here F is the original portfolio and the F_k are the available hedging contracts.

From now on we'll stick to the delta-gamma approximation and leave it to the reader to do the more robust and realistic whole-formulae approach.

THE MULTI-INDEX MODEL

In the same way that the CAPM model can accommodate multiple indices, so we can have a multiple-index CrashMetrics model. I will skip most of the details, the implementation is simple. We fit the extreme returns in each asset to the extreme returns in the indices according to

$$\delta S_i = \sum_{j=1}^{n} \kappa^j_i x_j,$$

where the n indices are denoted by the j sub/superscript.

The change in value of our portfolio of stocks and options is now quadratic in all of the x_j. Now we must decide over what range of index returns we will look for the worst case. Consider just the two-index case, because it is easy to draw the pictures. One possibility is to allow x_1 and x_2 to be independent, to take any values in a given range. Note there is no correlation in this between the two indices; fortunately, this difficult-to-measure parameter is irrelevant. Alternatively, if you believe there is some relationship between the size of the crash in one index and the size of the crash in the other, you may want to narrow down the area that you explore for the worst case.

CRASH DISPERSION

The crash coefficient does not capture the relationship between a stock and an index to perfection. A simple statistical analysis of the regression described above shows that some stocks are more closely modelled by the simple linear relationship than other stocks.

A more accurate representation of the relationship would accept that the link between the return on a stock and the return on the index is not completely deterministic. Accordingly, we propose the following model:

$$\delta S_i = x S_i (\kappa_i + \psi_i \varepsilon_i)$$

where κ_i, the crash coefficient, is a constant; ψ_i, the crash dispersion, is constant; and ε_i is a random variable with zero mean and standard deviation of one. We further assume that the ε are uncorrelated. Note that we have introduced a second parameter, the crash dispersion coefficient ψ_i, into our extreme-event model. We will see how this affects our analysis.

BIAS EFFECTS

Let us go back to our delta-gamma approximation for a single stock:

$$\delta \Pi = \Delta \, \delta S + \tfrac{1}{2} \Lambda \, \delta S^2.$$

With this new model, we have

$$\delta \Pi = \Delta x S (\kappa + \psi \varepsilon) + \tfrac{1}{2} \Gamma x^2 S^2 (\kappa + \psi \varepsilon)^2.$$

Although difficult to justify when we have a single stock, let us take expectations of this expression over the ε, to get

$$E[\delta \Pi] = \Delta x \kappa S + \tfrac{1}{2} \Gamma x^2 S^2 (\kappa^2 + \psi^2).$$

We can immediately see that the crash dispersion term has a major impact on the quadratic term. This bias effect can be very important in practice.

In the single-index, multi-asset case we obtain

$$\delta \Pi = x \sum_{i=1}^{N} \Delta_i \kappa_i S_i + \tfrac{1}{2} x^2 \left(\sum_{i=1}^{N} \sum_{j=1}^{N} \Gamma_{ij} \kappa_i S_i \kappa_j S_j + \sum_{i=1}^{N} \Gamma_{ii} \psi_i^2 S_i^2 \right).$$

There is a correction term to be added to our earlier model. Taking expectations is easier to justify for the multi-asset model if we assume there are many underlyings, by appealing to the central limit theorem.

ANALYSIS OF DATA

We will now examine the components of the Dow Jones Industrial Average (DJIA) to determine how this new model affects the analysis of extreme markets. Table 12.2 shows the results for the constituent stocks with the DJIA as the index. The far right column shows the old crash coefficients calculated without reference to the possible dispersion about the linear relationship. In the other columns are the new crash coefficients and the dispersions, as well as the important combination of the two.

Note how the old and the new crash coefficients are not that different from each other. But the combination, which is critical when looking at the second-order gamma effects, is generally much greater than originally estimated. Clearly, the bias effect is important.

Table 12.2 Old and new crash coefficients for the constituents of the DJIA and the crash dispersions

Stock	κ_i	ψ_i	$\sqrt{\kappa_i^2 + \psi_i^2}$	Old κ_i
AA	0.928 633 034	0.788 722 791	1.218 377 18	0.947 137 407
AXP	1.483 996 838	0.411 691 018	1.540 044 191	1.437 718 181
BA	0.977 286 242	0.604 455 706	1.149 110 569	0.838 730 826
C	1.100 877 49	0.871 926 447	1.404 345 747	1.116 907 788
CAT	0.928 996 832	0.595 831 998	1.103 653 425	1.003 232 169
CCE	0.723 227 329	0.569 902 136	0.920 785 651	0.896 244 344
DD	0.831 324 801	0.359 738 995	0.905 821 764	0.838 973 908
DIS	1.246 997 52	0.773 851 986	1.467 599 984	1.322 318 414
EK	1.111 819 767	0.768 626 593	1.351 639 758	1.209 976 697
GE	0.545 077 84	0.872 194 191	1.028 509 873	0.689 899 712
GM	1.102 204 469	0.569 803 32	1.240 778 189	1.009 146 58
HD	1.257 807 003	0.549 294 656	1.372 517 059	1.168 461 094
HON	1.252 408 773	1.013 763 605	1.611 286 561	1.333 608 778
HWP	1.313 206 737	0.659 879 672	1.469 677 895	1.112 396 695
IBM	1.117 511 015	0.452 848 901	1.205 779	1.106 380 462
INTC	1.456 132 994	1.218 585 271	1.898 755 74	1.208 902 253
IP	1.052 067 124	0.588 839 505	1.205 643 893	1.148 293 007
JNJ	0.909 311 16	0.489 213 335	1.032 558 218	0.884 596 919
JPM	1.107 612 454	0.840 486 286	1.390 403 734	1.177 106 697
KO	1.159 124 869	0.793 077 524	1.404 472 293	1.174 749 439
MCD	1.085 251 44	0.706 130 269	1.294 755 052	1.013 014 29
MO	0.725 974 397	0.630 195 681	0.961 345 631	0.723 649 066
MRK	0.890 195 447	0.587 750 241	1.066 723 151	0.784 920 33
MSFT	1.325 482 778	0.686 857 385	1.492 875 635	1.431 953 457
PG	0.977 887 052	0.758 311 09	1.237 456 583	1.095 306 218
SBC	0.737 210 095	0.466 752 273	0.872 545 935	0.648 272 019
T	1.021 423 771	0.477 599 618	1.127 567 256	1.069 152 359
UTX	0.758 232 697	0.553 177 782	0.938 574 707	0.715 845 046
WMT	1.076 926 56	0.633 739 796	1.249 558 7	0.908 968 945
XOM	0.896 538 871	0.636 959 689	1.099 772 518	0.990 309 581

Although an analysis of the correlation between the ε is certainly possible, the lack of data means that such an analysis would be highly suspect.

MARGIN CALLS AND MARGIN HEDGING

Stock market crashes are more common than one imagines, if one defines a crash as any unhedgeable move in prices. Although we have focused on the change in value of our portfolio during a crash, this is not what usually causes trouble. One of the reasons for this is that, in the long run, stock markets rise significantly faster than the rate of interest, and banks are usually net long the market. What causes banks, and other institutions, to suffer is not the paper value of their assets but the requirement to suddenly come up with a large amount of cash to cover an unexpected margin call. Banks can weather extreme markets provided they do not have to come up with large amounts of cash for margin calls. For this reason it makes sense to be 'margin hedged'. Margin hedging is the reduction of future margin calls by buying/selling contracts so that the net margin requirement is insensitive to movements in underlyings. In the worst-case crash scenario discussed here, this means optimally choosing hedging contracts so that the worst-case margin requirement is optimised. Typically, over-the-counter (OTC) options will not play a role in the optimal margin hedge since they do not usually have margin call requirements.

Recent examples where margin has caused significant damage are Metallgesellschaft and Long-Term Capital Management. LTCM suffered after a 'once in a millennium … 10 sigma event'. Unfortunately it happened in only their fourth year of trading.

What is margin?

Writing options is very risky. The downside of buying an option is just the initial premium, the upside may be unlimited. The upside of writing an option is limited, but the downside could be huge. For this reason, to cover the risk of default in the event of an unfavourable outcome, the clearing houses that register and settle options insist on the deposit of a margin by the writers of options. Clearing houses act as counterparty to each transaction.

Margin comes in two forms, the initial margin and the maintenance margin. The initial margin is the amount deposited at the initiation of the contract. The total amount held as margin must stay above a prescribed maintenance margin. If it ever falls below this level then more money (or equivalent in bonds, stocks, etc.) must be deposited. The levels of these margins vary from market to market.

Modelling margin

The amount of margin that must be deposited depends on the particular contract. Obviously, we are not too concerned with the initial margin since this is known in advance of the purchase/sale of the contract. It is the variation margin that will concern us since a dramatic market move could result in a sudden large margin call that may be difficult to meet.

We will model the margin call as a percentage of the change in value of the contract. We denote that percentage by the Greek letter χ. Note that for an over-the-counter (OTC) contract there is usually no margin requirement so $\chi = 0$.

The conclusion is that the CrashMetrics methodology will carry over directly to the analysis of margin provided that the Greeks are suitably redefined. We have therefore introduced the new Greeks, $\overline{\Theta}$, $\overline{\Delta}$ and $\overline{\Gamma}$, margin theta, margin delta and margin gamma, respectively. The reader who is aware of the Metallgesellschaft fiasco will recall that they were delta hedged but not margin hedged.

We've assumed a Taylor series/delta-gamma approximation that almost certainly won't be realistic during a crash. We are lucky when modelling margin that virtually every contract on which there is margin has a nice formula for its price. The complex products which require numerical solution are typically OTC contracts with no margin requirements at all. We leave it to the reader to go through the details when using formulae rather than Greek approximations.

COUNTERPARTY RISK

If OTC contracts do not have associated margin calls, they do have another serious kind of risk: counterparty risk. During extreme markets, counterparties may go broke, having a knock-on effect on other banks. For this reason, one should divide up one's portfolio by counterparty initially and examine the worst-case scenario counterparty by counterparty. Everything that we have said above about worst-case scenarios and Platinum Hedging carries over to the smaller portfolio associated with each counterparty.

SIMPLE EXTENSIONS TO CRASHMETRICS

In this section we briefly outline ways in which CrashMetrics has been extended to other situations and to capture other market effects. Because of the simplicity of the basic form of CrashMetrics, many additional features can be incorporated quite straightforwardly.

First of all, we haven't described how the CrashMetrics methodology can be applied to interest rate products. This is not difficult, simply use a yield (or several) as the benchmark and relate changes in the values of products to changes in the yield via durations and convexities. The reader can imagine the rest.

A particularly interesting topic is what happens to parameter values after a crash. After a crash there is usually a rise in volatility and an increase in bid/offer spread. The rise in volatility can be incorporated into the methodology by including vega terms, dependent also on the size of the crash. This is conceptually straightforward, but requires analysis of option price data around the times of crashes. If you are long vanilla options during a crash, you will benefit from this rise in volatility. Similarly, crash-dependent bid/offer spread can be incorporated but again requires historical data analysis to model the relationship between the size of a crash and the increase in the spread.

Finally, it is common experience that stocks bounce back shortly after a crash, so the real fall in price is not as bad as it seems. Typically 20% of the sudden loss is recovered shortly afterwards, but this is by no means a hard and fast rule. You can see this in the earlier tables; a date on which there is a very large fall is followed by a date on which there is a large rise. To incorporate such a dynamic effect into the relatively static CrashMetrics is an interesting task.

THE CRASHMETRICS INDEX

The results and principles of CrashMetrics have been applied to a *CrashMetrics Index* (CMI). This is an index that measures the magnitude of market moves and whether or not we are in a crash scenario. It's like a Richter scale for the financial world. Unlike

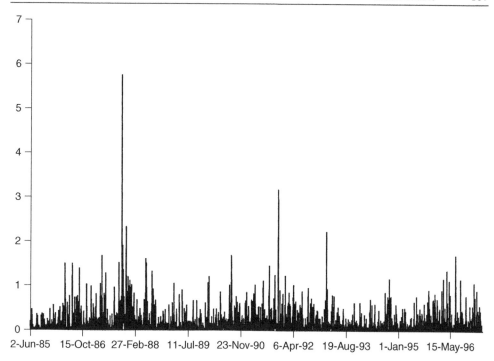

Figure 12.8 The S&P 500 CMI

most measures of market movements, this one is *not* a volatility index in disguise, it is far more subtle than that. However, being proprietary, we can't tell you how it's defined. Sorry. We can give you some clues: it's based on a logarithmic scale; it has only one timescale (unlike volatility which needs a long timescale such as 30 days, and a short one, perhaps 1 day); it exploits the effect shown in Figure 12.1. Figure 12.8 shows a time series of the CMI applied to the S&P 500.

SUMMARY

This chapter described a VaR methodology that is specifically designed for analysing market crashes and protecting against them. Such analysis is fundamental to the well-being of financial institutions and for that reason we have taken a non-probabilistic approach to the modelling.

FURTHER READING

- Download the CrashMetrics technical documents, data sets and demonstration software for CrashMetrics from www.crashmetrics.com
- CrashMetrics is currently being turned into commercial software by Xenomorph, see www.xenomorph.com
- See *Paul Wilmott on Quantitative Finance*, published by John Wiley & Sons, for more details and examples

SUMMARY

FURTHER READING

13

Herding in financial markets: a role for psychology in explaining investor behaviour?

Henriëtte Prast

INTRODUCTION

During the twentieth century, the focus in economic theory has moved away from philo-sophical, behavioural and psychological aspects toward physics and mathematics. In the 1920s, Keynes stressed 'animal spirits' as a determinant of investment. The later emphasis on quantification, econometrics and the 'homo economicus' (rational economic agent) has drastically reduced the attention paid to psychological and sociological influences on economic behaviour. Although informational aspects play a crucial role in models explaining economic decision making on a microeconomic level, the focus in economic and finance theory has been on the *availability* of information, not on how individuals *gather, process and interpret* it. Other disciplines, notably cognitive psychology, have long studied how the human mind searches for and processes information. Economics and finance theory have thus far only to a very limited extent used the results from those studies in explaining economic decision making. This may be one of the reasons why economists have had difficulties in explaining and predicting seemingly irrational behaviour, for example during financial panics.

The chapter investigates whether insights from psychology may shed new light on investor behaviour and can provide an explanation for (apparently) irrational phenomena observed in financial markets. Rather then modelling the behaviour of investors in a formal way, it aims at suggesting how research in behavioural finance might proceed in explaining herd behaviour. The conclusion is that the theory of cognitive dissonance developed by social psychologist Leon Festinger may prove to be useful in explaining investor behaviour both in normal times and during times of financial crisis and investor panics. In particular, it might clarify the behaviour that has become known as herding. First it defines 'herding' and pays attention to recent theoretical explanations of rational herding behaviour in financial markets. Then it takes a look at application of psychological concepts to financial market behaviour. It introduces the theory of cognitive dissonance and discusses its use in explaining investor behaviour in general and herding during financial crises in particular. It ends with concluding remarks and suggestions for further research. The views expressed in this chapter are those of the author.

HERDING IN ECONOMIC THEORY

Mathematical finance aims at finding optimal portfolio behaviour and deriving fair prices for financial instruments. The only individual (personality) characteristic that plays a role here is the investor's risk/return appetite. No matter how sophisticated mathematical finance models have become, they have not always been able to explain or predict observed behaviour in financial markets. This became clear with the debacle of the LTCM hedge fund in the United States in the autumn of 1998. The irony was that the fund benefited greatly from its knowledge about slightly irrational behaviour by investors, whereas its problems were due to the irrational psychological overreaction (flight to safety) of those same investors.[1] This example illustrates that economics and finance theory should take other determinants of investor behaviour into account. Without considering mathematical finance to be 'out', behavioural finance is obviously 'in' and can be expected to gain in importance in economics and finance theory in the years to come.

Behavioural finance aims at explaining and predicting analyst and investor behaviour from individual utility functions incorporating not only risk aversion, but taking other considerations at the individual level into account. The behavioural finance literature studies a number of phenomena observed in financial markets, one of which is herding. Scharfstein and Stein (1990) define herding as the mimicking of decisions of others, thereby ignoring substantive private information. According to this definition, individuals who copy the behaviour of others because it would be more costly to gather information themselves are not herding. It is not only the mimicking, but also the ignorance of own information that is crucial.[2] Herding behaviour is most visible during financial crises, when the direction in which the 'herd' is moving is suddenly reversed. But it may also occur during normal times, when investors, investment analysts and fund managers copy the behaviour of others, disregarding their own perhaps private information.

In their survey of rational herding models, Devenow and Welch (1996) distinguish three strands of literature: reputational models, models with pay-off externalities and cascade models. Reputational models focus on the behaviour of the investment analyst or fund manager. Crucial is the assumption that investment decisions are taken not (or not only) on the basis of expected risk and return, but also with the aim of affecting the analyst's future reputation. The investment analyst's reward (future wage) depends on his (ex post) reputation in the eyes of the public (his actual or potential clients). The reputation in its turn is assumed to depend on a performance evaluation which—and this is crucial—is based either on a benchmark or on relative performance.

An example of this strand of literature is the model by Scharfstein and Stein (1990). In this model it is assumed that analysts are either smart or dumb, i.e. they are or are not able to distinguish between informative and uninformative signals. There are two possible investment outcomes, high and low, and two signals about the investment project, good and bad. The analyst's type is unobservable to all including himself. The a priori probability that an analyst is smart is common knowledge, as is the a priori probability of a high investment pay-off. This information structure implies that the signals of smart analysts are correlated whereas those of the dumb ones are not. The investment analyst (or fund manager) uses his choice of investment to maximise his expected posterior reputation of being smart. He calculates the probability of an investment outcome using the common knowledge as well as the private signal he has received. Both the revision (by the public, i.e. the analyst's clients) of the analyst's reputation and the update of beliefs about the investment outcome by the analyst follow Bayes' rule.

The model assumes an exogenously imposed leader. When deciding on his strategy, the leader (the first to act) takes the rational reaction of the followers into account. The result is that both dumb and smart analysts are likely to herd because it is rational for them to do so: by joining the crowd, they can make believe that they act according to informative signals. The model therefore predicts that herding increases with the correlation between informative signals. The higher the signal correlation, the more likely it is that smart investors make the same choices, hence act as part of a group. This increases the incentive to joint the crowd.

Herding decreases with the ability of the smart analysts (the precision of the signal they receive), because this makes it more likely that an analyst's private information and his revised belief about the investment outcome are consistent. However, herding increases with initial reputation. This may seem counterintuitive, but it is because an analyst with a high reputation (and hence, given the assumptions, a high wage) has much to lose if he individually fails. Or, in the words of Keynes, commenting on investor behaviour: 'Worldly wisdom teaches that it is better for reputation to fail conventionally than to succeed unconventionally' (Keynes, 1936).

Scharfstein and Stein assume that the analyst's reward depends only on his reputation. However, the herding results also apply, although to a lesser degree, if the analyst is interested in both his reputation and the investment pay-off. This would be the case if the analyst's income depended not only on his reputation but also on the investment performance, either because his wage is directly performance-related (bonuses) or because he uses his knowledge for making private investments in line with his advice. In the reputational model, decisions are usually socially sub-optimal, because they are (partly) based on reputational considerations rather than investment quality. In the view of Scharfstein and Stein, the fact that agents use others' actions as informative signals complementing their private information is not the essence of herding. As they see it, herding occurs if *too much* weight is put on others' actions.[3]

The model has some flaws. The assumption that the analysts and fund managers do know the average quality of their profession, but not their own ability, is a bit far-fetched. It amounts to assuming that the used-car dealer in Akerlof's famous 'lemons problem' does not know the quality of the cars he has for sale (Akerlof, 1970). Furthermore, although the reputational approach explains herding behaviour during normal times, it does not endogenously model a reversal of the direction in which the crowd is moving. Finally, it may explain herding behaviour by fund managers and analysts, but not behaviour by private investors, who obviously do not have a reputation to think of but are merely interested in the expected pay-off of their private investment.[4]

Another strand in the herding literature concentrates on herd behaviour as a result of pay-off externalities. In this case, herding occurs because it is optimal to take an action simply because others do take that action as well.[5] Reputational and strategic considerations do not play a role, and neither does the gathering of information about fundamentals. The optimal behaviour during a bank run is a typical example: irrespective of whether a bank is solvent or not, once a run has started, perhaps because of a rumour that the bank may be insolvent, or because another bank has gone bankrupt, it is optimal for depositors to withdraw their money irrespective of whether (they believe that) the bank is insolvent or not. This is because even a solvent bank that becomes faced with a run will get into liquidity problems (and in the end probably into insolvency, unless the lender of last resort injects massive liquidity into the system) and the depositors who do not run in time lose their money (Diamond and Dybvig, 1983). Obviously, this type of herding (panicking) could be solved if individuals were able to coordinate their actions. However, it is impossible for individuals to credibly commit themselves not to run.[6]

The pay-off externalities view could explain why a rumour might result in rational herding behaviour. However, it does not make clear why some rumours are believed and others are not. A third class of rational herding models are the so-called informational cascades (Banerjee, 1992). Here it is assumed that some or all agents have limited private information and that publicly visible actions by others act as an additional source of information. This may lead to a situation in which the individual rationally ignores his private information or, rather, that the private information is overruled by the information received from the actions of others. In these models it is assumed that the prior probabilities (e.g. about the quality of an investment opportunity) are common knowledge. In addition, an individual may or may not (randomly) receive a signal about the investment quality. This signal does not need to be 'true' in the sense of reflecting the actual quality. Individuals do not know who receives a signal and who doesn't. It is assumed that agents act according to an exogenous ordering, and that the actions chosen by previous agents are public knowledge.[7]

Note that the actions by individuals are not intended to influence the decision by anyone coming after them: there is no strategic interaction. The individuals are assumed to maximise their expected pay-off, which depends on the investment outcome minus a fixed cost of investing. The outcome of this type of model is that extensive herding may occur, but obviously this result is already embodied in the (quite plausible) assumption that the actions of others are a source of information. The most important contribution of this line of research may be that it explains financial market fragility. Bikchandani *et al.* (1992) show that in this model convergence of behaviour can be fragile: the group tends to land on a borderline even on the basis of little information, and small changes in information can reverse the direction in which the crowd is moving. Therefore this model may be used to explain financial fragility and sudden panics and flights to safety.

Unlike the reputational approach, the cascade model explains the behaviour by both professionals (fund managers and analysts) and private investors. A drawback of the model is the exogenous ordering that is necessarily imposed, i.e. the assumption that individuals are unable to delay their decision. Also, there is the given and random distribution of signals: there is no possibility for the decision makers to actively seek information. In this respect, the model is similar to the reputational model by Scharfstein and Stein (1992).

PSYCHOLOGY IN FINANCE: EXISTING RESEARCH

The theories of rational herd behaviour described here have in common that they do not pay attention to the possibility that individuals may gather and interpret information in a biased way. This is a general flaw of economics and finance theory. For, in spite of the crucial role of information in economics and finance theory in general and especially in the theory of herding, economists have paid only slight attention to how people gather and treat information.[8] Other disciplines, notably cognitive psychology, have studied this subject intensively and have developed theories on information seeking and processing that are available to apply in economics and finance theory. Some of these have already been used to explain financial market behaviour.

In his analysis of capital allocation by banks, Herring (1999) uses the concept of availability heuristic developed by cognitive psychologists Tversky and Kahneman (1982). The concept is based on the hypothesis that an individual 'estimates frequency or probability by the ease with which instances can be brought to mind'. Hence the subjective probability of an event depends (partly) on recent experience, or in any case the individual behaves as if this is the case. Thus, an automobile driver who has just witnessed an accident drives more carefully, although he knows that the probability of having an accident has not increased. This increase of the subjective probability is temporary: as time goes by, driving behaviour becomes less cautious. If the estimated subjective probability of an event is a declining function of the availability of the memory of that event, it is obvious that the probability of low-frequency incidents falls to a very low level when a long time has gone by since its last occurrence.

As disasters happen with an extremely low frequency, the subjective probability can drop to practically zero. This leads to so-called disaster myopia.[9] People then behave as if the probability of such an event is indeed zero. Herring shows that disaster myopia in bank behaviour may have important implications for financial stability. His assumption is that a bank allocates its capital according to a subjective probability density function, which is a weighted combination of an objectively verifiable density function, based on historical losses, and a so-called disastrous distribution, namely a uniform density function defined over outcomes from zero to 100% loss. The weight placed on the disastrous distribution is the subjective probability that there will be a draw from this distribution. This is impossible to estimate. If disaster myopia applies and there has not been a market crash for a long time, this weight will then be zero. As Herring shows, a decrease in the subjective probability from 0.001 to zero leads to a dramatic reduction of the capital set aside by the bank to cushion itself against shocks (or to maintain its credit rating).[10] The existence of the availability heuristic and the existence of disaster myopia have been verified empirically both in experimental studies (laboratory experiments) and in real-world behaviour.

Barberis *et al.* (1998) use another concept introduced by Tversky and Kahneman, the representativeness heuristic, to analyse investor behaviour. This heuristic implies that people have a tendency to see patterns in random events. This may lead to overreaction in the sense that people draw far-reaching conclusions on the basis of only little evidence. The implication of the representativeness heuristic for investor behaviour may be an overreaction of stock prices to news. Barberis *et al.* admit that, although this assumption leads to model results that confirm some (but not all) of the empirical evidence, it is not clear why certain types of news are more relevant than others in the eyes of the investor. They conclude therefore that 'to push this research further, it is important to develop an a priori way of classifying events by their strength and weight' (Barberis *et al.*, 1998, p. 333). The theory of cognitive dissonance (see below) may prove to be useful in this respect.

Daniel *et al.* (1998) use the psychological concepts of overconfidence and biased self-attribution to explain under- and overreactions of security markets. Overconfidence among investors would imply that they overestimate their ability to value securities. Biased self-attribution relates to the dynamics of self-confidence: confidence is assumed to grow when public information confirms private information, but does not decline in case of a contradiction between the two. An interesting implication is that if, as some psychological evidence indicates, experts are more overconfident than inexperienced individuals, aggressive expert trading intimidates other traders and leads to higher returns.

The applications of psychological concepts to financial markets outlined here do not explicitly pay attention to herd behaviour or to explanations of financial crises (reversal of the direction of the herd). The next section suggests possibilities for further research on these phenomena using the psychological theory of cognitive dissonance.

THE PSYCHOLOGY OF CROWD BEHAVIOUR: THE THEORY OF COGNITIVE DISSONANCE

According to the founding father of psychoanalysis, Sigmund Freud, 'It is the very essence of a panic that it bears no relation to the danger that threatens it' (Freud, 1959). Mass behaviour, in Freud's view, is by definition irrational and as the defining characteristics of a crowd Freud mentions invincibility, irresponsibility, impetuosity, contagion, changeability, suggestibility, collective hallucination and intellectual inferiority (Chancellor, 1999). Still, Freud's theory of repression offers a useful background for the basic idea, that the human mind treats information in a biased way: unpleasant memories are locked away. Or as Freud puts it, 'The essence of repression lies simply in the function of rejecting and keeping something out of consciousness' (Freud, 1957, vol. 4, p. 86).

Whereas Freud's focus was on psychopathology, he believed that healthy individuals do also, to a certain degree, turn away from unpleasant information. Cognitive psychologists have further studied the way people in general gather and use information and knowledge, and how the memory works. Two concepts that may explain irrational financial market behaviour are the principle of congruity developed by Osgood and Tannenbaum (1955) and the principle of cognitive dissonance formulated by Festinger (1957).

Principle of congruity

Psychologists Osgood and Tannenbaum formulated the principle of congruity, which applies to the way people evaluate new information that has become available to them:

> Changes in evaluation are always in the direction of increased congruity with the existing framework of reference. (Osgood and Tannenbaum, 1955)

The existing framework of reference may be the individual's opinion or belief, which in its turn is likely to be based on information of the past. Thus, if an information source is regarded positively by an individual but produces information that the individual regards negatively (is contrary to his framework of reference), the individual either changes his attitude towards the source of information, or changes his attitude towards the information itself. If this principle held in reality, it would imply that people treat available information in a biased way. In its most extreme form, they will neglect information completely if it does not fit in with the existing belief. The congruity principle can be regarded as a first step toward Leon Festinger's theory of cognitive dissonance.

The theory of cognitive dissonance

Festinger (1957) defines cognitive dissonance as follows:

> Two cognitive elements are in a dissonant relation if, considering these two alone, the obverse of one element follows from the other.

Here cognitive elements may include opinions, information and beliefs. According to Festinger, individuals have the unconscious or subconscious psychological mechanism to diminish the dissonance they perceive. Thus:

> The presence of dissonance leads to seeking new information which will provide cognition consonant with existing cognitive elements and to avoiding those sources of

new information which would be likely to increase the existing dissonance. (Festinger, 1957, p. 264)

In Festinger's view, individuals may diminish dissonance in a number of ways.[11] Thus, when faced with dissonance, individuals engage in actively seeking out information that confirms their belief and the choices they have made. Also, they tend to avoid information that would suggest they have made the wrong choice. Finally—and here crowd psychology, or herd behaviour, enters the picture—they may try to find support and comfort in the fact that other people have made the same decisions.

When the dissonance between the existing framework of reference becomes so large that it becomes impossible to reduce it by selective gathering and interpretation of information and by finding social support, the individual switches to the opposite method of dissonance reduction: instead of trying to find evidence that his opinion is correct, he will now, faced with too much unfavourable information, make an effort to change his belief or opinion.[12] He does so by actively seeking out *dissonance-increasing* information.[13] The dissonance then disappears because the large amount of dissonance between the individual's opinion and the information received has enabled him to change his existing belief. The reversal in the biased information-seeking behaviour occurs when the dissonance perceived by the individuals equals the resistance to change his framework of reference (his opinion or belief).

According to Festinger, efforts to reduce dissonance are undertaken more actively, the more the individual benefits from the dissonance reduction. Obviously, this depends on the importance of the decision. Interestingly, Festinger uses an economic decision, namely the purchase of a car, to illustrate his theory. After the purchase, the buyer is likely to expose himself to any information confirming the advantages of this particular type of automobile, whereas he tends to avoid reading advertisements about cars that once were an alternative but that he chose not to purchase. Investment decisions are different in the sense that asset markets are more liquid. Still, the mechanism by which information gathering is biased is likely to be at work in essentially the same way.

Festinger pays special attention to what he calls, in a neutral fashion, mass phenomena. Assume that, for one reason or another, many people suffer from the same cognitive dissonance. According to Festinger:

> Under such circumstances, the striking and dramatic aspects of mass phenomena exist not because something exceptional or unique is brought to the situation, but only because social support is particularly easy to find in the pursuit of dissonance reduction. (Festinger, 1957, pp. 233–34)

In this respect, Festinger recognises the role of rumours, especially in situations in which fear is widespread, but evidence justifying fear is not available.

The theory of cognitive dissonance, when applied to financial markets, would explain 'sequential herding': the phenomenon that investors, analysts and fund managers 'herd' on previous behaviour. Furthermore, the theory predicts that investors, when faced with dissonance, find comfort in the fact that they are part of a group. This may explain crowd behaviour and reinforces the bias in information gathering in situations where many investors have previously made similar decisions. When time goes by, and despite this bias, unfavourable information about pay-offs of investments made (bad fundamentals, increased probability of default) may grow in intensity and frequency, up to the point where it cannot be disregarded anymore, not even by an individual who is part of a crowd. Investors start paying attention to it, first gradually, but when the cognitive dissonance between the new (unfavourable) information and the existing (optimistic) mood becomes too large, they start actively seeking information that increases dissonance, enabling them to change their framework of reference (optimistic mood) about the investments made.

Obviously, the dissonance is reinforced when the group starts falling apart. This happens when for some investors the dissonance has become too large, but this mere fact—their departure from the crowd—increases the dissonance of the remaining investors, who in their turn will start seeking out dissonance-increasing information. The theory would therefore predict a sudden reversal of the crowd, which once it has started will proceed at a high speed. The timing of the reversal is unpredictable, because although the reversal ultimately depends on the fundamentals, the timing depends on the (subjectively perceived) dissonance and resistance to change of some investors.

The theory of cognitive dissonance does not consider strategic behaviour by individuals. However, incorporation of strategic and reputational considerations may reinforce some mechanisms outlined by the theory, with implications for financial markets. This is through the behaviour not of investors, but of analysts and fund managers.

Suppose investment analysts and fund managers take into account that, as a result of the principle of congruity and because of the incentive to reduce dissonance, their clients 'suffer' from a selectivity bias in gathering and interpreting information. Thus, if they are regarded by their clients as a reliable source of information (they are part of the framework of reference), they can to a certain degree make mistakes without being 'punished', especially if their decisions seem to indicate that previous investments were sound. This could induce them to make investment recommendations and choices that are in line with earlier decisions, even if they know that new information would justify a change of direction. Also, they know that the principle of 'shooting the messenger' holds. This may make them reluctant to be the first to break the news to their clients that times are getting worse.

This chapter aims merely at suggesting in an informal way how the theory of cognitive dissonance might explain a variety of behavioural patterns in financial markets, especially the herding behaviour during financial panics. Future research should concentrate on modelling investor behaviour along the lines suggested by the cognitive dissonance theory. Formalisation should pay attention to some of the following aspects implied by the theory:

- A measure of dissonance should be constructed, most probably in terms of discrepancy between past investment decisions and new information
- Efforts of information gathering would have to be modelled as increasing with perceived dissonance
- A threshold of dissonance would have to be defined, below which information gathering is biased toward news confirming earlier investment decisions, and above which the bias is toward bad news about investments undertaken
- A critical level of dissonance equal to the resistance to changing the framework of reference should be defined
- Dissonance reduction by being part of a crowd would have to be incorporated, for example by assuming that efforts to gather information vary inversely with the size of the crowd

These aspects, taken together, may explain both crowd behaviour and the fact that the crowd suddenly (in the sense that it does not rationally react to fundamental news and in the sense that it happens very quickly) moves in the opposite direction.

When modelling not only the behaviour of investors but also that of analysts and fund managers, these aspects may need to be supplemented by decision making of investment analysts and fund managers reflecting reputational considerations, as they are incorporated in the rational herding theory.

In addition to this, studies could be set up analysing investor behaviour in an experimental context, focusing on cognitive dissonance and seeking support in the crowd. A drawback of experimental studies is of course that the decisions the participants must take in this context are by far not as important as real-life (investment) decisions. This is especially relevant as the theory assumes that dissonance and the behaviour to diminish it increase with the importance of the decision (Festinger, 1957, p. 262).[14]

A first look at financial market developments during the Asian crisis indicates that the facts may well be explained by the theory of cognitive dissonance. Kaminsky and Schmukler (1999) have studied financial market reactions to news during the Asian crisis. They try to explain the 20 largest one-day swings in stock prices in nine Asian countries during 1997 and 1998. They find that some of these swings cannot be sufficiently explained by economic or political news. Their evidence indicates that with the deepening of the crisis, stock prices overreact more and that during the crisis episodes, investors react more strongly to bad news than to good news. They suggest that bad news in crisis episodes may increase uncertainty and accentuate herding behaviour, but they do not explain what kind of mechanism would be at work here. The theory of cognitive dissonance may provide the answer. Thus, the finding of Kaminsky and Schmukler that in crisis episodes investors react more strongly to bad news than to good news, would fit in with the theory of cognitive dissonance. In crisis periods the framework of reference is pessimistic and investors actively seek bad news because this confirms their opinion. Thus, it is not so much the overreaction to bad news, as the overexposure to it (and the underexposure to good news) that would explain the irrational stock price movements.

CONCLUSIONS

This chapter has argued that psychological mechanisms regarding information gathering and interpretation should be taken into account when explaining investor behaviour. Thus far, economists have relied too greatly on how much information is available, and have paid only little attention to how people gather and process information and why they do so. Herding behaviour can only partly be explained by rational behaviour. Various attempts have been made recently to incorporate psychological concepts in models explaining certain features of investor behaviour. The theory of cognitive dissonance, developed by Festinger, may be able to explain most empirical evidence. Crowd behaviour (herding), mood swings and investor reactions to news in various circumstances can be explained by this theory. Strategic and reputational considerations, as studied in the rational herding literature, may, combined with individuals' pressure to reduce dissonance, reinforce the mechanisms of overreaction and crowd behaviour.

This chapter has presented the theory of cognitive dissonance in an informal way and has argued that it seems to have the ingredients to explain herding behaviour. Further research would have to focus on modelling the behaviour implicit in the theory, possibly complementing it with strategic behaviour. Still, one conclusion can be drawn from the intuitive approach taken here. Even if the theory of cognitive dissonance can explain herding behaviour and investor behaviour during financial panics, it is still impossible to predict its timing, as too many psychological factors influence the mechanism that ultimately leads to a reversal of the direction in which a crowd is moving. This makes it difficult to base policy prescriptions on the theory. One possible implication may be that policy-makers who care about financial stability should engage in careful information dissemination.

NOTES

1. LTCM's models were based on the empirical finding that there was a structural preference for the most recent US Treasury bonds. Knowing that the overvaluation of these titles would quickly disappear, LTCM could earn a profit by taking large positions. However, the Asian crisis in 1997 and the financial distress in Russia in 1998 led to a psychological overreaction by investors that had not been foreseen by LTCM: a flight to quality and an increase in price of those titles that were, according to the LTCM models, already overvalued.

2. Otherwise this type of behaviour could be explained by conventional rational expectations theory, in the sense that people gather information up to the point that the marginal cost equals the marginal benefit.

3. A version of the model by Scharfstein and Stein has been tested empirically by Graham (1999) in an application to the announcements by investment newsletters, where *Value Line*, being the best-known investment newsletter in the United States, acts as the leader. Graham concludes that his evidence supports the model's predictions. Thus, for example, analysts who are longer in the business (have greater ability) herd less than less experienced colleagues with the same income level (reputation).

4. Unless private investors merely follow an analyst's advice; but then this assumption should itself have to be motivated.

5. Devenow and Welch (1996) mention driving on the right-hand side of the road as an example, but in my view this is inappropriate because this is legislation as a result of coordination, whereas the phenomenon we would like to explain occurs precisely because coordination is absent.

6. This is why governments view it as their task to regulate the banking sector. Deposit insurance is introduced to prevent depositors from running.

7. When the individuals are indifferent between acting according to their own signal and following the others, they follow their own signal.

8. Exceptions include Herring (1999) and Barberis *et al.* (1998) (see next section). Barberis *et al.* use this concept in a model of investor sentiment and show that it results in under- and overreaction of stock prices to news.

9. Guttentag and Herring (1986) demonstrate that this decline in subjective probability is consistent with Bayesian decision making, provided that the disaster did happen a very long time ago.

10. An implication is that a bank that is not disaster-myopic and charges an appropriate credit risk premium for a low probability is driven from the market if other banks and market participants suffer from myopia (Herring, 1999).

11. Using his own words: by changing one or more of the (cognitive) elements involved in the dissonant relation, by adding new cognitive elements that are consonant with already existing cognition and, finally, by decreasing the importance of elements of the dissonant relation itself. From these three 'strategies', the second and third are the most important for our purpose, as they both have to do with information gathering and information interpretation on an individual basis and with finding social support for the decision that has been taken.

12. Examples abound both in the realm of mass psychology and in daily life. Religious fanatics try to reduce the cognitive dissonance between their belief and real-world evidence by attracting new souls to their group. 'Shooting the messenger' is a well-known stereotype reaction, especially at a group level. Wishful thinking by a person who is in love, but also any interpretation of the real world that is stereotypical. For example, both men and women do unconsciously have the stereotypical 'dumb blonde' as their framework of reference. Hence the individual does not easily process information that a blonde is not dumb. Empirical research in the field of social psychology has verified this theory.

13. Think of the man who initially refuses to deny any signs of his wife's infidelity (explains them away) but suddenly, when he feels this becomes too difficult, switches to hiring a private detective determined to find proof that his wife betrays him.

14. This may have further implications for financial markets in situations where the population of investors changes, for example because technology and new financial instruments enable the less wealthy to enter the market.

REFERENCES

Akerlof, G. (1970) The market for 'lemons': quality, uncertainty and the market mechanism. *Quarterly Journal of Economics* **84**, 488–500

Banerjee, A.V. (1992) A simple model of herd behavior. *Quarterly Journal of Economics* **93**(3), 797–817

Barberis, N., A. Shleifer and R. Vishny (1998) A model of investor sentiment, *Journal of Financial Economics* **49**, 307–43

Bikchandani, S., D. Hirschleifer and I. Welch (1992) A theory of fads, fashion, custom and cultural change as informational cascades. *Journal of Political Economy* **100**, 992–1026

Chancellor, E. (1999) *Devil take the hindmost: a history of financial speculation*. Macmillan, London

Daniel, K., D. Hirshleifer and A. Subrahmanyam (1998) Investor psychology and security market under- and overreactions. *Journal of Finance* **LIII**(6), 1839–85

Devenow, A. and I. Welch (1996) Rational herding in financial markets. *European Economic Review* **40**, 603–16

Diamond, D. and P. Dybvig (1983) Bank runs, deposit insurance and liquidity. *Journal of Political Economy* **91**(3), 401–19

Festinger, L. (1957) *A Theory of Cognitive Dissonance*. Stanford University Press

Freud, S. (1959) Repression. In E. Jones (ed.), *Sigmund Freud, Collected Papers*, Hogarth Press, New York, and Institute of Psychoanalysis, London

Graham, J.R. (1999) Herding among investment newsletters: theory and evidence. *Journal of Finance* **LIV**(1), 237–67

Guttentag, J.M. and R.J. Herring (1986) *Disaster Myopia in International Banking*. Princeton University Press

Herring, R.J. (1999) Credit risk and financial instability. *Oxford Review of Economic Policy* **15**(3)

Kaminsky, G.L., and S.L. Schmukler (1999) What triggers market jitters? A chronicle of the Asian crisis. Unpublished paper, World Bank

Keynes, J.M. (1936) *The General Theory of Employment, Interest and Money*. Macmillan, London

Osgood, C.E. and P. Tannenbaum (1955) The principle of congruity and the prediction of attitude change. *Psychological Review* **62**, 42–55

Scharfstein, D.S. and J.C. Stein (1990) Herd behavior and investment. *American Economic Review* **80**(3), 465–79

Tversky, A. and D. Kahneman (1982) Availability: a heuristic for judging frequency and probability. In D. Kahneman, P. Slovic and A. Tversky (eds) *Judgement under Uncertainty: Heuristics and Biases*, Cambridge University Press

Further reading

Here is a collection of miscellaneous books, which for some reason never got mentioned in the text but should be on every quant's reading list. (Other references may be found at the end of the individual chapters in this book.)

Cox, J. and Rubinstein, M. (1985) *Options Markets*. Prentice Hall

Elton, E.J. and Gruber, M.J. (1995) *Modern Portfolio Theory and Investment Analysis*. John Wiley

Embrechts, P., Klüppelberg, C. and Mikosch, T. (1997) *Modelling Extremal Events*. Springer-Verlag

Haug, E.G. (1997) *The Complete Guide to Option Pricing Formulas*. McGraw-Hill

Ingersoll, J.E. Jr (1987) *Theory of Financial Decision Making*. Rowman & Littlefield

Malkiel, B.G. (1990) *A Random Walk Down Wall Street*. Norton

Neftci, S. (1996) *An Introduction to the Mathematics of Financial Derivatives*. Academic Press

Peters, E.E. (1991) *Chaos and Order in the Capital Markets*. John Wiley

Peters, E.E. (1994) *Fractal Market Analysis*. John Wiley

Sharpe, W.F. (1985) *Investments*. Prentice-Hall

Soros, G. (1987) *The Alchemy of Finance*. John Wiley

Taleb, N. (1997) *Dynamic Hedging*. John Wiley

Thomson, R. (1998) *Apocalypse Roulette: the lethal world of derivatives*. Pan

Thorp, E.O. (1962) *Beat the Dealer*. Vintage

Thorp, E.O. and Kassouf, S. (1967) *Beat the Market*. Random House

Wilmott, P. (2000) *Paul Wilmott on Quantitative Finance*. John Wiley

Wilmott, P., Dewynne, J. and Howison, S.D. (1993) *Option Pricing: mathematical models and computation*. Oxford Financial Press

Author biographies

Paul Wilmott is a researcher, writer, consultant and editor. His best-selling textbooks include *Paul Wilmott on Quantitative Finance* and *Paul Wilmott Introduces Quantitative Finance*. The former is a two-volume work aimed at practitioners and covers almost every conceivable area of finance. The latter is a condensed version aimed at the student market. It only covers the classical side of finance. Both books are published by John Wiley & Sons. Paul is the editor in chief of *Wilmott*, a quantitative Finance e-zine.

Henrik Rasmussen is a quantitative analyst at Schroder Salomon Smith Barney (Citigroup) in London, developing models and pricing tools for traders of exotic fixed-income and hybrid derivatives. He joined Citigroup in 2001 from a similar position at Bank of Montreal. Henrik did his undergraduate studies at the Technical University of Denmark, then continued with Part III and a PhD at the University of Cambridge. He has held post doctoral positions at universities in Britain, France and Italy. Currently, he is a visiting research fellow at OCIAM (Oxford Centre for Industrial and Applied Mathematics), Mathematical Institute, University of Oxford.

Antony Penaud is currently an associate in the Research and Product Development team at Tokyo Mitsubishi International (London), for whom he has worked since November 2000. He is involved in pricing options on equities, FX and commodities, and is also involved in CDO modelling. He holds an MSc in mathematical modelling and numerical analysis (1997) and a DPhil in mathematical finance (2000) from Oxford University, Somerville College. His DPhil supervisor was Paul Wilmott.

David Bakstein holds degrees from the London School of Economics and Oxford University, where he worked under the supervision of Paul Wilmott and Sam Howison and with whom he published a number of papers on dividend and liquidity modelling. He now works in a financial institution in London.

Christer Borell was born in Sweden in 1945. After studies in mathematics at the University of Uppsala and the Mittag-Leffler Institute in Stockholm, he is now a professor in mathematics at the Chalmers University of Technology in Gothenburg. Christer Borell's former publications in mathematics mostly concern geometric properties of Brownian motion with applications to heat conduction, potential theory, Wiener chaos, and finance.

Isabelle Bajeux-Besnainou obtained her PhD in 1989 from the University of Paris 9. She is a former student from the mathematics department at the Ecole Normale Superieure. She has taught Finance at ESSEC (rated one of the top two French business schools) from 1989 to 1993, and Montreal University from 1993 to 1994. She has been teaching at the George Washington University from 1994, where she is currently in charge of the PhD programme for the finance department. Her teaching assignments are currently investment (for the MBA programme), financial theory (for the Master of Science in Finance programme) and continuous-time finance (for the PhD programme). She is currently researching the dynamic aspects of portfolio management and has published numerous articles in academic journals.

Roland Portait is professor of finance at both CNAM and ESSEC (Paris) and is also a member of the Commission des Opérations de Bourse (COB), the French equivalent of the Securities and Exchange Commission (SEC). He is editor of *Finance* and holds a PhD in finance from the Wharton School, University of Pennsylvania. He also holds degrees in mathematics, electrical engineering and political sciences from the University of Paris. He is the author of several respected French-language books on finance and has also published numerous articles in academic journals.

Philip Hua is a freelance consultant currently working for Merrill Lynch Investment Management. Prior to this, he worked at Bankers Trust for 12 years in the global risk management department and on various trading desks. He is the co-inventor of Crash-Metrics with Paul Wilmott and is also completing his PhD in applied Mathematics at Imperial College, London.

David Epstein is a market risk analyst at Credit Agricole Lazard Financial Products (CAL FP) Bank and a visiting research fellow at the Oxford Centre for Industrial and Applied Mathematics (OCIAM), Oxford University. He holds a DPhil in applied mathematics from Oxford University.

Aldo Nassigh has a PhD in plasma physics. He is quantitative analyst at UniCredito Italiano Holding in Milan, Italy, in the Market Risk Management & Capital Markets Unit of the Corporate Group Treasury. From 1998 to 2000 he was member of the team that studied and implemented the market risk management system of UBM, the investment bank controlled by UniCredito Holding.

Henriëtte Prast is a senior economist at the Nederlandsche Bank (Dutch Central Bank), Section Banking and Supervisory Strategies, and is associate professor in money, credit and banking at the University of Amsterdam. She has published on various subjects in academic journals, including central banking, inflation and unemployment, financial sector regulation and stability, and the role of psychology in financial markets. Currently she is specialising in 'emotionomics', a term she has coined to describe the area of research that concentrates on the role of emotions in economics. She writes a weekly column on emotionomics in Dutch financial newspaper *Het Financieele Dagblad*.

Ferdinando Samaria graduated in 1991 in electrical engineering from Trinity College, Cambridge, and, in 1994 he also obtained an MA and a PhD. He worked for Credit Suisse Financial Products in the areas of risk management and product development until 1998, when he joined UBM, the investment banking arm of the UniCredito Italiano group, as a founding member. He is currently a managing director in charge of risk technologies and product development.

Andrea Piazzetta graduated in economics in 1997 from Universita' Ca' Foscari, Venice. In 1999 he obtained an MA in economics and finance from Venice International University and an MA in finance from the London Business School. He has worked at UBM, the investment banking arm of the UniCredito Italiano group since 1999, where he is vice president in charge of market risk management.

Paul Wilmott   Antony Penaud   Henriëtte Prast   Aldo Nassigh

Ferdinando Samaria   David Bakstein   Christer Borell   Isabelle Bajeux-Besnainou

Roland Portait   Andrea Piazzetta

Index

Other Wiley Editorial Offices

John Wiley & Sons, Inc., 605 Third Avenue,
New York, NY 10158-0012, USA

WILEY-VCH GmbH, Pappelallee 3,
D-69469 Weinheim, Germany

John Wiley & Sons Australia Ltd, 33 Park Road, Milton,
Queensland 4064, Australia

John Wiley & Sons (Asia) Pte Ltd, 2 Clementi Loop #02-01,
Jin Xing Distripark, Singapore 129809

John Wiley & Sons (Canada) Ltd, 22 Worcester Road,
Rexdale, Ontario M9W 1L1, Canada

Library of Congress Cataloging-in-Publication Data

New directions in mathematical finance/edited by Paul Wilmott and Henrik Rasmussen.
    p. cm.
  Includes Index.
  ISBN 0-471-49817-3
    1. Securities–Mathematical models. 2. Investments–Mathematical models. 3. Risk
management–Mathematical models.   I. Wilmott, Paul. II. Rasmussen, Henrik O., 1996

HG4515.2.N49 2002
332.6′01′5118–dc21   2001055797

British Library Cataloguing in Publication Data

A catalogue record for this book is available from the British Library

ISBN 0-471-49817-3

Typeset in 10/12pt Times by Laserwords Private Limited, Chennai, India
Printed and bound in Great Britain by TJ International Ltd, Padstow, Cornwall
This book is printed on acid-free paper responsibly manufactured from sustainable forestry,
in which at least two trees are planted for each one used for paper production.

Printed and bound by CPI Group (UK) Ltd, Croydon, CR0 4YY

23/04/2025

14660968-0005